Grades 9 - 12

Teaching Mathematics with PentaBlocks™

by

Sheldon Berman

Cuisenaire Company of America, Inc.
White Plains, New York

Dedication

Some of us believe that work, play, and education can be integrated, appreciated, and enjoyed. The PentaBlocks and their use in the classroom can achieve this integration. This book is dedicated to those teachers who strive to share the joy of mathematics with their students, and to those students who enthusiastically work, play, and learn.

Acknowledgments

I am most thankful to my wife, Susie Q. Mastrobermanardo, for her continual and complete support of this and all of my professional endeavors. Without her encouragement and devotion to our family, this project would probably never have been completed.

From the initial conception to the writing of the investigations, I have appreciated the personal and professional support of E.Y. Murphey. As a mentor, colleague, and friend, he continues to have a profound influence on me and my work.

Bringing the PentaBlocks from an idea to a commercial product has been a fascinating experience. The people at Cuisenaire, especially Al Verdeschi, Doris Hirschhorn, Maggie Holler, and Rosemary Calicchio, have all been wonderful to work with.

Most recently and most importantly for the writing of this book, working with Al MacDonell has been a real treat. His quick wit, sensitivity, acuity with language and mathematics, and editorial savvy have made this production a blend of work, play, and education I hope your students will enjoy.

In addition, I offer a sincere thanks to my son Zach, other relatives, colleagues, and friends for their support and understanding throughout the writing period.

Managing Editor: Alan MacDonell
Acquisitions Manager: Doris Hirschhorn
Reviewer/Editor: John Nelson

Text and Cover Design: Phyllis Aycock
Line Art and Production: Joan Lee

Printed in the United States of America.
ISBN 1-57452-024-5

1 2 3 4 5 -VG- 01 00 99 98 97

Table of Contents

Introduction

Brief Description of the PentaBlocks

The classic Pattern Blocks were introduced in the early 1960s as part of the Elementary Science Study (ESS) materials developed by the Educational Development Center in Newton, MA. The six classic shapes share one common characteristic: All of the angle measurements are multiples of 30°. These shapes include the regular triangle, square and hexagon; the isosceles trapezoid or "half-hexagon"; the {60°, 120°} rhombus; and the {30°, 150°} rhombus. All side lengths are the same except the long side of the trapezoid, which is twice the other length.

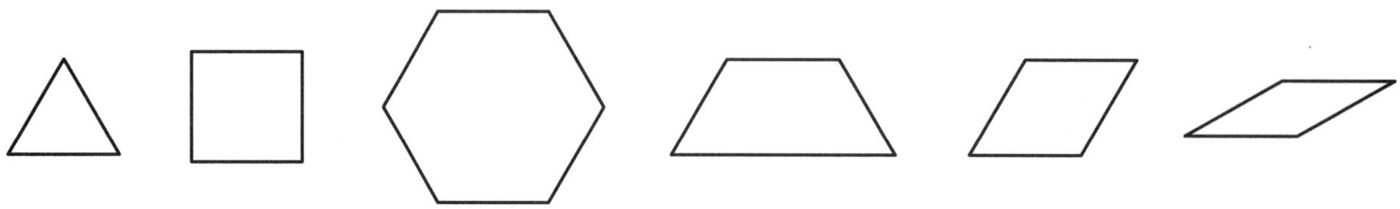

With this minimum inventory of shapes it is possible to create an amazing diversity of patterns. This is partly because the basic 30° angle is a factor of 90, 180, and 360, leading to a variety of complementary and supplementary relationships at the vertices. Thus, many combinations fall together readily to tile the plane nicely without gaps.

Yet it seems that something is missing. The regular polygons with three, four, and six sides are all included, but where is the regular five-sided polygon?

The PentaBlocks Shapes

The regular pentagon* was not included with the classic shapes because its 108° vertex angle was not compatible with the 30° family. That is, 108° does not form a complementary or supplementary pair with any multiple of 30°, so the pentagon interferes with the tiling ability of the group.

What was needed to help the pentagon generate "well-behaved" patterns was a family of its own, with compatible angles that would yield supplementary relationships. The basic angle would have to be one that divided evenly into 108 (for the pentagon) and 180 (for supplementary relationships). The PentaBlocks were created to meet this need, with shapes whose angles are multiples of 36°.

Constructing the two diagonals from one vertex of a regular pentagon creates three isosceles triangles, one with angles of {36°, 72°, 72°} and two with angles of {108°, 36°, 36°}.

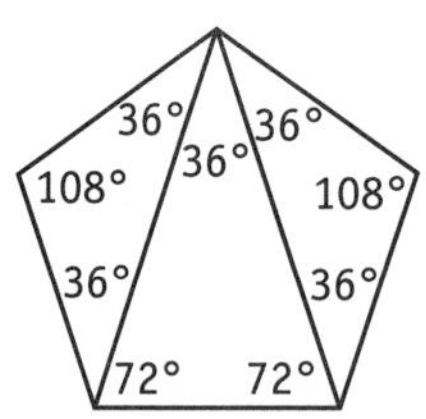

Each of these triangles can be described as a golden triangle, because the side lengths are related to a number called the *Golden Ratio*, often represented as the Greek capital Φ (*phi*). This number, whose

* Unless stated otherwise, *pentagon* will refer to the *regular* pentagon.

value is about 1.6, is the ratio of the longer side to the shorter side of a golden triangle. The Golden Ratio and its related geometry occur frequently in a wide variety of phenomena in the botanical and biological sciences.

Each type of golden isosceles triangle can be joined at the base with an identical triangle to form a related rhombus, one with angles of {72°, 108°}, and the other with {36°, 144°} angles.

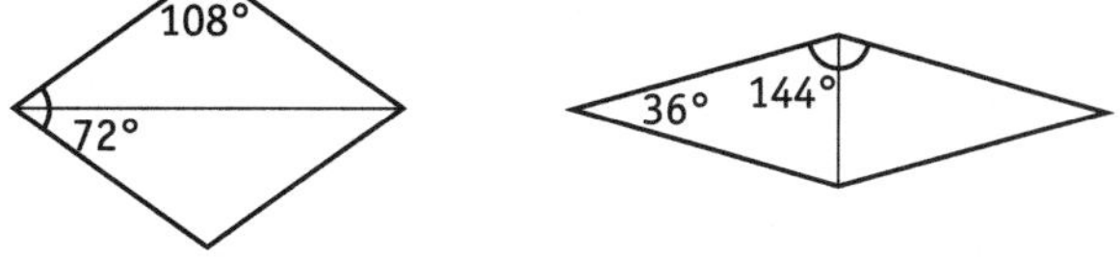

When all of the diagonals in a regular pentagon are constructed another important shape emerges: the five-pointed General's Star, or pentacle. The angles at the "points" are 36°, while the angles at the "dents" are 252°. (We're talking about *interior* angles, so the measure is 360 – 108 = 252°.)

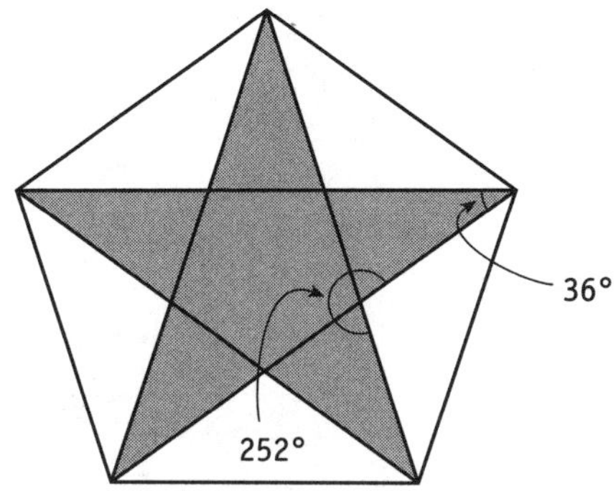

Thus, the PentaBlock family consists of the regular pentagon, two golden isosceles triangles, two rhombuses, and a five-pointed star, all of whose angles are multiples of 36°.

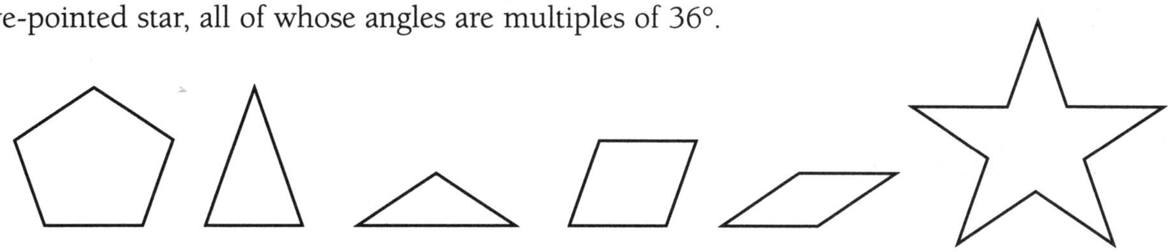

It is worth mentioning that if the pentagon is the parent of the PentaBlock family, then the regular decagon should be considered the grandparent, with its central angle of 36° and vertex angle of 144°.

What's So Special About the Pentagon?

The regular pentagon has a number of important properties:

- It is the only polygon with an equal number of sides and diagonals.

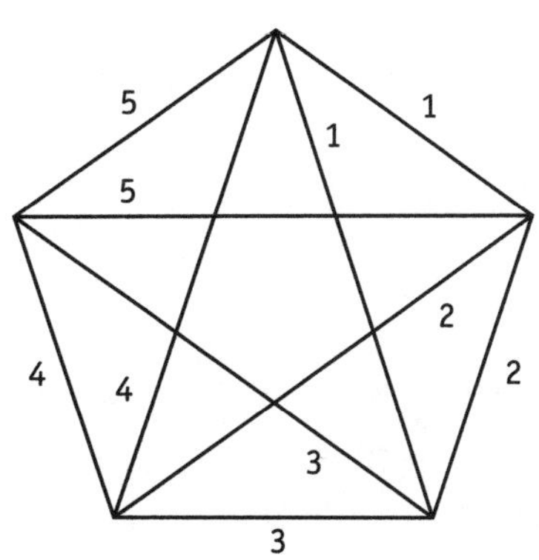

- If you extend nonadjacent sides beyond the pentagon, the resulting triangle is congruent to the triangle formed by the diagonals from a vertex.

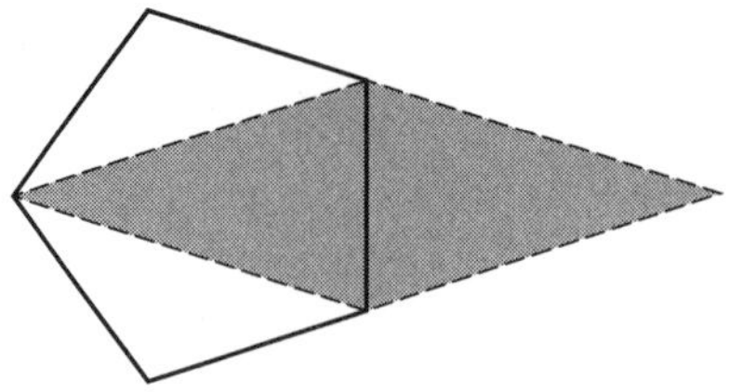

- It is the first (least n) regular n-gon that does not tile the plane by itself.

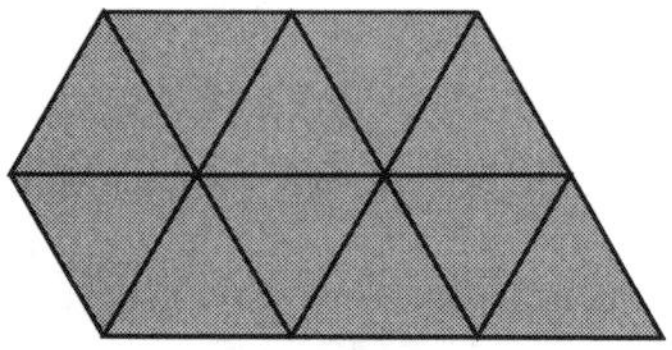

$n = 3$

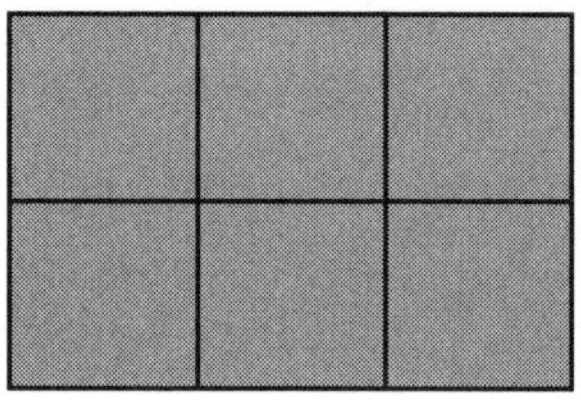

$n = 4$

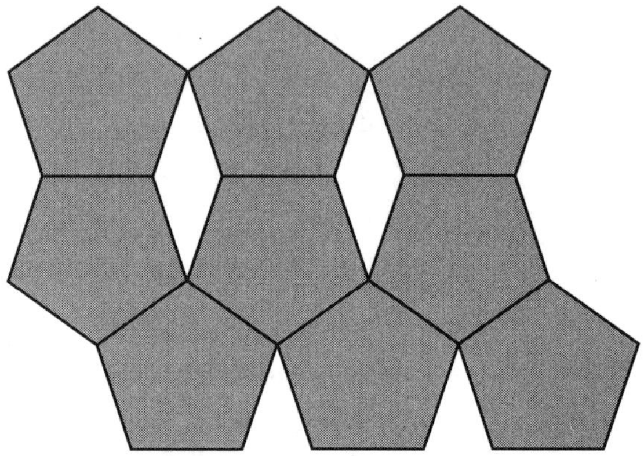

$n = 5$

- It is the last (greatest n) regular n-gon that is the face of a regular solid.

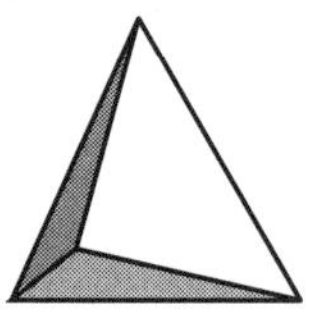

$n = 3$

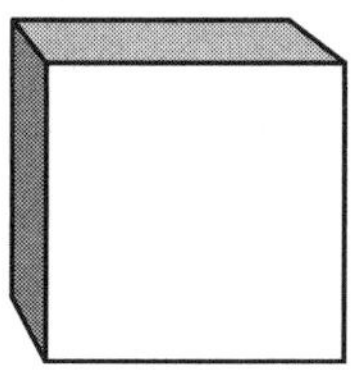

$n = 4$

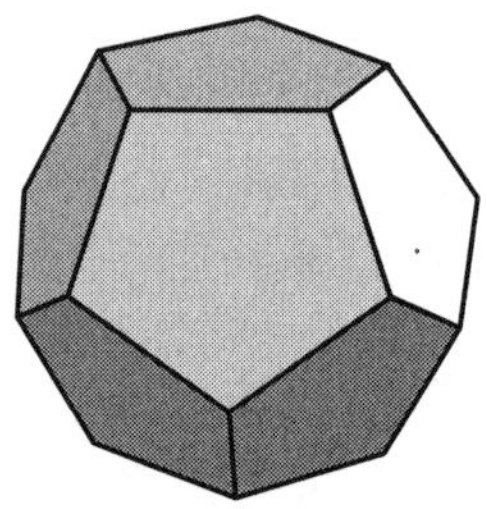

$n = 5$

- It is the last (greatest n) regular n-gon whose diagonals all have the same length.
- The Golden Ratio, Φ, appears frequently in the relationships between segments formed by the diagonals. (More on this on page vii.)

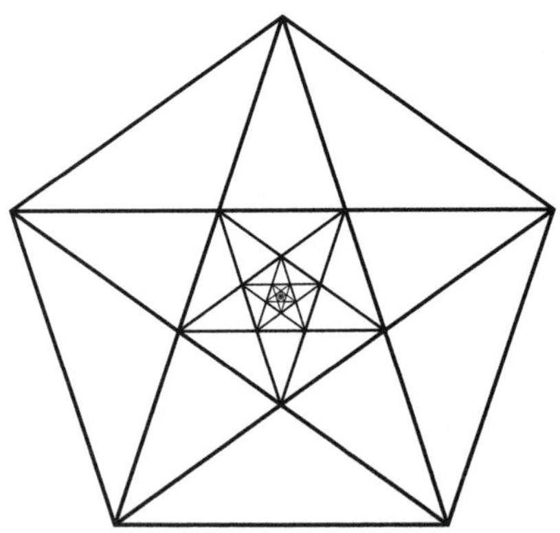

It is the inherent presence of similarity, harmony, and beauty within the regular pentagon that made it important to the ancient Greeks. Simply constructing the diagonals of the regular pentagon provides insight into its uniqueness:

Notice that the diagonals create a five-pointed star, and within the star yet another pentagon, which can again create another star and inner pentagon, and so on. This infinite series of similar shapes can be seen as a sort of representation of the mystery of life—the ability to regenerate, creating new and self-similar forms.

This connection between the pentagon and life is reinforced by prolific examples in nature. Cross sections of apples, pears and many other fruits and vegetables reveal their five-fold symmetry, as do the shapes of sand dollars, starfish, the leaves and flowers of many plants, and the hands, paws, and claws of so many creatures.

The Golden Ratio

In many ways, the geometry of the regular pentagon is a byproduct of the presence of the Golden Ratio. This ratio expresses a very special relationship. Like π, the Golden Ratio is an irrational value that was understood and appreciated even in antiquity. It is generated by solving the following proportion: a smaller number is to a larger number as that larger number is to the sum of the two numbers.

$$\frac{\text{smaller number}}{\text{larger number}} = \frac{\text{larger number}}{\text{smaller number} + \text{larger number}}$$

To the ancient Greeks, this proportion represented an understanding of one's place in the universe: *I am to my world as my world is to the universe.* Looking at this idea geometrically, the challenge is to find the point on a segment that separates it into two parts, so that

{the ratio of the smaller segment's length to the larger segment's length}

is the same as

{the ratio of the larger segment's length to the whole segment's length}

That is:

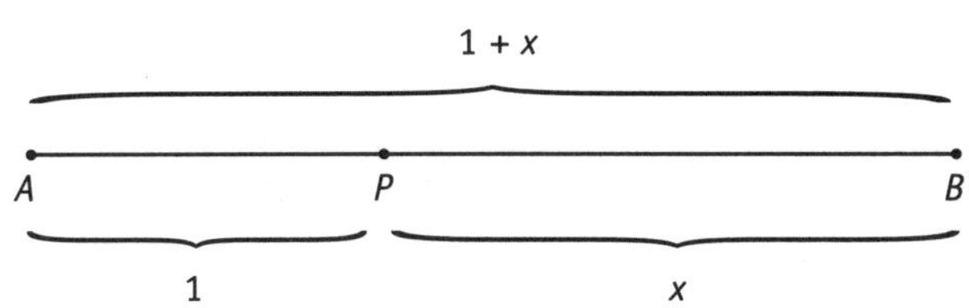

$$\text{where} \quad \frac{AP}{PB} = \frac{PB}{AB}$$

If we assume $AP = 1$ and let $PB = x$, then

$$\frac{1}{x} = \frac{x}{1+x}$$

$$x^2 = 1 + x$$

$$x^2 - x - 1 = 0$$

Using the quadratic formula, we discover the positive root as

$$x = \Phi = \frac{1+\sqrt{5}}{2} \approx 1.618$$

This value, named "Φ" in honor of the master Greek artist, Phidias, who incorporated this ratio into many of his works, appears frequently in natural settings and in many mathematical connections.

One connection of special interest is that Φ appears repeatedly within the segments formed by the diagonals of the pentagon, as seen here.

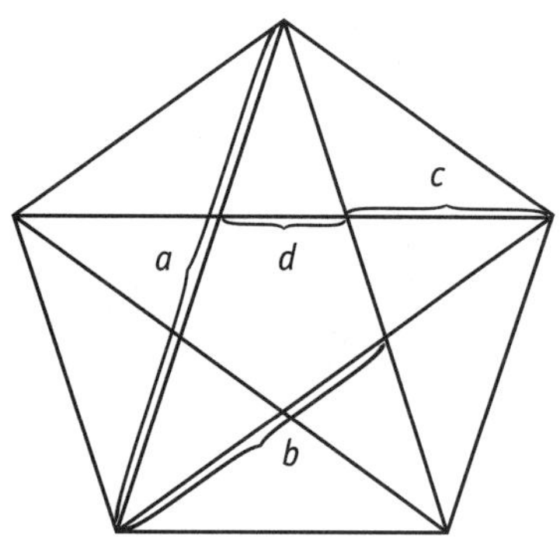

$$\frac{a}{b} = \frac{b}{c} = \frac{c}{d} = \Phi$$

This relationship can be expressed another way:

If $d = 1$, then

$c = \Phi$

$b = (\Phi + 1) = \Phi^2$

$a = (2\Phi + 1) = \Phi^3$

Additional unique properties of Φ are shown below.

$$\Phi - 1 = \frac{1}{\Phi}$$

$$\Phi^n = \Phi^{n-1} + \Phi^{n-2}$$

$$\Phi^n = F_n\Phi + F_{n-1}$$

(where F_n is the nth term of the Fibonacci sequence: 1, 1, 2, 3, 5, 8, ...)

What' s So Special About the PentaBlocks?

The set of shapes in the PentaBlocks family were specifically chosen to take full advantage of the similarity relationships in figures derived from pentagons. They repeatedly lead back to pentagons, stars, golden triangles, and decagons of different sizes. Also, because their angles are compatible, the small inventory of PentaBlocks shapes combine to form an infinite variety of patterns.

The pentacle star is arguably the most interesting shape. Not only is it the first *concave* pattern block, but its compelling shape appeals to nearly everyone at an almost subconscious level. Think about stars and the associations people make with them:

- In sports and the performing arts, a star is someone who is clearly outstanding, who shows brilliance or excellence, as in the phrases *rising star* and *superstar*.
- There is no symbol more widely used on flags than the regular five-pointed star. It appears on the flags of more than sixty nations.
- The five-pointed star has been used since antiquity to represent authority and power, appearing in law enforcement and military decorations and symbols from many unrelated cultures. Here are three examples from the United States.

Air Force Military Insignia

United States Marshals Service Badge

Army Medal of Honor

Historical Note About Colors

The Pythagoreans valued the pentagon and its related star because of the power and philosophical meaning they saw in the shapes. To honor this connection of value and mathematics, the PentaBlocks are colored to represent jewels and materials that were of particular value to the ancient Greeks.

The pentagon is the color of amber. The Greeks called amber *elektron*, a word associated with the sun, for amber represented crystallized sunlight. In Greek mythology, after Phaeton, the son of the sun god Helios, was killed by lightning, his grief-stricken sisters were turned into poplar trees, continually weeping tears of amber.

The "tall" triangle is ivory colored. Ivory was greatly valued by the ancient Greeks and had been traded for centuries before that in many of the African and other early cultures. It enjoyed widespread popularity with the Egyptians. In contrast, the star is black for ebony, a valued wood that was appreciated for both its color and its hardness.

The "short" triangle is purple to represent amethyst. Amethyst, a type of quartz, was used extensively in jewelry by the Greeks and Romans. The Greeks regarded quartz as water which had been frozen forever by the gods. Their word for ice was *krystallos*, from which the word "crystal" is derived. According to Greek mythology, the god Bacchus had been angered by some insult and decided to set tigers upon the next person he saw. That person was Amethyst, on her way to worship at the shrine of Diana. As the tigers sprang to attack, Diana turned the young girl into clear crystal. Sorry about the results of his actions, Bacchus poured wine as a tribute over the crystallized Amethyst, giving the stone its deep purple color. The Greeks believed that amethyst would prevent intoxication and, in later legend, could relieve frustrated passion.

The "thin" rhombus is colored pink for rose quartz. Because of its scarcity in Greece, rose quartz was highly valued. The "fat" rhombus, on the other hand, has the color of malachite. Known for its vivid green, the relative softness of malachite made it easy to carve, and it was frequently used for beads, or powdered to use as eye shadow.

The Changing View of Teaching Mathematics:

The Student-Centered, Activity-Based Classroom

"What should students know and be able to do?" This perennial issue is at the core of the current "Standards" movement. It addresses not only the content issue of *what,* but also the process issues of *how:*

- *How* can we best teach the content?
- *How* can we best assess the depth of students' understanding?

This Standards movement began in earnest with the 1989 release of the National Council of Teachers of Mathematics (NCTM) *Curriculum and Evaluation Standards for School Mathematics*, which stimulated professional discussion about the *what* and *how* of teaching mathematics. A headline summary of this important document might be

TASKS and DISCOURSE

LEAD STUDENTS TO MAKE THEIR OWN MEANING OF MATHEMATICS

In the NCTM vision of an engaging classroom, the teacher creates an activity-based environment and orchestrates enticing discussion. To respond effectively, students need to make connections, look for patterns, use reasoning, and apply a variety of problem-solving approaches. Students must also be able to communicate mathematically, presenting problems and their resolutions in verbal, written, symbolic, graphical, and tabular forms. Students need to create models—intellectual and physical models—and use them in their work.

According to the *Standards*, geometry is basic to how we "represent and make sense of the world." It is so important that two of the fourteen standards for grades 9–12 are dedicated to its study:

- *Geometry from a Synthetic Perspective,* which focuses on shapes, their properties, and real world applications; and
- *Geometry from an Algebraic Perspective,* which analyzes figures and properties by using coordinate systems, transformations, and vectors.

The NCTM is not alone in focusing on the student-centered, activity-based classroom model.

- Important ideas about teaching and learning geometry have been expressed by Pierre and Dina Van Heile and by Alan Hoffer. Summaries of their work appear in the appendices. Howard Gardner's "multiple intelligences" also relate specifically to the use of manipulatives.
- The motto of the Coalition of Essential Schools, "Student as Worker, Teacher as Coach," suggests that teachers create the game plan and suggest or guide what might be done, but the students are the ones playing the game—through active participation and hard work.
- Many noted writers are focused on the importance of classroom dialogue. One example is Jay McTighe, director of the Maryland Assessment Consortium, who has developed strategies for extending student thinking. Some of these strategies are given in the appendices.
- Constructivists believe that students construct their own meaning from their experiences and explorations, in a sequence that may be summarized as Play → Inquiry → Investigation → Personal Discovery → Conjecture → Personal Understanding → Personal Mastery.
- Cooperative or collaborative learning, especially in small groups, encourages students to communicate about mathematics, and it helps create a classroom community of learners, in which everyone helps everyone to understand as much as possible, as deeply as possible.

- The idea of making connections is a primary issue in the AAAS *Benchmarks for Science Literacy* and the ASCD Program *Dimensions of Learning*. A problem that seems small and simple can become a rich source of exploration when time and attention are given for extracting as much math as possible from the situation. Finding connections means following the threads that connect this kind of problem to a widening web of relationships and applications, both mathematical and otherwise. This often requires thinking deeply about (or *unpacking*) specific situations and/or generalizations, which leads to a greater understanding at all levels.

Planning for Instruction With Manipulatives

Recent researchers have investigated how students learn geometry. They conclude that physical exploration with manipulatives is a vital element of student learning. It provides concrete ways for students to discover and understand mathematical concepts. PentaBlocks (and pattern blocks in general) connect abstract ideas about numbers, shapes, and patterns to something students can see, touch, count, and measure. Students get involved in *doing* mathematics in a natural way that integrates visual, kinesthetic, and analytical thinking. Because of this, PentaBlocks make mathematical ideas easier to internalize, and their actual manipulations allow students to find relationships, patterns, and an esthetic to which they would not otherwise have access.

The most important element of your instructional planning for using these blocks is how you investigate them yourself. First, think about the topics you need or want to discuss. Then preview the investigations to familiarize yourself with the mathematics in the suggested activities, and determine which ideas are worthy of your class time. The more you play creatively and purposely with the PentaBlocks yourself, the easier it will be to predict how your students will respond to working with them.

The way you use PentaBlocks will depend on how much time you have and how much of your course you find embedded within the activities. Pattern blocks in general are particularly valuable in that

- they are visually stimulating
- they foster individual creativity
- they encourage exploration with patterns
- they provide opportunity for communicating mathematical information
- they let students compare angle measures and lengths concretely and directly
- they clearly illustrate subdivision of areas
- they can be used to illustrate symmetry operations
- their manipulation allows for accidental discoveries (about patterns, and about size/shape relationships)
- they stimulate inquiry: "What happens to the pattern when I do this?"; "Why do (or don't) these shapes combine this way?"; "Why does (or doesn't) this work the way the other example did?"

The use of pattern blocks is only one of many tools for exploring geometrical ideas. The blocks work best in a high school course when you integrate them with direct instruction and link them to other hands-on activities—activities like compass-and-straightedge constructions, mirrors, paper folding, the use of dynamic geometry software (like the *Geometer's Sketchpad*™), constructing string sculptures and models of solids, and other types of challenges.

A Note About Assessment

As suggested by NCTM, curriculum, instruction, and assessment are all threads that are interwoven into a complete course of study. The fact that you are incorporating PentaBlocks into your instruction already indicates that you are using an activity-based approach.

In many ways, each of the investigations provided in this guide is like a performance task.

1. Students usually work as part of a pair or group.
2. Students communicate results in writing, drawings, and tables. One approach might be group lab reports with student entries under columns marked *Date*, *Work Done*, and *Questions*, and a teacher' s response column as well. You could also ask for a *Summary of Learnings* statement focused on relationships, conjectures, and conclusions.
3. Each student could maintain an individual journal to be used as part of a portfolio, especially if that is the format students use to record their learnings.
4. The questions and activities posed in the Students' Guides range from analytical to open-ended and creative. Try to be clear about how the items will be assessed or used in grading: You may want to use one method for the open-ended activities and a more quantifiable approach for analytical questions. One possible analytical scoring scale is shown here:

Analytic Scoring Scale

Understanding the Problem	0: Complete misunderstanding of the problem 1: Part of the problem misunderstood or misinterpreted 2: Complete understanding of the problem
Planning a Solution	0: No attempt, or totally inappropriate plan 1: Partially correct plan based on part of the problem being interpreted correctly 2: Plan could have led to a correct solution if implemented properly
Getting an Answer	0: No answer, or wrong answer based on an inappropriate plan 1: Copying error, computational error; partial answer for a problem with multiple answers 2: Correct answer and correct label for the answer

Using This Book

This guide provides a collection of structured activities, suggestions, and resources to help you integrate the use of PentaBlocks into a high school level geometry course.

The instructional material is organized as three sets of investigations focused on three different domains: Properties and Set Relationships, Similarity, and Patterns. Within each of those domains, the first few investigations include basic terminology. Additional vocabulary is introduced in subsequent investigations to describe more complex concepts. For each domain there are advanced topics and/or special projects described in the Teacher's Guides and the appendices.

The investigations are designed to give students an integrated mathematical learning experience:

- The investigations explore mathematical content at a variety of levels of complexity.
- The challenges and questions are mostly open-ended, so there are a variety of appropriate responses.

- Students are encouraged to develop their own approaches and strategies.
- Students create their own designs, some within a variety of constraints.
- Students must communicate about mathematical relationships through talking, writing, drawing, and creating symbol systems.
- Students can (and should) work in a variety of groupings—as individuals, in pairs, in quads (groups of four) or other small groups, and as larger groups like octas (groups of eight) or the class as a whole.

The first investigation, *Getting Started*, is specifically designed to be used *first* in any continuing program. It allows students to engage with the PentaBlocks immediately, starting with the most basic and important notions and terminology, and exploring relationships among the shapes. The *very first* lab session is your best opportunity to

- set the appropriate tone, and describe expected behaviors
- introduce the general format of a lab session
- establish start-up, distribution, collection, and wind-down procedures
- establish the grouping processes and create initial pairs and quads
- define what is meant by *doing* an investigation: exploring both generally and with a purpose, and seeking to understand connections and relations enough to state a conjecture
- describe your expectations about the use of the *Investigations Journal* or other lab report formats
- describe how students' work from the lab session will be assessed and how that assessment will be used in grading.

Each investigation has two parts, a Teacher's Guide and a Students' Guide. The Teacher's Guide highlights organizational and pedagogical issues and is structured in this way:

ORGANIZATION

- *Mathematical Focus*
- *Special Materials:* a list of any required material *other than* the Students' Guide and a set of PentaBlocks per group. Templates for recording block outlines are not required, but they are extremely helpful for keeping illustrations neat and compact.
- *Approximate Time:* suggested times only. Like most hands-on activities, these investigations continue to teach even after several repetitions, and the pace will depend on the group as well as the teacher.
- *Suggested Group Size:* When several are listed, they are listed in order of preference.

INSTRUCTION

- *Lesson Summary:* a brief description of what the students and teacher will be doing
- *Terminology:* a list highlighting the terms described or defined in the Students' Guide
- *Specific Notes to Teachers:* general hints, strategies, and focus points that should help in planning for doing the investigation in the classroom
- *Activity Sequence:* step-by-step suggestions for orchestrating the activity
- *Possible Responses:* typical reactions or answers to the ***Action*** tasks outlined for students. Since many of the task questions are open-ended, this list of responses is intended to suggest, not to be comprehensive.

- *Possible Extensions:* suggested opportunities for further pursuit, deeper understanding, and more challenging items that are related to the investigation

The Students' Guide provides background information as well as the sequence of tasks that make up the investigation. This is the structure of the Students' Guide:

Background Information

- new terminology and definitions
- some introduction to the general topic and basic concepts

Action

- the specific sequence of tasks designed to practice, use, show, or apply the related mathematics in the context of the PentaBlocks
- a reminder to write an entry into the *Investigations Journal* (see Note 3 below)

Note 1. For many of the investigations it may be helpful to provide large sheets of newsprint for groups to record and post their illustrations and/or conjectures.
Note 2. It is always helpful to make sure that students know exactly what the task is and what they must do. You might have one or more students describe the specific task or question in their own words before launching them into their group work.
Note 3. Students should maintain some form of *Investigations Journal*, in which they can record

- how they felt about the directions or the activity itself
- what they learned from the activity, including conjectures
- questions that were raised but not fully answered
- anything that was confusing
- comments about interactions within their group or between groups.

A Note About Terminology

This set of investigations is intended to supplement your work with the textbook. Even though most necessary vocabulary is defined in the Students' Guides, there are certain basic geometric terms that are assumed to be part of a student's working vocabulary. Because of this, words like *segment* and *angle,* or *acute* and *obtuse* are not defined.

When students are exchanging ideas in a limited time period, it's important to create an atmosphere that promotes easy and rapid communication. To help create that kind of environment, this book introduces a number of "shortcut" terms—terms that communicate quickly. An example is *descriptor*, which means any descriptive word that categorizes or defines attributes. So if you hold up a polygon in front of the class and asks for descriptors, students can immediately launch into responses like *Convex! Equiangular! Pentagonal!* Likewise, the term *supersupplementary* is introduced to describe two angles whose measures add up to 360°. Terms like these save time.

For similar reasons, this book uses the term *equal* rather than *congruent* to relate angles or segments that have the same measure. In informal group work, it's important to exchange ideas quickly and neatly; and in an eager dialogue, much may be lost by spending valuable time on precision of language. Idea takes precedence over form in these groups, and you can determine how much time should be used later to address details.

Hints on Managing Activities, Movement, and Materials

Using pattern blocks creates a certain degree of noise and movement in a classroom. The following hints will help keep the noise level tolerable and provide enough structure to capitalize on the full instructional value of the PentaBlocks.

- Use a Math Lab environment, with clearly defined expectations about behaviors. When you add your own activities to the ones in these investigations, define your tasks and questions carefully. Make sure students understand what they are to do.
- Have a regular storage location for the blocks that is known to all of the students.
- Have clearly defined distribution and cleanup procedures (including a floor check). These might include rules about setting up tables, students moving into work groups, assigned responsibilities for getting and returning blocks and other materials. Plan time for this movement.
- Use small groups to increase the range of creative responses and to provide communications opportunities. Research and experience suggests that a group of four students is ideal and is appropriate for one set of PentaBlocks. You may choose to combine groups progressively during an investigation, moving from pairs to quads to octas. Work groups could be deliberately assigned with students of differing abilities and strengths. Groups should last long enough for comfortable working relationships to form (maybe a marking period or a semester).
- Require a written lab report or investigation report summarizing the explorations and/or conclusions from each lab session or from a series of labs. Have students record patterns they create; using the templates makes this quick, easy, and accurate.
- Make it clear to students how the blocks are being used to explore mathematics. Many secondary students feel uncomfortable about "playing with blocks", which they perceive as an elementary school activity. Use the blocks appropriately, with limited "free play" time; they become trivial when overused with instructions like "Create a pattern", especially if the patterns are not used in any instructional way.
- Orchestrating conversation (what NCTM calls *discourse*) is important within and among groups. Here are some specific strategies:
  - *The Jigsaw*
    1. Within a group—each member gets a specific task or question to do; the learnings are shared and the work is compiled.
    2. Between groups—each group presents its approach or result to a question or problem.
  - *Sending An Emissary*
    One member of a group is sent over to another group to get or give help, a suggestion, etc.
  - *The Round Robin*
    In turn, each group or person either contributes *one* new idea or else passes; keep going around until there are no more new ideas.
  - *Gallery Exhibits*
    Each group or individual posts work in an exhibit area. In this way, everyone gets to see the work done by all, making it easier to identify general trends or to compare and contrast results.

Creating Thought-full Classrooms

Strategies to Extend Student Thinking

(adapted by Shelly Berman from Jay McTighe, Maryland State DOE)

Use "Wait Time" 1 and 2

Leave at least *3 full seconds* between asking a question and giving a prompt, and *another 3 full seconds* between getting a student response and giving approval, or correction, or asking for the reactions of other students.

Use "Think-Pair-Share"

Allow individual thinking time and talking with a partner time before orchestrating any whole class discussion.

Ask Follow-ups

"Tell me more." "Can you give an example?" "Can you elaborate?" "Why?" "What might be the consequences of that?"

Play the Devil's Advocate

Require students to defend their reasoning against different points of view, or to propose debate challenges.

Make Thinking Visible with "Think Aloud" and "Unpacking"

Describe your own thinking, and try to make students' thinking and thought sequences visible and accessible to others. Graphic organizers also always help.

Prompt Additional Student Responses

"How many other responses can we generate?" or "Who has a different idea?"

Respond Without Immediate Judgment

Respond to student answers without immediately giving *your* approval or correction, so other students can react to their peers' responses.

Ask Students to Summarize

"John, could you please summarize Mary's point?" or "Who can summarize our discussion today?" This promotes active listening.

Survey the Class

"How many people agree with the author's point of view?" This could be a simple but visible "thumbs up" or "thumbs down."

Allow Students to Call on Students

"Shawn, will you please call on someone else to respond?"

Call on Students Randomly

This gets more students to be active participants and avoids the pattern of calling on only the few who always volunteer.

Encourage Student Questioning

Have students develop their own questions that are about facts, that require inference, or that ask for an opinion.

Ask Students, "What's Interesting to You?"

Students may be motivated by topics that they develop themselves.

Teacher's Guide

ORGANIZATION

- *Mathematical Focus:*
  Reviewing basic terminology related to polygons
- *Special Materials:*
  All investigations in this book will require PentaBlocks; templates of PentaBlocks shapes are optional, but they keep illustrations neat and accurate.
- *Approximate Time:* 50 minutes
- *Suggested Group Size:* Quads

INSTRUCTION

- *Lesson Summary:*
  - Students describe each shape completely using appropriate terminology.
  - Students explore area relationships by looking for simple combinations that cover blocks exactly.
  - Students do an organized search to explore how pairs of shapes fit together.
- *Terminology:*
  - See the Students' Guide for specific descriptions and definitions of these words:

    complementary, supplementary, supersupplementary
    congruent, similar
    interior angle, diagonal
    isosceles, equilateral, equiangular, regular
    polygon, convex, concave
    rhombus, rectangle, square
    star, regular star, point, dent
- *Specific Notes to Teachers:*
  This investigation is designed to be used *first* in any continuing program. It allows students to use the PentaBlocks immediately, starts with the most basic and important notions and terminology, and explores the relationships among the shapes. The very first lab session is your best opportunity to
  - set the appropriate tone and describe expected behaviors
  - introduce the general format of a lab session
  - establish start-up, distribution, collection, and wind-down procedures
  - establish the grouping processes and create initial pairs and quads
  - define what is meant by "doing" an investigation: exploring both generally and with a purpose, and seeking to understand connections and relations enough to state a conjecture
  - describe how you expect students to use the *Investigations Journal*
  - describe how students' work from lab will be assessed and used in grading.

- *Activity Sequence:*
  1. Introduce the "lab session" format. Describe the procedures, use of cooperative pairs and quads, and expected behaviors. Get students into their quads. Point out that the work they will be doing may be different from what they're used to, but emphasize that they are graded for their lab work, and that they are responsible for completing a written *Lab Report* or an *Investigations Journal* entry.
  2. As soon as possible, distribute the PentaBlocks and name each block for the class (pentagon, star, tall triangle, short triangle, thin rhombus, fat rhombus). Give students about five minutes of (unannounced) "free" play.
  3. Distribute the Student Guides. Point out the descriptive terminology and provide a few minutes for people to talk within their group about the words as they work on the first *Action* item. Review vocabulary directly only as needed. Make sure students understand the task. Have students record illustrations and descriptors (for example, "isosceles" or "convex") for each block on newsprint and display their work. Compare lists as a class so there is conversation and (perhaps) consensus among groups.
  4. Students should work on ***Action* 2** only briefly, spending more time on ***Action* 3**. ***Action* 4** could go fairly quickly if each group is assigned one or more specific pairs of shapes. You may use the PentaBlock Combination Cards (pages 24-26) to assign pairs of blocks.

     Another way to assign pairs is to use a matrix like the one shown here. You will need only half of the matrix: the other half is duplication. Also, the shaded cells along the diagonal have been discussed already in ***Action* 3**; this leaves fifteen pairs of shapes. Assign a group to explore each pair and put their group number in the appropriate cell(s). Have students illustrate ways the pairs of blocks fit, and display their results for the class.

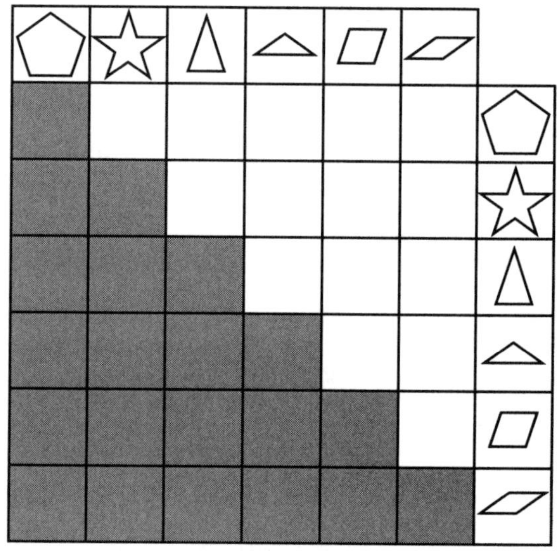

  5. Clarify the writing assignment as needed.
  6. Leave time for collection of materials and clean-up.

- *Possible Responses:*
  1. *Pentagon:* regular; convex; all angles obtuse; all five diagonals the same length.

     Star: concave; regular star; decagon; alternating between angles greater than 180° and less than 180°; five distinct diagonal lengths; the tall triangle fits over it to show a diagonal the length of a short PentaBlocks side; the thin rhombus fits over it to show that there are two different diagonal lengths shared by both rhombus and star.

     Tall triangle: isosceles, base shorter than legs; all angles acute; fits inside pentagon so they have the same height; no diagonals.

     Short triangle: isosceles, legs shorter than base; acute base angles, obtuse vertex angle is supersupplementary with the star dent; two of them fit inside pentagon with the tall triangle; no diagonals.

Thin rhombus: equilateral quadrilateral, but not equiangular; angles alternate between acute and obtuse; diagonals are perpendicular.

Fat rhombus: equilateral quadrilateral, but not equiangular; angles alternate between acute and obtuse; obtuse angle is supersupplementary with the star dent; diagonals are perpendicular.

The star differs most from the others, being concave and having ten sides. Either the pair of triangles or the pair of rhombuses could be considered most alike, because their respective sets of characteristics match closely.

2. The fat rhombus is a simple combination of two short triangles; the pentagon is a simple combination of a tall triangle and two short triangles.

3. Illustrations show several combinations using just the tall triangle. Students will not be able to surround a vertex completely using just the pentagon or the star, but they may come up with unexpected solutions to the problem: for example, they may create a necklace of stars that "surrounds a point" by circling it from a distance.

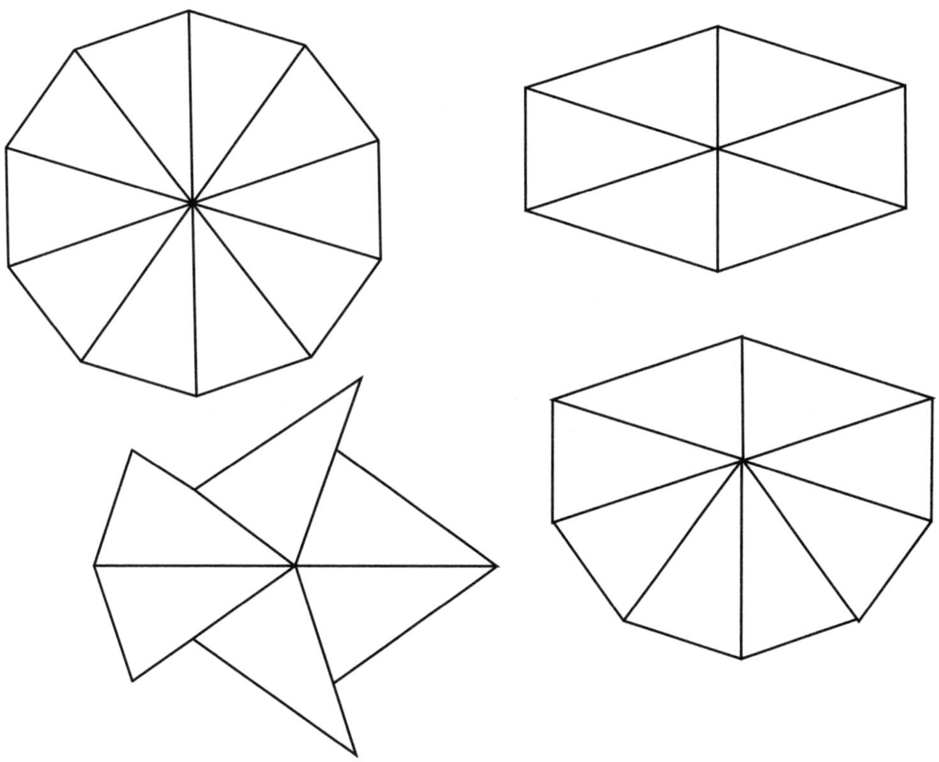

4. Here are two possible solutions using pentagons and short triangles.

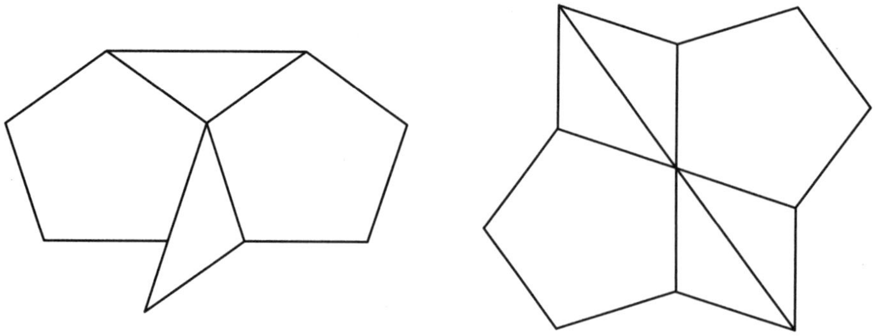

- *Possible Extensions:*
  1. The regular pentagon was well studied by the ancient Greeks, who associated it with the creation of life. Research and report on their fascination with the pentagon, examining its presence in other cultures as well.
  2. The regular five-pointed or pentacle star has a long history and has often been associated with authority and excellence. Find out what you can about this history and prepare a presentation for the class.
  3. Many types of polygonal stars have been used in the designs of many cultures throughout history. Find examples of these stars in the art of as many cultures as you can. Cite your references.

Student's Guide: Investigation

Investigation 1: Getting Started

Background Information:

Much more than mere child's play, PentaBlocks were designed to make the study of geometry and patterns enjoyable and understandable. You will be using the blocks to explore mathematical relationships, and you will need mathematical terms to describe what you notice.

The list below defines and describes many words that you have used before, and a few words that may be new to you. Refer to this list as you go through the investigations in Part I.

- A **polygon** is a closed path of connected line segments that lie in a plane and do not cross each other. The segments are its **sides**, and any two consecutive sides meet to form an **interior angle** at a **vertex**.

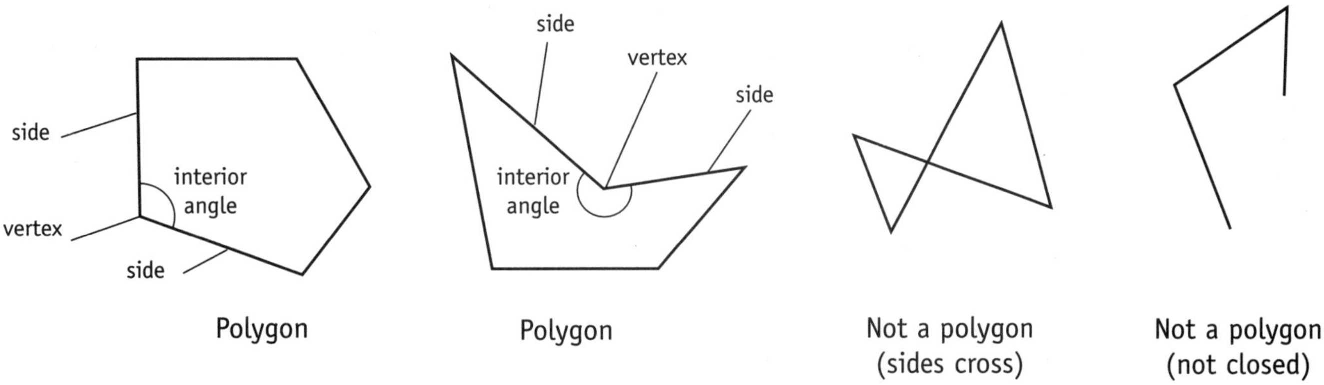

- A polygon is named generally by the number of sides it has:

  3 sides = triangle; *4 sides = quadrilateral;* *5 sides = pentagon;* *6 sides = hexagon;*
  8 sides = octagon; *10 sides = decagon;* *12 sides = dodecagon;* *N sides = N-gon.*

- Polygons are **similar** if they have exactly the same shape. Polygons are **congruent** if they have exactly the same shape *and* size.

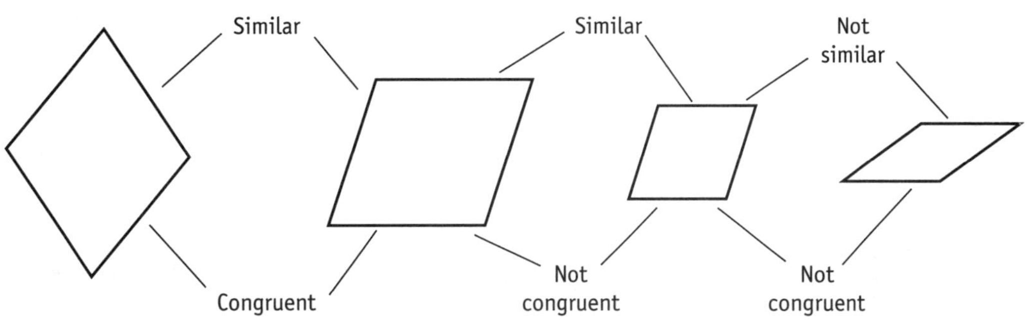

- A **diagonal** is any segment joining nonconsecutive vertices. A polygon is **convex** if all diagonals are within the interior, and **concave** if any diagonal is outside the polygon.

Dashed lines represent diagonals.

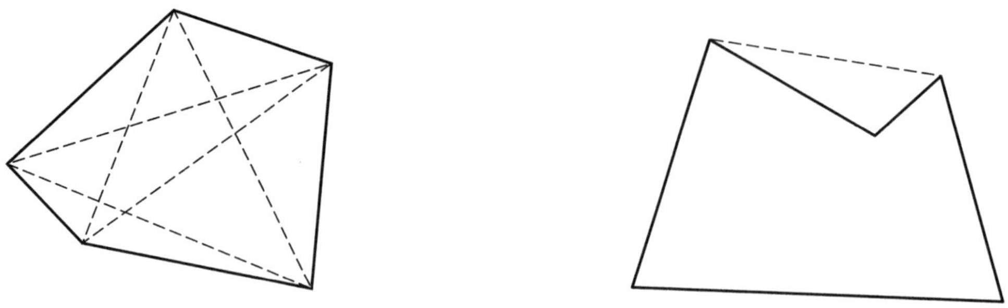

Convex polygon

Concave polygon
(a diagonal outside polygon)

- A polygon with at least two sides equal is described as **isosceles**. If *all* sides of a polygon are equal it is **equilateral**; if *all* angles are equal it is **equiangular**. A **regular** convex polygon is both equilateral *and* equiangular.
- A **rhombus** is an equilateral quadrilateral; a **rectangle** is an equiangular quadrilateral; and a **square** is a regular quadrilateral (both equilateral *and* equiangular).

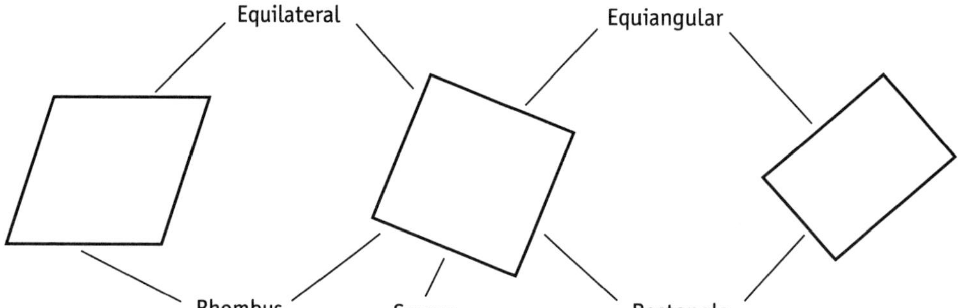

- A **star** is a concave polygon that alternates between "**points**" (with interior angles less than 180°) and "**dents**" (with interior angles more than 180°). In other words, consecutive vertices are . . . point, dent, point, dent . . . . A star is **regular** if it is equilateral and all point angles are equal and all dent angles are equal.

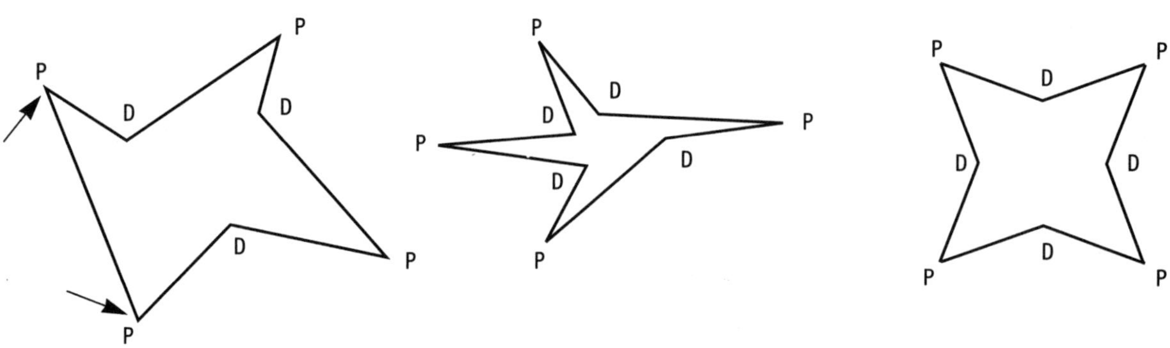

Not a star
(consecutive points)

Star
(not regular)

Star
(regular)

- When *two* angles add up to 90°, they are **complementary**, or complements of each other. When *two* angles are **supplementary**, they add up to 180°. And *two* "**supersupplementary**" angles add up to 360°.

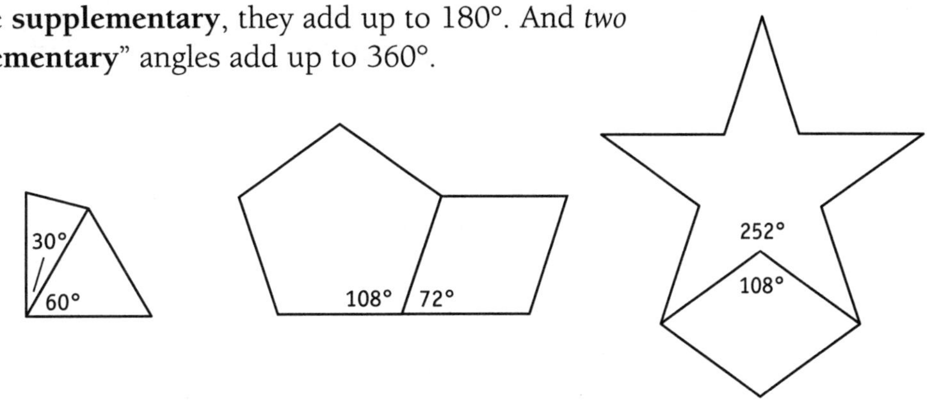

Complements Supplements Supersupplements

There are two Basic Rules to keep in mind when combining PentaBlocks to create a design:

The **Lie Flat Rule**: Blocks must be placed flat on the table, not standing up on their edges.

The **Fit Flush Rule**: Adjacent blocks must fit flush, with at least one vertex in common.

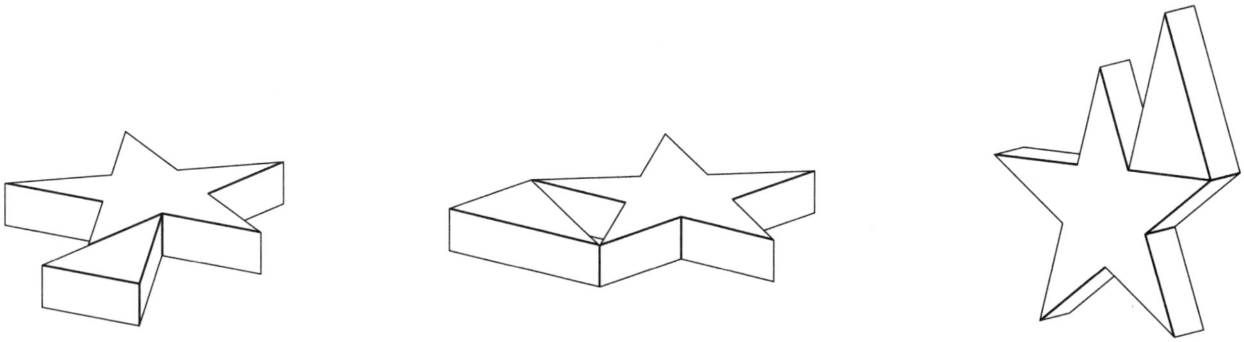

Okay

Not okay: Vertices do match, but sides are not flush.

Not okay: Tiles are not flat on the table.

Action:

Part I

1. Use the correct terminology to describe each of the PentaBlocks shapes as specifically and completely as you can. Which are most alike? Which are most different? Why?
2. Which PentaBlocks shapes are simple combinations of other PentaBlocks shapes? Illustrate any such discoveries.
3. Illustrate several ways you can use one kind of PentaBlock to surround a point, while following the two Basic Rules. Try this with each of the PentaBlocks shapes.
4. Illustrate several ways you can use two kinds of PentaBlocks to surround a point, following the two Basic Rules. Try this with every possible pair of shapes.

Part II

5. Write an entry in your *Investigations Journal* summarizing what this activity has helped you discover about the PentaBlocks and how the shapes relate to each other. Write each statement or conjecture as simply and precisely as possible.

Investigation 2: Length and Angle Measure

ORGANIZATION

- *Mathematical Focus:*
  Measuring length and angles; standard units of measure
- *Special Materials:*
  Protractors and rulers (showing millimeters)
  Optional: Hinged mirrors (1 per group, for use with Extension 3)
- *Approximate Time:* 50 minutes
- *Suggested Group Size:* Quads

INSTRUCTION

- *Lesson Summary:*
  Students manipulate the blocks physically to compare lengths and angle measures.
- *Terminology:*
  - See the Students' Guide for specific descriptions and definitions of these words:
    standard; degree
- *Specific Notes to Teachers:*
  - The *essential* elements of polygon shape are *lengths of sides* and *measures of angles.* The goal of this investigation is to have students understand more about the specific relationships among the PentaBlocks shapes due to their side and angle measurements.
  - The longer side is *not* a rational multiple of the shorter side, so students will not be able to line up a series of short sides against a series of long sides and get an exact match. This idea could form a useful introduction to the meaning of *irrational* numbers. Introduce the use of the symbol Φ, the Golden Ratio, to represent the length of the longer side if the shorter side is set at 1.
  - ***Action* 2a** establishes the important connection between a) the 360° measure of a full rotation and b) the 360° sum of the angles of the polygons surrounding a point in a tessellation. Also, manipulating combinations of shapes can help students figure out the measures; they aren't restricted to using only one shape at a time.
  - In answering ***Action* 2d**, it helps to represent the angle measures as multiples of the base angle ($\alpha = 36°$). Then, using a chart to show all possible combinations of 1α, 2α, 3α, 4α, and 7α that add up to 10α helps students approach the problem in an organized and thorough manner.
  - A hinged mirror can be created using a pair of cosmetic mirrors. Place them face to face with the edges aligned. Use a strip of vinyl tape along one common edge to make a flexible hinge so that the mirrors can be opened like a book. The Reflect It™ hinged mirror is a well designed and safer alternative.

- *Activity Sequence:*
  1. Introduce the use of *measurement* and *standard units.*
  2. Discuss the importance of side length and angle measurement as the *essential characteristics that determine shape,* especially for polygons.
  3. Distribute Students' Guides.
  4. If you distribute hinged mirrors, you should illustrate their proper handling and use.

- *Possible Responses:*
  1. a. There are only two different side lengths found in the set of PentaBlocks shapes.

     b. The larger length is close to 1.6 times the shorter length. You can show it is greater than 1.5 times by placing two of the larger lengths next to three of the shorter lengths.

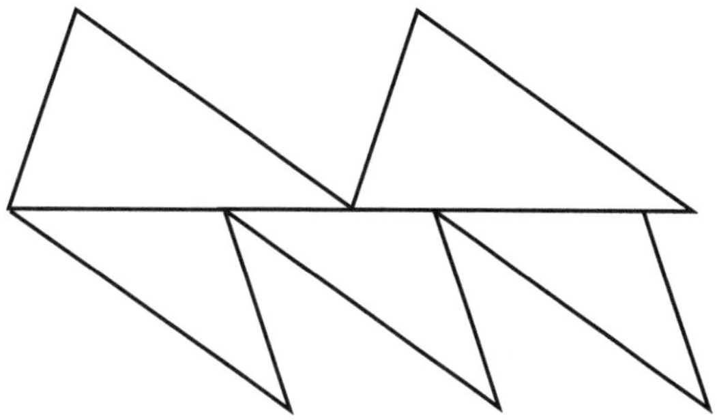

This idea might be represented algebraically to show yet another mathematical connection:

$$2L > 3S$$

$$L > \frac{3}{2}S$$

$$L > 1.5S$$

Placing 10 of the larger lengths next to 16 of the shorter lengths is a much closer fit, implying the following calculation:

$$10L \approx 16S$$

$$L \approx 1.6S$$

Because the ratio of long side to short side is irrational, the match will never be exact, no matter how many blocks are used.

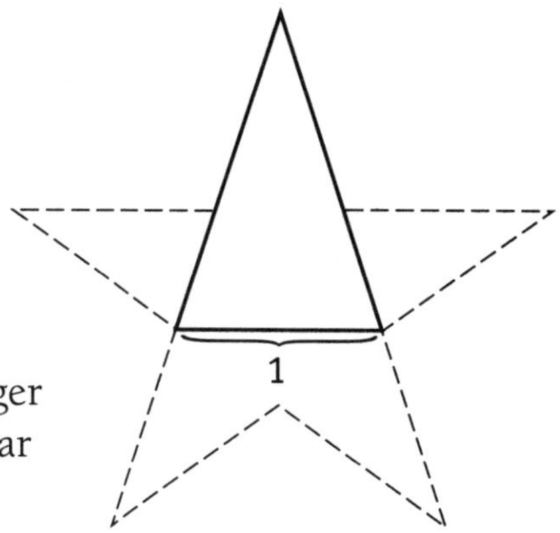

c. The diagonal of the pentagon is the same length as the longer side of either triangle, and placing a tall triangle over the star shows that one of the diagonal lengths of the star is 1, the length of the short side of the tall triangle.

2. a PentaBlock arrangements will vary.

   b. The angle measures are 36°, 72°, 108°, 144°, and 252°. They are all multiples of 36°. If you use the symbol α to represent the 36° fundamental angle, then the angle measures are 1α, 2α, 3α, 4α, and 7α. The illustration on the next page shows the PentaBlocks shapes and their angles in degrees and as multiples of α.

PentaBlocks angles as multiples of α

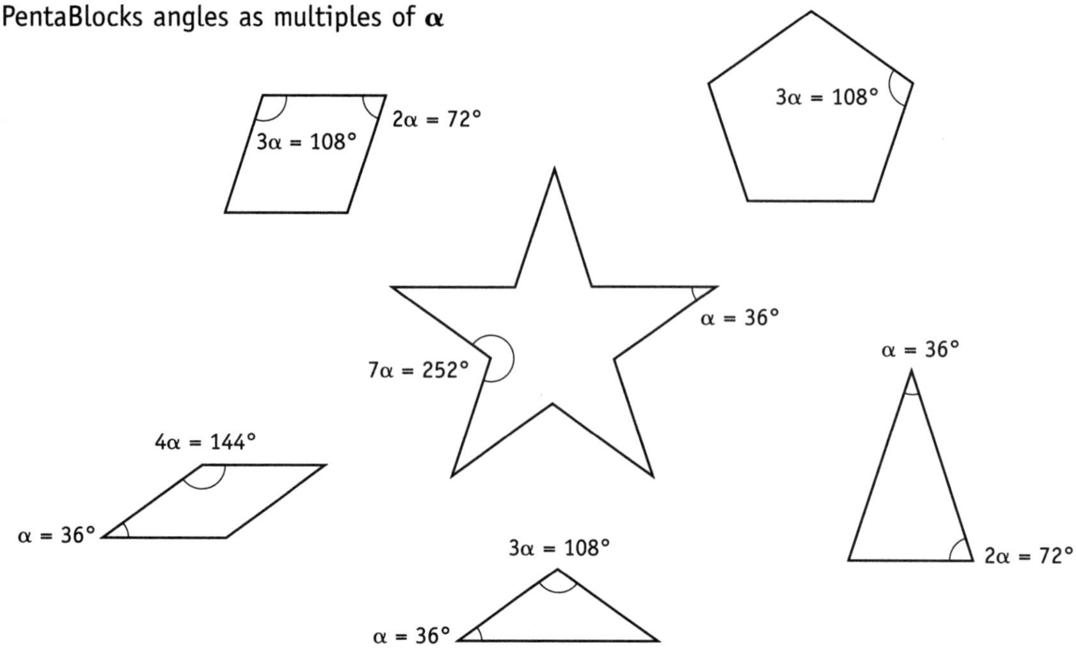

c. There are no complementary pairs. In fact, there are no combinations of angles at all that add up to 90°, so you won't get perpendicular lines in any pentagonal design. (You may, however, get perpendicular lines of symmetry.)

The two supplementary pairs are found in the two rhombuses: {36°, 144°} and {72°, 108°}.

The only supersupplementary pair is 108° and 252°.

d. Finding combinations of angle measures that add up to 360° can be simplified by looking for the combinations of 1α, 2α, 3α, 4α, and 7α that add up to 10α. These are represented as rows in the chart below. For example, Row F represents the fact that a point could be surrounded by five 36° angles, one 72° angle and one 108° angle.

	1α (36°)	2α (72°)	3α (108°)	4α (144°)	7α (252°)
A	10	-	-	-	-
B	8	1	-	-	-
C	7	-	1	-	-
D	6	-	-	1	-
E	6	2	-	-	-
F	5	1	1	-	-
G	4	3	-	-	-
H	4	1	-	1	-
I	4	-	2	-	-
J	3	2	1	-	-
K	3	-	1	1	-
L	3	-	-	-	1
M	2	4	-	-	-

	1α (36°)	2α (72°)	3α (108°)	4α (144°)	7α (252°)
N	2	2	-	1	-
O	2	1	2	-	-
P	2	-	-	2	-
Q	1	3	1	-	-
R	1	1	1	1	-
S	1	1	-	-	1
T	1	-	3	-	-
U	-	5	-	-	-
V	-	3	-	1	-
W	-	2	2	-	-
X	-	1	-	2	-
Y	-	-	2	1	-
Z	-	-	1	-	1

This means that the only combinations of PentaBlocks shapes that could surround a point must have angles in the combinations listed above. For example, Row E could be describing the combination shown at right:

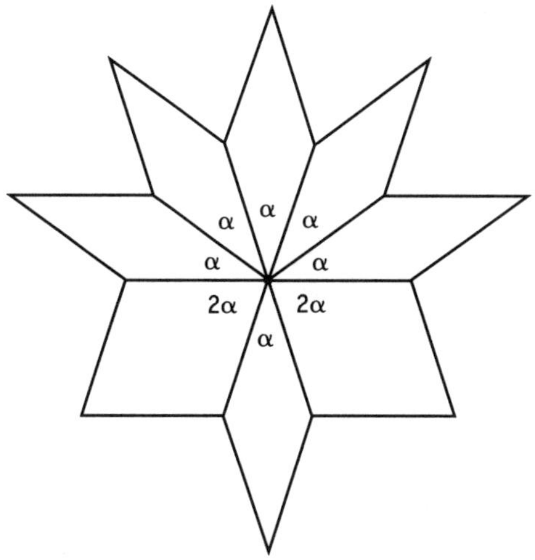

- *Possible Extensions:*

1. The Golden Ratio, or Divine Proportion, has a well-documented presence in many disciplines. The symbol **Φ** is used to represent this number, in honor of the ancient Greek artist Phidias, who incorporated it into his works. A number of the books listed in the bibliography provide ample material for an in-depth study of the historical, cultural, philosophical, and mathematical connections related to **Φ**. Research as many interesting connections as you can find.
2. The adjacent placement of the short and long side lengths shows that they do not have a 2:3 ratio. In fact, we know that they have an **irrational** relationship. The Greeks and other early mathematicians were fascinated with the "incommensurate" values, which included π, square roots of nonsquare numbers, and the Divine Proportion. Research the early approaches to studying what we now refer to as irrationality. This should include the cultural and philosophical implications as well as mathematical connections.
3. An exploration with a hinged mirror or Reflect It™ will generate a design with
   - 5-fold rotational symmetry when the 72° angle of a block is at the vertex of the hinge
   - 10-fold rotational symmetry when a 36° angle of a block is at the vertex of the hinge
   - simple bilateral symmetry when the angles of a combination of blocks have a sum of 180° and meet at the vertex of the hinge.

   Illustrate some of these designs.

Investigation 2: Length and Angle Measure

Background Information:

The most basic functions of mathematics are counting, measuring, and calculating. Measurement is the process of assigning a number in terms of a **standard unit value**. Angles, sides, and diagonals are things you can measure directly for any polygon.

For your preliminary explorations you need to know only that:

Angles are measured in **degrees** (°).

There are 360° in a full rotation about a point.

Equal angles coincide. (The vertex and sides fit over each other exactly.)

Equal lengths coincide. (The sides match up exactly.)

Action:

Part I

1. **a.** How many different side lengths are found in the set of PentaBlocks shapes?
   b. Assign the value 1 to the smallest side length. Illustrate how to use the blocks themselves to find or estimate any other side lengths. After estimating using only the blocks, compare your results to what you measure with a ruler.
   c. Is the length of a side of any block the same as the length of a diagonal of any other block?
2. **a.** You can find the measure of any PentaBlocks angle by arranging the blocks to make an appropriate physical model. For example, this figure shows fat rhombuses meeting in such a way that five of the acute angles completely surround a point. Because the sum of these five equal angles is 360°, each angle must measure (360° ÷ 5), or 72°.

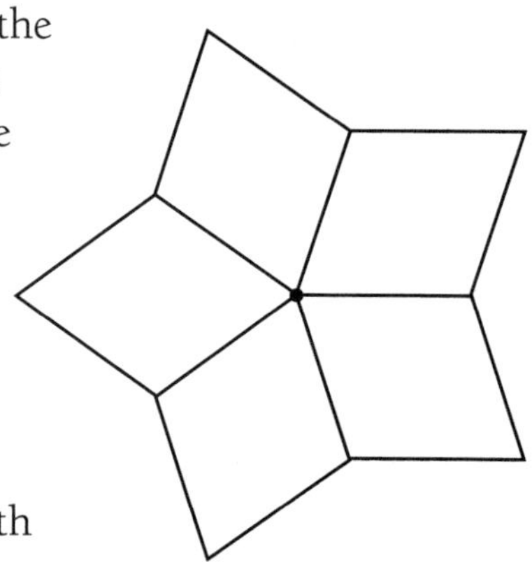

   Make and record arrangements of PentaBlocks that will help you find each different angle measure in the set. Of course, once you know the measure of one angle, you can use it to find other measures. After doing your calculations, compare your results with what you measure using a protractor.
   b. List the different angle measures from smallest to largest. What is the greatest common factor? List the angle measures as multiples of the greatest common factor.
   c. Which pairs of angles, if any, are complementary? supplementary? supersupplementary (a *pair* with a sum of 360°)?
   d. What combinations of angle measures add up to 360°? What does this tell you about how the PentaBlocks shapes might combine to surround a point?

Part II

3. Write an entry in your *Investigations Journal* summarizing what this activity has helped you discover about the side lengths, diagonal lengths, and angle measures of the PentaBlocks, and how they fit together. Write each statement or conjecture as simply and precisely as possible.

ORGANIZATION

- *Mathematical Focus:*
  Measuring or comparing area; Area Addition Postulate; approximating the area of irregularly shaped objects by counting covered squares on a grid.
- *Special Materials:*
  Quarter-inch grid paper (optional: a second size of grid paper)
- *Approximate Time:* 50 minutes
- *Suggested Group Size:* Quads, pairs, or individuals

INSTRUCTION

- *Lesson Summary:*
  Students approximate the areas of the blocks by counting squares on grid paper, and they compare the approximated areas. They also look for block combinations that have equivalent areas.
- *Terminology:*
  - See the Students' Guide for specific descriptions and definitions of these words:

    Area Addition Postulate; area
- *Specific Notes to Teachers:*
  - In this activity, students explore the idea of area addition and use it to approximate areas of the blocks.
  - Area equivalence is used to generate equations. Students then manipulate the equations to verify the relative values of areas.
- *Activity Sequence:*
  1. Distribute the Students' Guides.
  2. Make sure students are confident with their understanding of area, the difference between measuring area and measuring length (or distance), and the use of square units.
  3. Before students read the Background Information for this investigation, you may want to cut up a piece of paper and ask how the total area was affected (if at all). After reading the Background Information, ask students to discuss the Area Addition Postulate within their group.
  4. You might want students to make their lists in ***Action* 2a** before distributing the grid paper. To bring the issue of standard units clearly into focus, consider distributing different-sized grids to different groups, guaranteeing different sets of approximate values and the need for discussion.
  5. Students may need some help in creating ways to symbolize the shapes for equations in ***Action* 3**. You may want each group to create their own, or it may be helpful for the whole class to use the same symbols. One suggested symbol system is this: Pentagon = P; Star = S; Tall triangle = TT; Short triangle = sT; Fat rhombus = FR; Thin rhombus = tR.
  6. You may want to discuss real-world approximation procedures, how calculations with estimation errors magnify inaccuracy, significant figures, etc.

- *Possible Responses:*
  1. $\dfrac{\text{Area of short triangle}}{\text{Area of fat rhombus}} = \dfrac{1}{2}$
  2. **a.** Answers vary.

     b. Star: about 2 square inches or 4 short triangles
     Pentagon: about 1.7 square inches or 3.5 short triangles
     Fat rhombus: about 1 square inch or exactly 2 short triangles
     Tall triangle: about 0.8 square inch or 1.5 short triangles
     Thin rhombus: about 0.6 square inch or 1 short triangle

     c. Using quarter-inch grid paper, the following estimates are in terms of quarter-inch squares:
     star: 31; pentagon: 27; fat rhombus: 16; tall triangle: 12.5; thin rhombus: 8; short triangle: 8.

     The smaller the grid, the more accurate the approximations will be.
  3. **a.** There are many possible responses. Some of them are shown below:

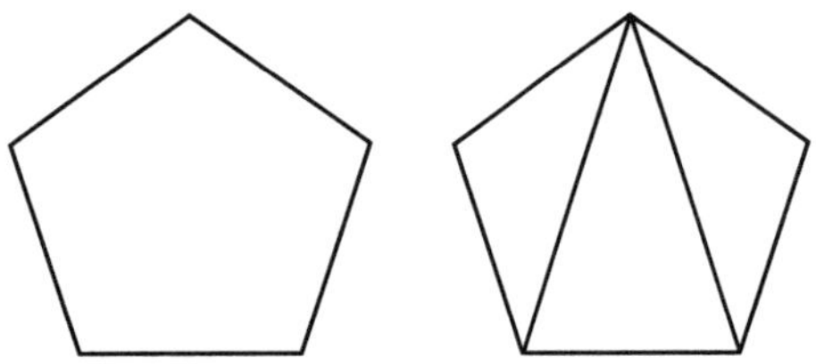

1 pentagon = 1 tall triangle + 2 short triangles

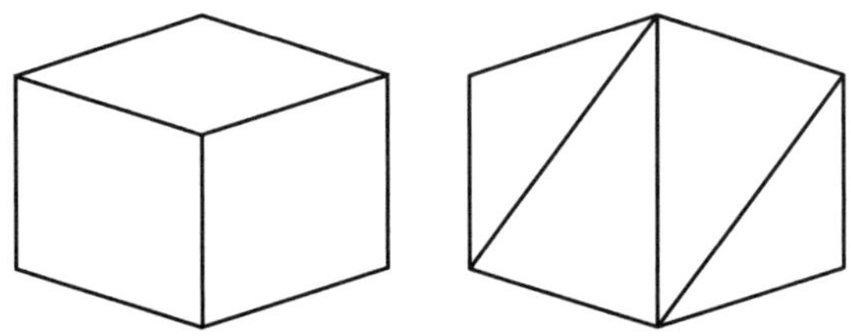

2 fat rhombuses + 1 thin rhombus = 2 tall triangles + 2 short triangles

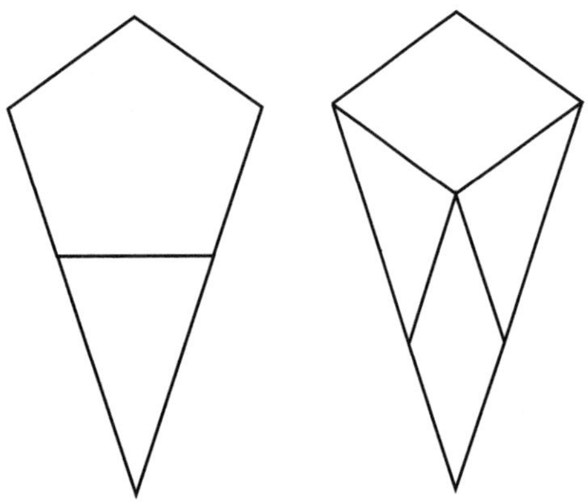

1 pentagon + 1 tall triangle = 1 fat rhombus + 1 thin rhombus + 2 short triangles

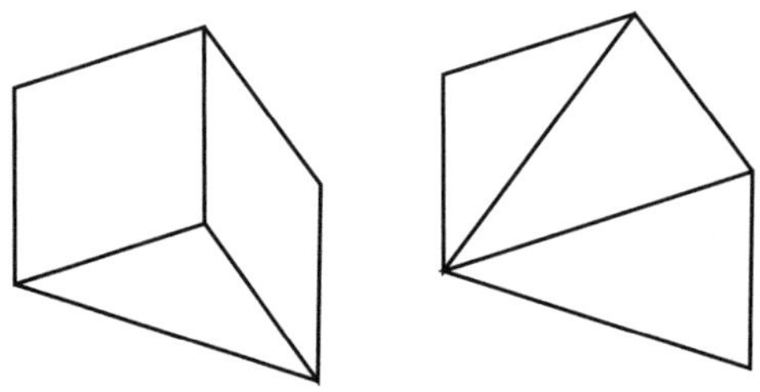

1 fat rhombus + 1 thin rhombus + 1 short triangle = 2 tall triangles + 1 short triangle

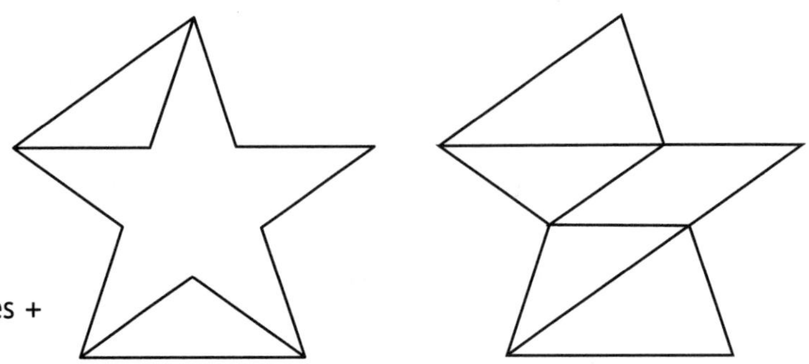

1 star + 2 short triangles = 1 thin rhombus + 2 tall triangles + 2 short triangles

b. The sides of students' equations should be nearly the same. Using the first sample response for **3a** and the approximate quarter-inch values in **2c**:

$$\begin{aligned} 1 \text{ pentagon} &= 1 \text{ tall triangle} + 2 \text{ short triangles} \\ 27 &\approx 12.5 + 2\,(8) \\ 27 &\approx 28.5 \end{aligned}$$

- *Possible Extensions:*

1. Research the use of square units for standards of area measurement. Is this universal or cultural? For example, are there cultures where area is measured in hexagons or equilateral triangles?

Investigation 3: Comparing Areas

Background Information:

The **area** of a bounded region on a surface is a measure that tells *how much surface* is enclosed within that region. Unlike distance or perimeter, which is a description of one dimension, area is two-dimensional. Historically, area has been expressed in *square units*. For example, a square centimeter is a square that measures 1 centimeter on each side. Most pushbutton telephones have buttons that are square centimeters. A floor tile is usually made as a square foot, and carpet is often sold by the square yard.

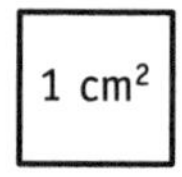

Cutting up a piece of paper does not change how much surface area it covers. You could cut it up into rectangles, triangles, or irregular shapes, and this still wouldn't change the amount of surface area the paper has. That is the idea behind the **Area Addition Postulate**, which states

> *If a bounded region on a surface is subdivided into a set of smaller bounded regions, the sum of the areas of the separate regions is equal to the area of the original region.*

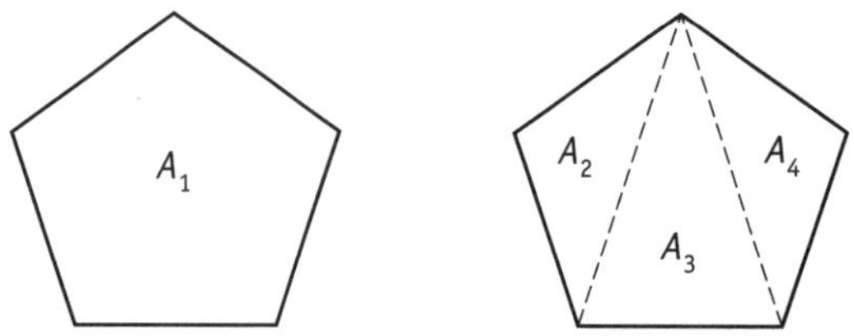

$$A_1 = A_2 + A_3 + A_4$$

One way to find the *approximate* area of an irregularly shaped flat region is to place it on a square grid and count how many squares it covers. Because of its irregular shape, it would probably cover some squares only partially. You could count a partially covered square in the following way:

- Count it as a whole square if clearly more than half is covered.
- Count it as a half if just about half is covered and half is uncovered.
- Don't count it at all if clearly less than half is covered.

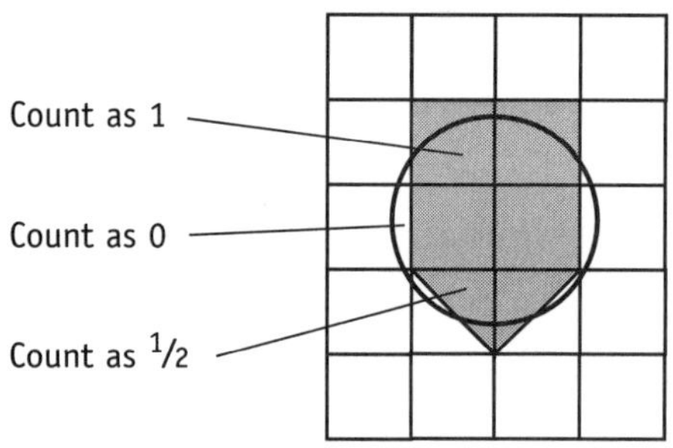

$1 + 1 + 1 + 1 + 1/2 + 1/2 = 5$ square units

Area of circle is approximately 5 square units.

Another way to deal with partially covered squares is to try to combine pieces of squares in your mind's eye to get whole squares.

Action:

Part I

1. According to the notion of area addition, any two combinations of PentaBlocks shapes that coincide (fit exactly within the same outline) have equal areas. In fact, if the same outline can be filled with a given number of blocks of one shape as well as with a different number of blocks of another shape, you can represent the area relationship between the two different blocks as a simple ratio. For example, 2 short triangles coincide exactly with 1 fat rhombus.

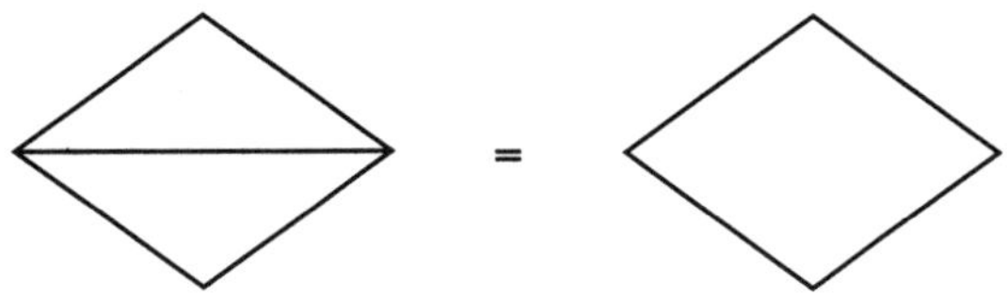

   Using this fact, create an equation or statement comparing the areas of the two shapes.

2. **a.** Arrange the PentaBlocks shapes in order from largest area to smallest area simply by "eyeballing" them. Record your estimation of their size order.

   b. In your group, have one pair use a square inch as one standard unit of area; the other pair should use the area of a short triangle as the standard unit. Express the area of each of the PentaBlocks shapes in terms of these standards. The first pair might have *1.5 square inches* as one of its measures, while the second pair would have something like *4.5 short triangles* as one measure. Compare your results to the list you made in ***Action* 2a** above.

   c. Use square grid paper in units smaller than one square inch to determine the approximate area of each of the different PentaBlocks shapes. How will using grid paper with smaller squares affect your approximations?

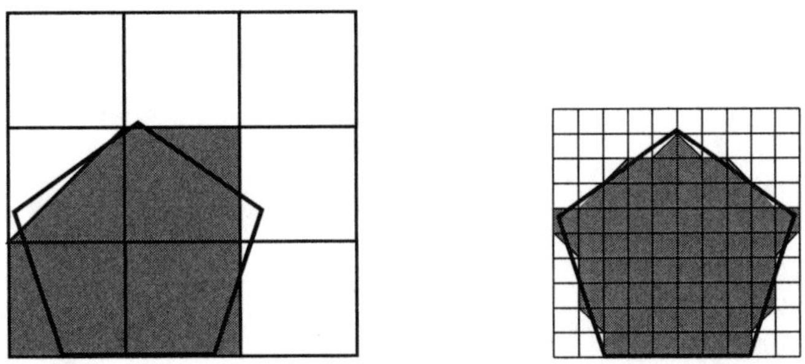

3. **a.** The figure below shows that a combination of two tall triangles coincides with a combination of two short triangles and a thin rhombus. The areas of the two combinations must be the same, by the Area Addition Postulate.

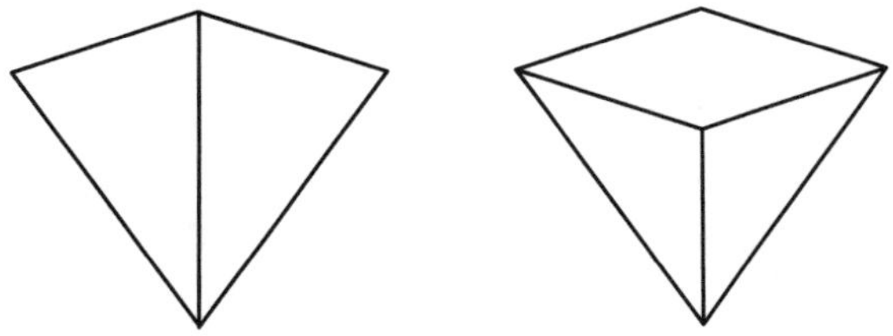

2 tall triangles = 2 short triangles + 1 thin rhombus

Find as many pairs of combinations as you can that show a relationship among a few PentaBlocks shapes. Express each relationship in an equation.

b. Substitute the "standardized" values you created in ***Action* 2c** into the equations you wrote in ***Action* 3a** to check yourself for accuracy.

Part II

4. Write an entry in your *Investigations Journal* summarizing what this activity has helped you discover about area. Write each statement or conjecture as simply and precisely as possible.

ORGANIZATION

- *Mathematical Focus:*
  - Describing properties of sides, angles, and diagonals of the PentaBlocks shapes
  - Using combinations of attributes to define set and subset relationships
- *Special Materials:* none needed
- *Approximate Time:* 50 minutes
- *Suggested Group Size:* Quads

INSTRUCTION

- *Lesson Summary:*
  - Students explore the attributes of the different shapes through two game or challenge formats.
- *Specific Notes to Teachers:*
  - The emphasis of this investigation is the recognition of attributes and combinations of attributes. This type of thinking forms the basis of classification systems. You may wish to formalize this idea by having students represent their understanding of the relationships among sets by using Venn diagrams. For example, the intersection of the two sets

    {PentaBlocks that are convex polygons}

    and

    {PentaBlocks with alternating acute and nonacute angles}

    is

    {both rhombuses}

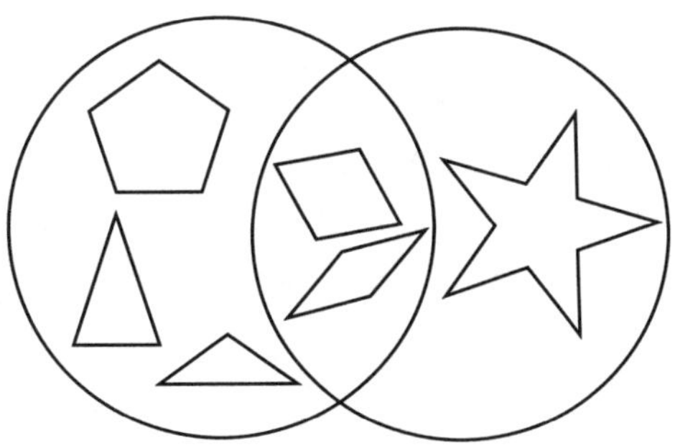

  - If students have trouble solving the challenges in Part III, don't give them the answers right away; you could use Part III instead as an extra credit challenge, posting submitted answers the following week.
- *Activity Sequence:*
  1. Distribute the Students' Guides and materials.
  2. Make sure students understand the vocabulary imbedded within the attributes lists. You might do this by asking students to work in their groups to answer ***Action 1*** together.
  3. Go over the results of ***Action 1*** as a class, and establish this list as the *Acceptable Attributes* list.

4. Before students try the Attribute Game, be sure to define
   a. the time for a turn;
   b. whether or not they'll be using the dice to find multipliers;
   c. how to add attributes to the *Acceptable* list; and
   d. which of the three options you will establish for ending the game.
5. You might want to do ***Action* 4** as a class, to be sure that students understand how it works. You could do this by asking, "What combination of attributes do *all* of these (on the left) have *in common*?" and then listing them. For each attribute ask, "Do *any* of those (on the right) also have this attribute?" Eliminate any attribute that is exhibited on both sides.

- *Special Notes About the Attribute Game*

This game is intended to help students differentiate attributes or properties. The game is described in the Students' Guide, but these notes may help you in setting up the game.

Setup: Prepare the Combination Cards. Use the forms at the end of this investigation as blackline masters and copy onto cardstock if possible. Each pair of players or teams will need a deck.

Timer: Define the time span of each play. Try starting with 4 minutes and adjust as appropriate for your group. An automatic timer with a count-down function and a bell works best, but a student using a watch with a second hand is a reasonable alternative. Establish a "Pencils Down!" rule when time is called.

Adding Attributes: Each player should have a basic set of six PentaBlocks and a list of *Acceptable Attributes* (taken from the results of ***Action* 1**). Be sure to leave room in each category for students to list additional *Acceptable Attributes* they have discovered. You may want to stop play after a few rounds and have students share attributes they have added to their list.

Optional Cards: You may (or may not) wish to use the "Double Score" and "Triple Score" cards. They add chance and more excitement to the game aspect of this activity.

Because the total number of possible combinations is 15 (an odd number), the first team will normally have one more turn than the second team. You can avoid this by using the Joker as a 16th card. Or you may want to eliminate the Joker and stop the play after each team has had seven turns (leaving the last card unturned).

- *Possible Responses:*

  1. *Attributes related to SIDES:* being equilateral, or not; having the number of sides equal to the number of diagonals.

     Attributes related to ANGLES: having angles that alternate between acute and nonacute; containing supplementary angles.

     Attributes related to DIAGONALS: having (all, any, or none) of the diagonals bisecting an angle; having (all, any, or none) of the diagonals acting as a line of symmetry.

     Other mathematical attributes of shapes: tessellating the plane by itself, or not; having (all, one, no) vertex angle bisectors perpendicular to opposite side; being constructible by combining other PentaBlocks.

  2. Shapes are listed by attribute number. Added attributes are given in italics after each section.

     (1) 3 sides: both triangles; 4 sides: both rhombuses; 5 sides: pentagon; 10 sides: star

(2) isosceles: both triangles

(3) opposite sides parallel: both rhombuses
equilateral: both rhombuses, pentagon, star
number of sides equalling number of diagonals: pentagon

(4) all: tall triangle; any: both triangles, both rhombuses, star; none: pentagon

(5) all: pentagon; any: short triangle, both rhombuses, pentagon, star; none: tall triangle

(6) equiangular: pentagon
alternating acute-nonacute angles: both rhombuses, star
containing supplementary angles: both rhombuses

(7) no diagonals: both triangles; 2 diagonals: both rhombuses; 5 diagonals: pentagon; 35 diagonals: star (some of these diagonals are collinear)

Note: Since triangles have no diagonals, students may list the triangles for "none" in items involving diagonals.

(8) all: pentagon; any: star; none: both rhombuses

(9) no: pentagon; one: both rhombuses; more than one: star
having diagonals bisect an angle: all: both rhombuses; *some:* star; *no:* pentagon
having diagonals act as mirror: all: both rhombuses; *some:* star; *no:* pentagon

(10) pentagon; star is a regular *concave* polygon, which is not the same thing.

(11) concave: star; convex: all the others

(12) both rhombuses, star
tessellating by itself: both triangles, both rhombuses
being constructible from other PentaBlocks: pentagon, fat rhombus

4. In each case, other answers are possible.
   - **a.** four sides; containing supplementary angles; all diagonals act as line of symmetry; all diagonals bisect angles; one pair of perpendicular diagonals
   - **b.** all angles are acute; no obtuse angles
   - **c.** five sides; no acute angles; all obtuse angles; equiangular; 5 diagonals; same number of diagonals as sides; all diagonals congruent; regular
   - **d.** ten sides, concave; more than one pair of perpendicular diagonals; number of diagonals is greater than the number of sides
   - **e.** three sides; isosceles; not equilateral; no diagonals
   - **f.** more than two diagonals; not tessellating the plane; having at least two congruent diagonals; five "points"; regular (remember the distinction between regular polygons and regular stars!)
   - **g.** alternating between acute and nonacute angles; having at least one pair of perpendicular diagonals; having no vertex angle bisectors perpendicular to the opposite side; having collinear angle bisectors
   - **h.** can be formed by combining PentaBlocks

- *Possible Extensions:*
  1. Have students make exhaustive lists of PentaBlock shapes that fit each descriptive attribute. (Some students may already have done this in ***Action 1***.)
  2. Have students create additional Set Relationship challenges.

Investigation 4: Geometrical Attributes

Background Information:

In this investigation you will be asked to observe and think about the similarities and differences among the PentaBlock shapes. This will mean thinking about their geometrical characteristics or attributes. Since the PentaBlock shapes are all polygons, you will be most concerned about the properties of their sides, angles, and diagonals. Here is a starter list of geometric attributes. You will be asked to come up with more.

Attributes related to SIDES:

1. Having a certain number of sides
2. Being isosceles, or not
3. Having opposite sides parallel, or not

Attributes related to ANGLES:

4. Having (all, any, or no) acute angles
5. Having (all, any, or no) nonacute angles
6. Being equiangular, or not

Attributes related to DIAGONALS:

7. Having a certain number of diagonals
8. Having (all, any, or none) of the diagonals congruent
9. Having (more than one, one, no) pair(s) of perpendicular diagonals

Other mathematical attributes of shapes:

10. Being a regular polygon
11. Having a convex or concave shape
12. Having collinear angle bisectors

Action:

Part I

1. Working with your partner, find one or two additional attributes for each category.
2. Working with your partner, identify at least one PentaBlock shape that exhibits each attribute, including the attributes you added. The more shapes you list, the easier the Attribute Game will be for your team.

Part II

3. **The Attribute Game** (directions follow)

Start Up and Play:

1. This is a game for for two individuals or two teams of two people each. For simplicity, these directions use the term "player" rather than "team or individual player."

2. Players take turns drawing a card from the top of a shuffled deck of PentaBlocks Combination Cards. Players decide in advance how long a turn will last.
3. As one player turns up a card, the other player begins keeping time. If the combination on the card has already been played, the player loses that turn. If the combination has not been played, *both* players make a *Same* list and a *Different* list.
   - The *Same* list names attributes that the two pictured blocks have in common.
   - The *Different* list names attribute differences between the two pictured blocks.
4. (optional) If the Joker is drawn, the player may choose any combination of PentaBlocks that has not already been chosen and then makes the lists.
5. (optional) If a Double or Triple Score card is drawn, the player draws another combination card and makes the lists. The player's final score for the turn is then doubled or tripled.
6. Most *Same* and *Different* attributes will come from the *Acceptable Attributes* list created in ***Action* 1**. However, if either player comes up with a new attribute that the other player agrees to, that attribute can be added to the *Acceptable Attributes* list.
7. When the timer rings or time is called, players compare their lists and cross off any attributes that both players found. Then players get a point for each item they listed but the other player did not list.
8. The play then moves to the other player.
9. Players continue to take turns until the game ends. There are three ways to end the game. (This should be decided before the game begins!) The game ends
   1. at the end of the lab session; or
   2. when all the cards have been used; or
   3. after each player has had seven turns.
10. The player with more points at the end of the game wins.

Part III

4. Each lettered item below represents an individual challenge. For each challenge, *all* of the shapes on the left exhibit some combination of attributes that *none* of the shapes on the right exhibits. The challenge is to describe that combination of attributes.

a.	both rhombuses	pentagon, star, both triangles
b.	tall triangle	pentagon, star, short triangle, both rhombuses
c.	pentagon	star, both triangles, both rhombuses
d.	star	pentagon, both triangles, both rhombuses
e.	both triangles	pentagon, star, both rhombuses
f.	pentagon, star	both triangles, both rhombuses
g.	star, both rhombuses	pentagon, both triangles
h.	pentagon, fat rhombus	star, both triangles, thin rhombus

Part IV

5. Write an entry in your *Investigations Journal* summarizing what this activity has helped you discover about defining subsets. Write each statement or conjecture as simply and precisely as possible.

Combination Cards I

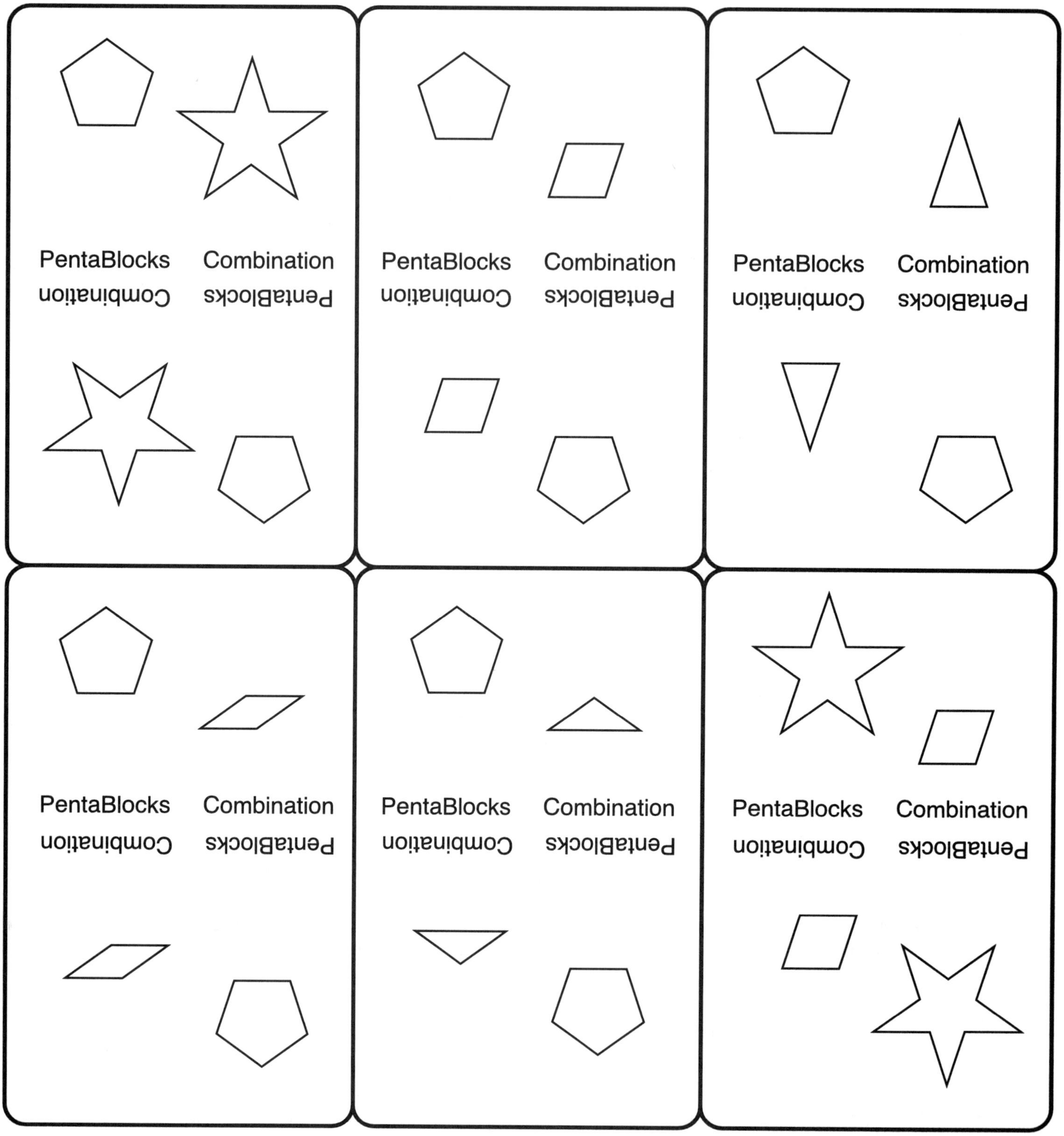

Combination Cards II

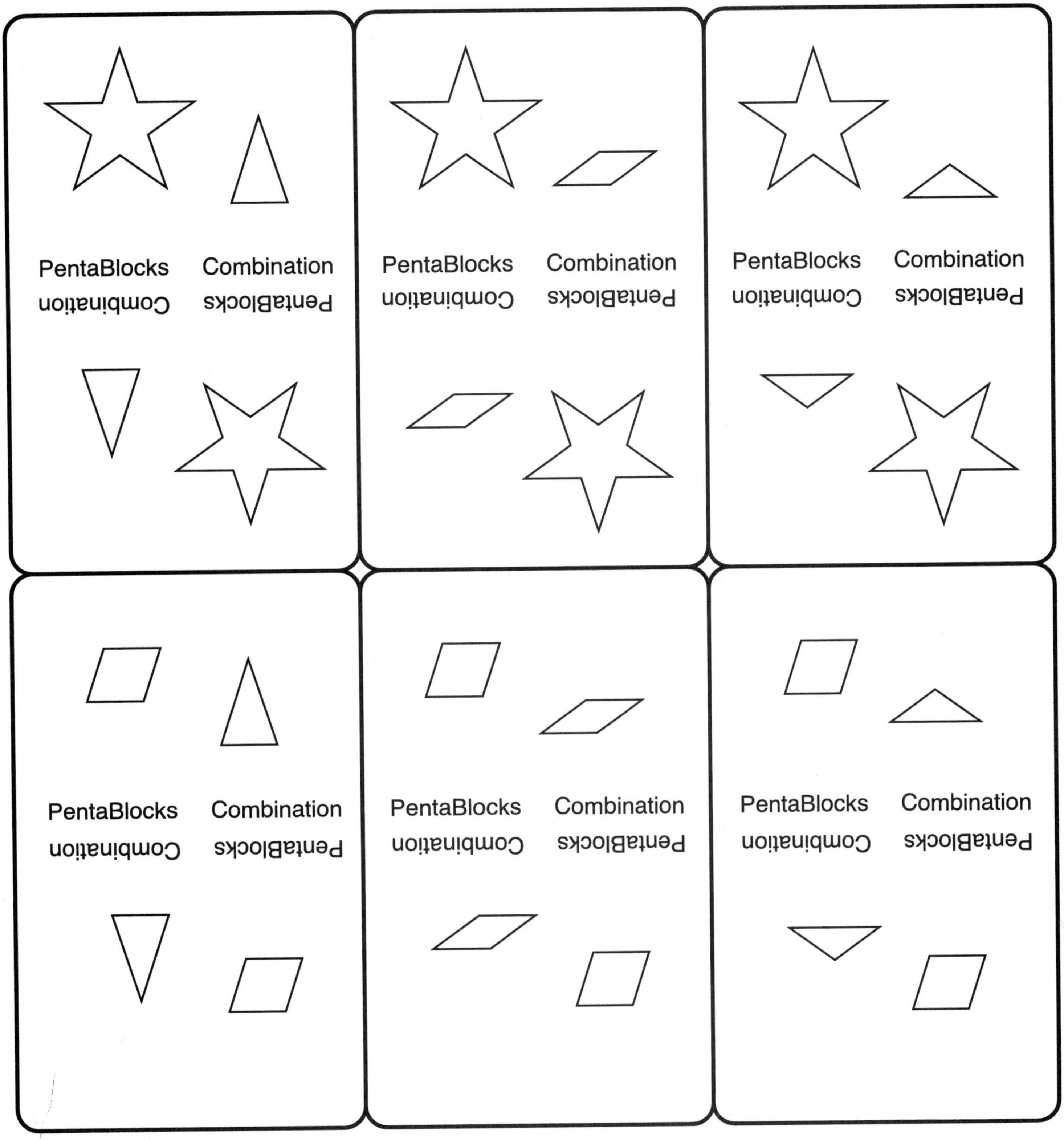

Combination Cards III

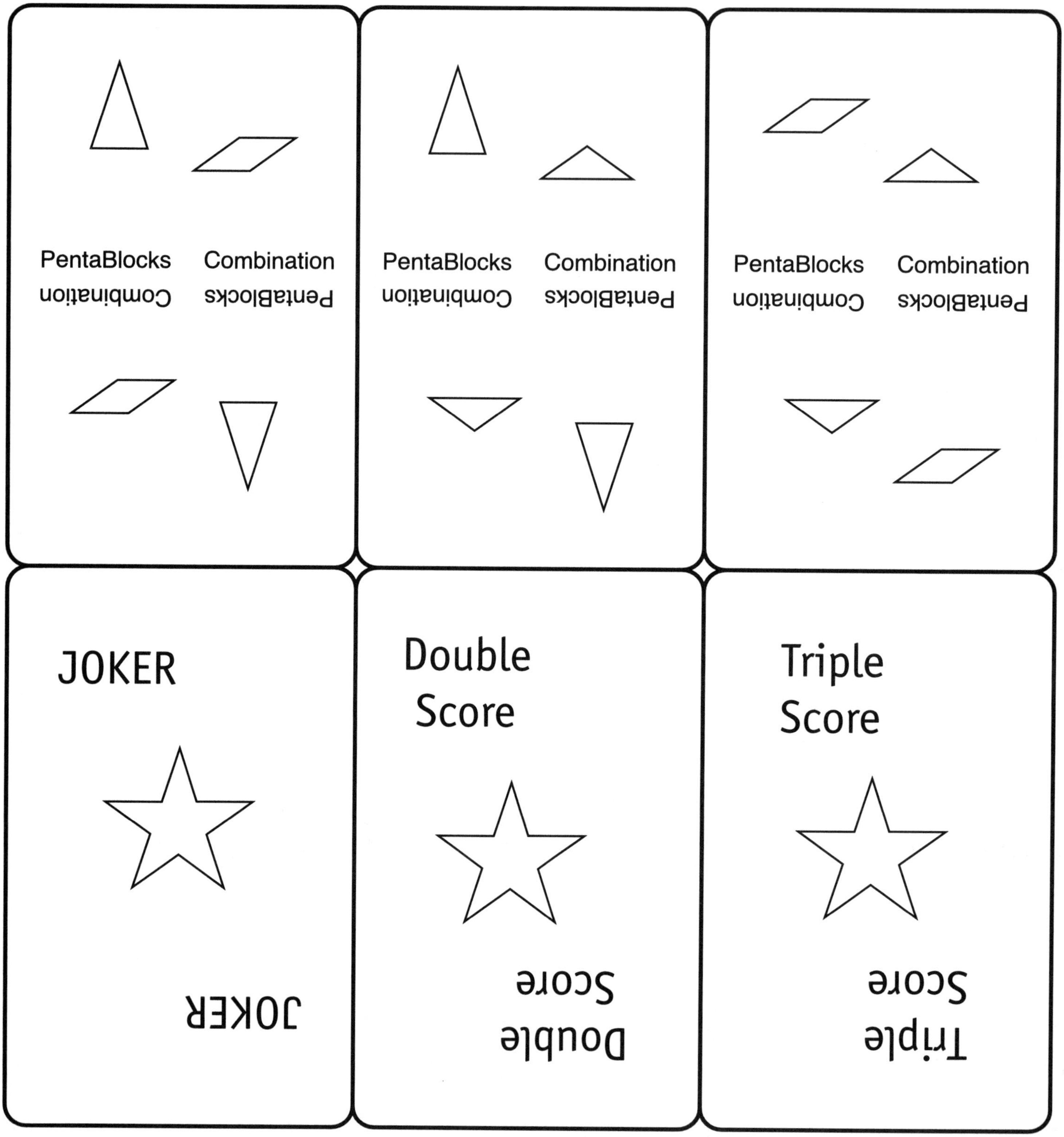

Teacher's Guide

Investigation 5: Similarity

ORGANIZATION

- *Mathematical Focus:* Similarity and proportion
- *Special Materials:* none needed
- *Approximate Time:* One or two 50-minute sessions
- *Suggested Group Size:* Quads

INSTRUCTION

- *Lesson Summary:*
  - Students set up and solve proportions based on similar polygons. Students examine existing similar figures and create their own designs similar to existing shapes, using given multipliers.
- *Terminology:*
  - See the Students' Guide for specific descriptions and definitions of these words:

dilation factor	proportion
multiplier	similar polygons

- *Specific Notes to Teachers:*
  - Students need to be familiar with solving proportions in order to benefit most from the mathematics inherent in this investigation. It may be helpful to spend some class time setting up and solving proportions before having students begin the investigation.
- *Activity Sequence:*
  1. Hand out Students' Guides. It may be helpful to look first at a few pairs of similar figures and create proportions as a class. This technique will then be reinforced in ***Action* 1**.
  2. Have students do ***Action* 2**. This may generate some discussion about the Golden Ratio. If so, consider allowing time for the discussion before continuing with the rest of the ***Action*** sequence, because the Golden Ratio plays an integral part in the rest of the activity.
- *Possible Responses:*

1. $\frac{1}{x} = \frac{x}{1+x}$; $x^2 = x + 1$; $x = \frac{1+\sqrt{5}}{2}$

2. a. It's always a pentagon, smaller than the previous one and upside-down. The actual ratio is $1/(\Phi^2)$.

b. It forms a star. You could form the same star by surrounding a pentagon with five tall triangles.

When you connect the vertices you get another, larger pentagon. The ratio is the same as the ratio from ***Action* 2a**—that is, $1/(\Phi^2)$.

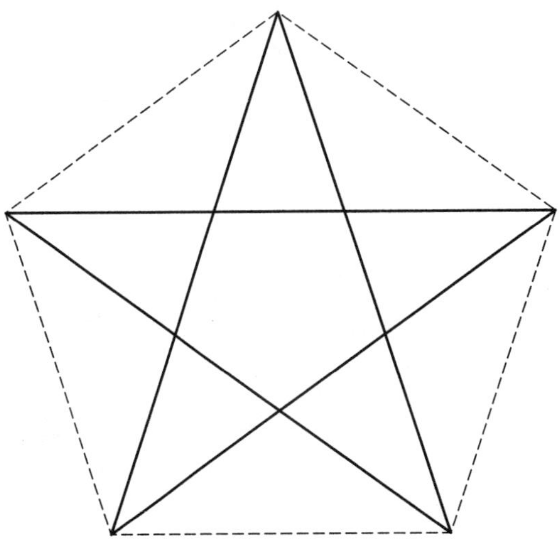

3. a.

Squares	Perimeter	Area
Generation 1	4	1
Generation 2	8	4
Generation 3	12	9
Generation 4	16	16

b.

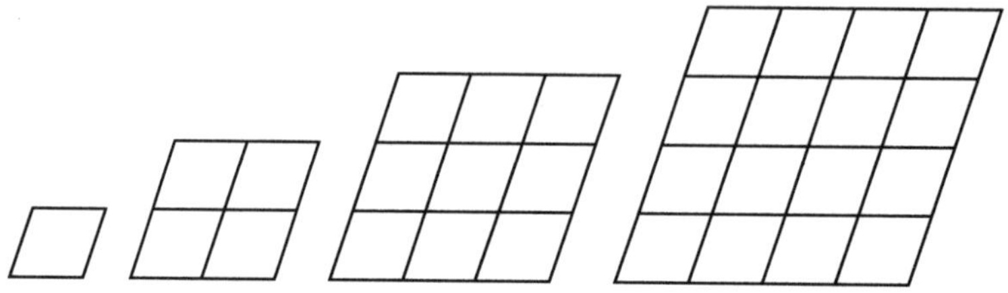

Fat rhombus (FR)	Perimeter	Area
Generation 1	4	1FR
Generation 2	8	4FR
Generation 3	12	9FR
Generation 4	16	16FR

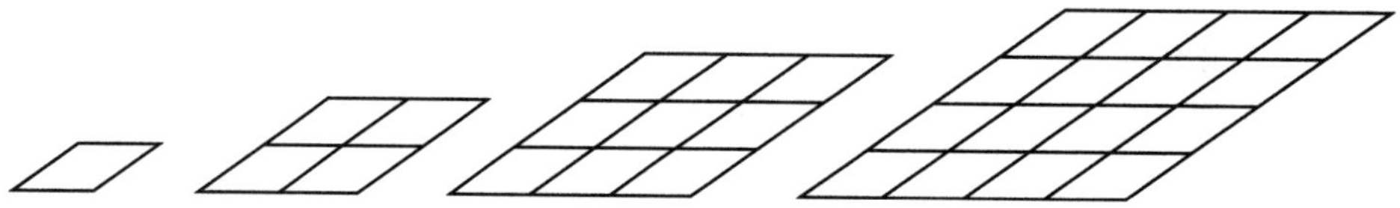

Thin rhombus (tR)	Perimeter	Area
Generation 1	4	1tR
Generation 2	8	4tR
Generation 3	12	9tR
Generation 4	16	16tR

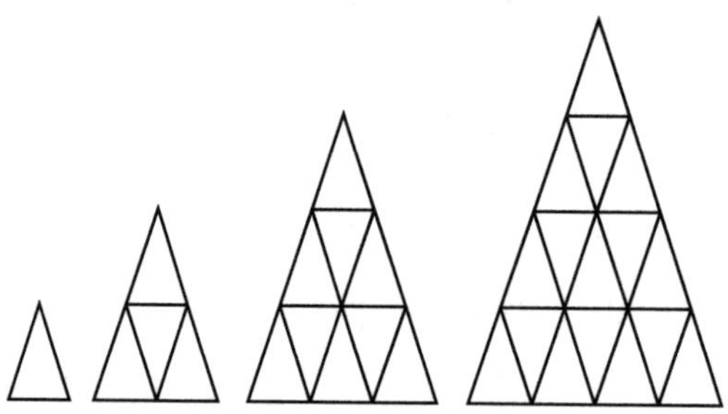

Tall triangle (TT)	Perimeter	Area
Generation 1	$1 + 2\Phi$	1TT
Generation 2	$2 + 4\Phi$	4TT
Generation 3	$3 + 6\Phi$	9TT
Generation 4	$4 + 8\Phi$	16TT

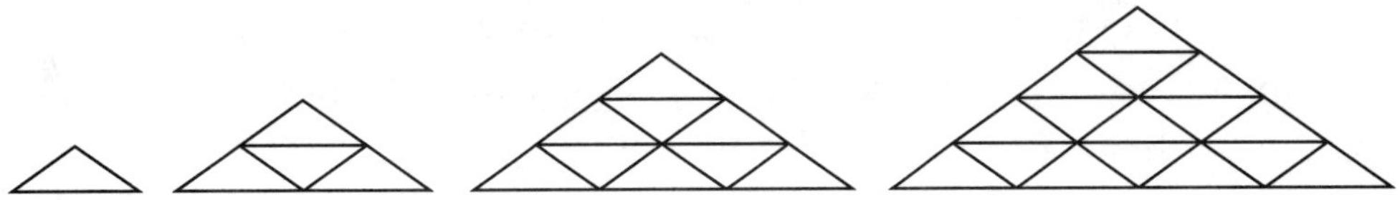

Short triangle (sT)	Perimeter	Area
Generation 1	$2 + \Phi$	1sT
Generation 2	$4 + 2\Phi$	4sT
Generation 3	$6 + 3\Phi$	9sT
Generation 4	$8 + 4\Phi$	16sT

c. Pentagons and stars are more difficult because they do not tessellate by themselves to form similar shapes. Students may create a compromise in which similar shapes are made up of different PentaBlocks, and areas are established by area equivalents. For example, at the right are shown the first two generations of a pentagon RepTile.

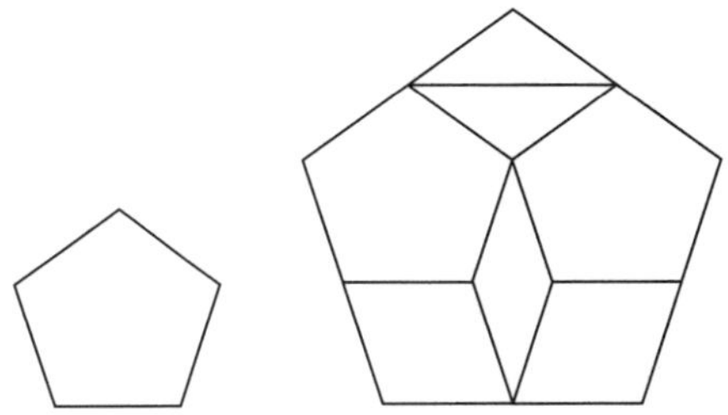

By Area Addition, you can see that 2 fat rhombuses + 2 short triangles + 1 thin rhombus = 2 pentagons. Therefore the area of Generation 2 of the pentagon RepTile is 2P + (2FR + 2sT + 1tR) = 2P + 2P = 4P. Using this method for pentagons and stars, students can obtain the values given in these charts.

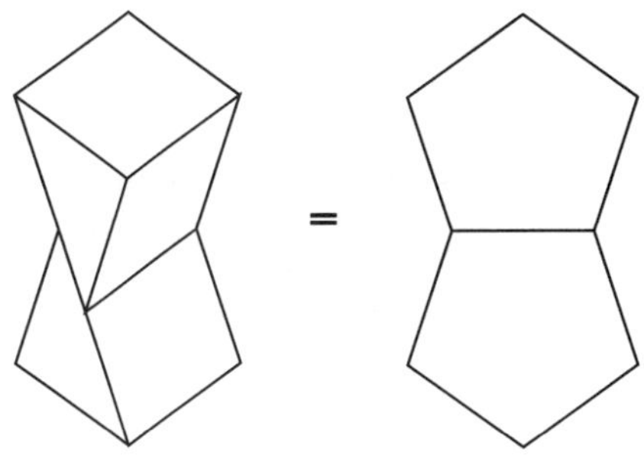

Pentagon (P)	Perimeter	Area
Generation 1	5	1P
Generation 2	10	4P
Generation 3	15	9P
Generation 4	20	16P

Star (S)	Perimeter	Area
Generation 1	10	1S
Generation 2	20	4S
Generation 3	30	9S
Generation 4	40	16S

4. **a.** Pentagon: 2, 3, 4, Φ, 2Φ, (Φ + 1), (Φ + 2), (Φ + 4), (2Φ + 1)
   Star: Φ, 2Φ, (Φ + 1), (Φ + 2) [this is a challenging one; one solution is shown here], (Φ + 3), (2Φ + 2), (3Φ + 1)
   Tall triangle: 2, Φ, (Φ + 1)
   Short triangle: Φ, (2Φ + 2)
   Thin rhombus: Φ, (2Φ + 2)
   Fat rhombus: 2, Φ, 3Φ, (Φ + 1), (Φ + 2), (2Φ + 1), (2Φ + 2)

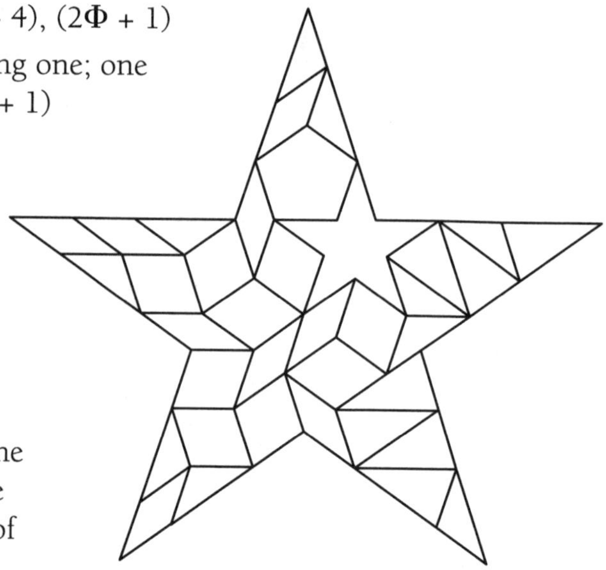

   b. Rhombuses and pentagons are especially easy because they are equilateral. The star is also equilateral, but it can be more difficult because the pentagon at its center and the star itself have side ratios of 1/Φ. The triangles also have side ratios of 1/Φ and may be tricky to construct.

   c. Regular decagon: 2, Φ, (Φ + 2)
   "Fat Star": Φ, (Φ + 1), (2Φ + 1)

• *Possible Extensions*

1. Once you've discovered in ***Action* 1** that the longer length is Φ, substituting that value into the equation from the cross product of the proportion of corresponding sides gives the unexpected outcome that

$$\Phi^2 = \Phi + 1$$

Show how this fact leads to the generalizations that:

- any power of Φ can be represented as the sum of the two lesser powers of Φ
- any power of Φ can be represented as $a\Phi + b$, where a and b are consecutive Fibonacci numbers.

2. The notion of a geometric progression is that each successive term in a series is generated by multiplying the last term by a constant. The figure at right shows how stars and pentagons grow from one another, as described in ***Action* 2**.

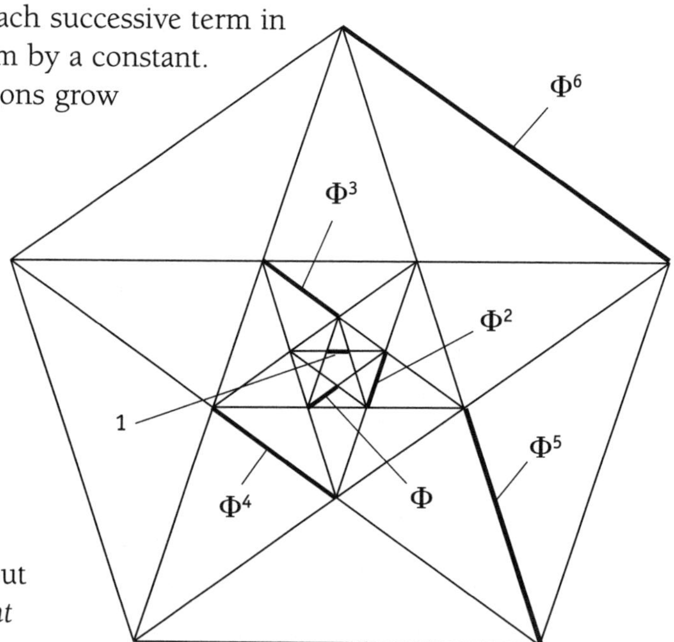

   In fact, the lengths of corresponding sides in successive similar figures (either the stars or the pentagons) form a geometric progression. Investigate the history and mathematics within this figure. Research the "Lute of Pythagoras": How is it related to the geometric progression demonstrated in this figure?

3. The "enlargements" you made in this investigation are examples of *dilation*, a transformation operation that changes lengths proportionally but does not change angle measure. Investigate *point inversion* and *projection*, two operations that may affect both length and angle measure.

Background Information:

Proportionality was a central focus of the study of mathematics in antiquity and still pervades many fields of mathematics and science. Over the years, it has been perhaps the most continuously important topic in the formal study of mathematics, largely because of its practical applications in commerce, architecture, and the arts. The close connection between proportionality and aesthetics is reflected in the use of the phrase "being in proper proportion" to mean "being in balance or harmony" or "looking or feeling right."

Ratios are **in proportion** if their decimal values are the same or if the ratios are equivalent fractions.

Similarity is the geometrical counterpart of proportionality. **Similar figures**—that is, figures with exactly the same shape—give rise to proportions in a very specific way. Similar polygons are defined by two relationships, often abbreviated in this way:

CASPE: Corresponding **A**ngles of **S**imilar **P**olygons are **E**qual

CSSPP: Corresponding **S**ides of **S**imilar **P**olygons are **P**roportional

With the PentaBlocks, it's easy to show that corresponding angles are equal by showing that they physically coincide.

Similar figures are generated by an operation called a **dilation**. For a given pair of similar figures, the ratio of corresponding sides defines a **dilation factor** or **multiplier**. This multiplier is easy to show when one side length is a simple multiple of a corresponding side length. In the illustration below, the multiplier is 2 when you are moving from the left figure to the right figure. If you are moving from right to left, the multiplier is $1/2$. In general, a dilation factor (multiplier) greater than one *increases* the size of the figure. A dilation factor less than one *decreases* the size.

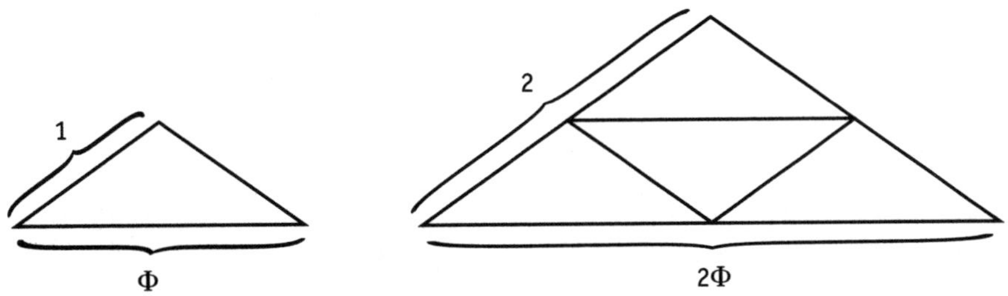

$$\frac{\Phi}{2\Phi} = \frac{1}{2}$$

right triangle to left triangle

$$\frac{2\Phi}{\Phi} = \frac{2}{1}$$

left triangle to right triangle

In some cases, PentaBlocks make it easy to show similar designs with an irrational multiplier.

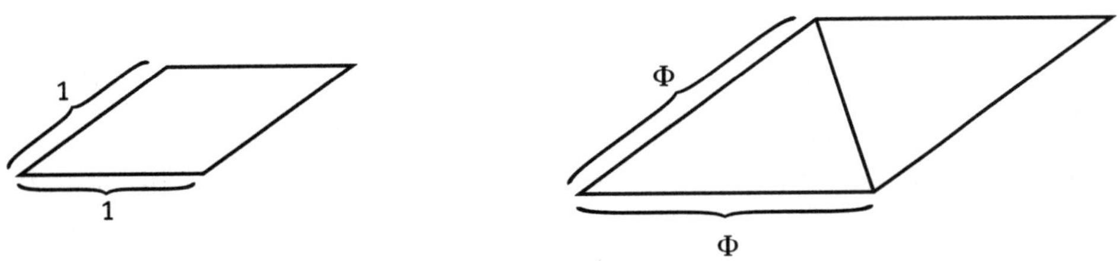

$$\frac{1}{\Phi} = \frac{1}{\Phi} \quad \text{or} \quad \frac{\Phi}{1} = \frac{\Phi}{1}$$

PentaBlocks readily illustrate dilations because of the angles and proportions within each shape. They combine to generate similar shapes in a variety of different sizes.

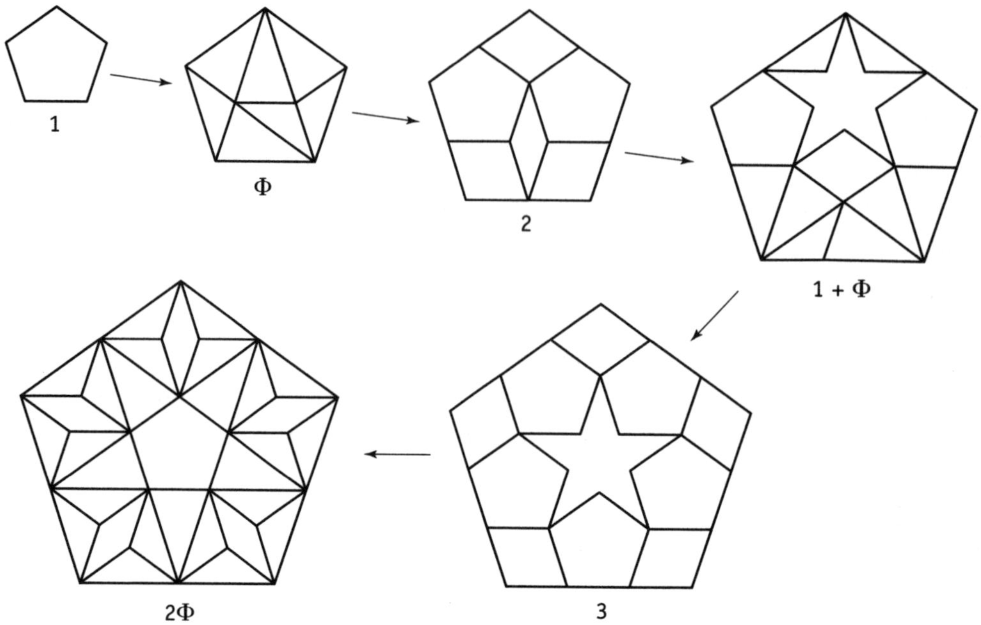

Action

Part I

1. Finding the Length of a Diagonal of a Regular Pentagon

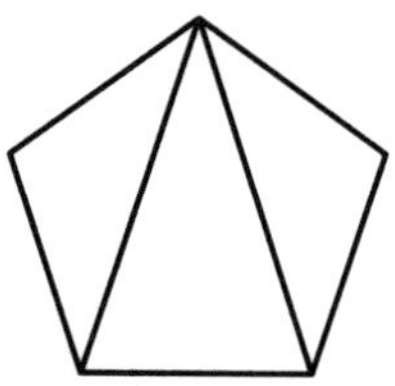

Figure A

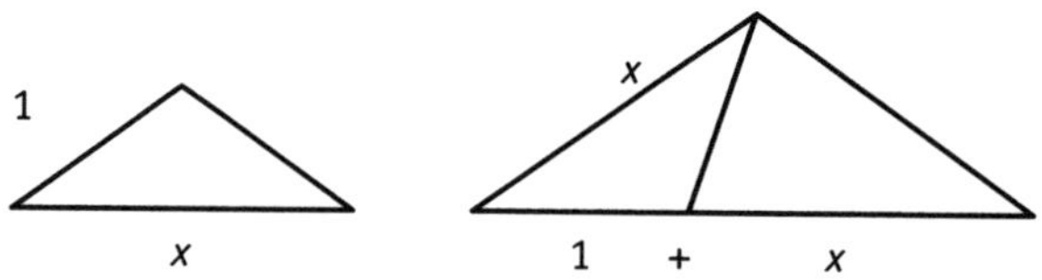

Figure B

Note from Figure A that the diagonal of the regular pentagon is equal to the longer side length of the PentaBlocks triangles. Figure B shows a pair of triangles that seem to be similar. You can easily verify this by showing that the corresponding angles are equal. You can use the similarity and a little algebra to find the length of the first triangle's longer side, which is also the length of the pentagon's diagonal. Here's how: If you label the lengths in the first triangle as 1 unit for the short sides and x units for the long side, you can set up a proportion using the lengths of the corresponding sides of the two triangles. Use this proportion to find the value of x.

2. Pentagons and Stars: A Growing Relationship

a. Start with an outline of the pentagon and draw all the diagonals. What do you notice about the center figure created within the intersecting diagonals? How does the length of a side of the center figure compare to the length of a side of the PentaBlocks pentagon? If you repeat this process, does the same thing happen again? What is your best guess about the ratio of the sides of each successively smaller central figure?

b. Start with an outline of the pentagon and extend the sides of the pentagon until they meet. What figure does this form? How could you have produced this same figure using only the

PentaBlocks? What figure results if you connect the outer vertices of the new figure? How does the length of a side of the center pentagon compare to the length of a side of the newly formed outer figure? How is this sequence related to the one described above?

3. **Growing "RepTiles"**

 a. Examine this growth sequence formed with square tiles:

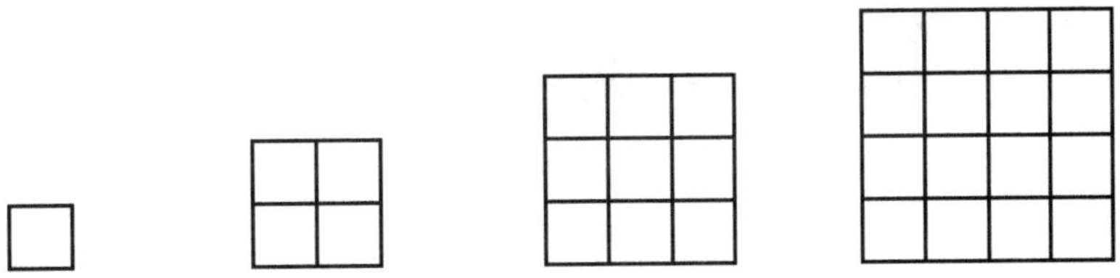

Refer to the single square on the left as the first generation, the next larger square as second generation, and so on. Chart the data this sequence generates for perimeter (in units of side length) and the area (in units of area of the original square). Notice how the perimeter and area change as a readily describable function (or multiple) of the generation. This could be called "growing RepTiles," since each generation is larger and exactly similar to the original square tile.

 b. Now try to grow a few generations of each of the PentaBlocks shapes, recording perimeter and area data in a separate chart for each shape. Do all of the PentaBlocks shapes grow as readily as the squares? Which shapes don't seem to work?

 c. Examine the shapes that don't easily form RepTiles. Try to create the larger, similar versions of these shapes using combinations with other PentaBlocks shapes. Chart the perimeter as you did with the other RepTiles. Use the Area Addition Postulate to find the new areas in terms of the original shape.

4. **a.** Use PentaBlocks to construct each of the PentaBlocks shapes in a variety of sizes. Since the length of the shortest side of each block is 1, and since every length is either 1 or Φ, you will be able to find the dilation factor or multiplier directly: it will be the side length of the larger figure. For example, this illustration shows a pentacle star with a side length of (Φ + 1); that is, it is similar to the black PentaBlocks star and has a multiplier of (Φ + 1).

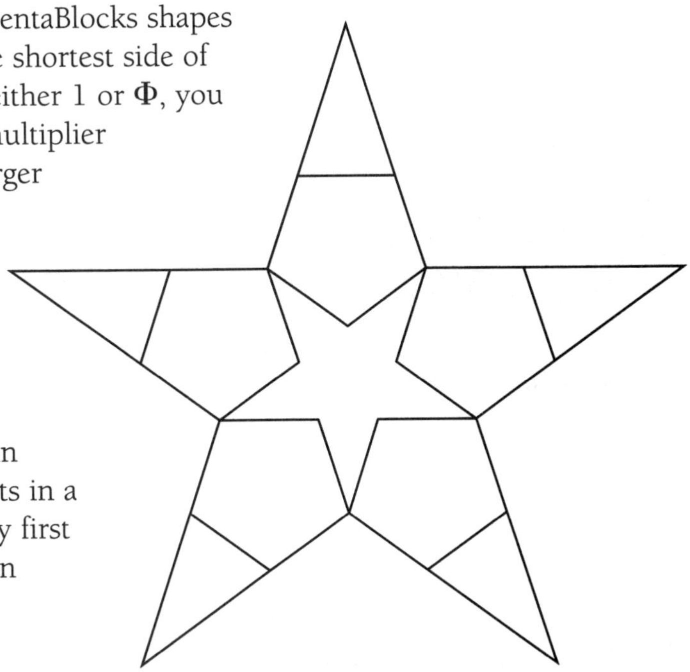

 Record your similar figures. (You have already constructed some of these figures in ***Action*** 3.) You might also show your results in a table; organize the list of dilation factors by first showing integers, then multiples of Φ, then combinations in the form ($x\Phi + y$).

 b. Do any multipliers appear on most or all lists? How might this be explained? Which shapes, if any, seem to be easily created in many sizes? Is it difficult to construct similar forms of any shapes? Why?

c. In addition to the standard PentaBlocks shapes, two other figures emerge in various sizes from PentaBlocks constructions. The regular decagon is one, the other is a "regular fat star": one can be made by placing five fat rhombuses so that their acute angles meet at a point. Record dilation factors you find with figures similar to these two shapes.

Part II

5. Write an entry in your *Investigations Journal* summarizing what this activity has helped you learn about similarity and proportion. Write each statement or conjecture as simply and precisely as possible.

Investigation 6: Spatial Reasoning: Solving Outlines

ORGANIZATION

- *Mathematical Focus:* Spatial Reasoning
- *Special Materials:* Newsprint for posting outlines, PentaBlocks templates
- *Approximate Time:* 50 minutes
- *Suggested Group Size:* Individuals, then pairs, then quads

INSTRUCTION

- *Lesson Summary:*
  - Students fill the outlines of a pentagon, decagon, and star.
  - Students create their own designs, using a given number of blocks, and draw outlines of their designs.
  - Students are challenged to fill outlines created by other groups.
  - Students compare outlines and designs, considering such characteristics as symmetry, aesthetic appeal, and number and types of blocks used.

- *Specific Notes to Teachers:*
  - You should first show an outline and then a number of its solutions, so students can easily visualize different ways of filling the same area. A sample is found on Blackline Master 1 in the appendices.
  - Decide how you want to count designs that use the same block combinations but are, for example, left- and right-handed versions (reflections), or that have only slightly different placements of some of the blocks. You might show a simple table as a way of keeping count of each block type used and the total for each outline design. This table describes the designs found on the next page:

	Tall triangle	Short triangle	Fat rhombus	Thin rhombus	Pentagon	Star	Total number of blocks
Outline 1	0	0	3	1	2	0	6
Outline 2	9	8	1	2	1	0	21
Outline 3	4	2	6	11	6	2	31

  - As students get practice with creating and solving outlines, you might want to increase the maximum number of blocks incrementally to about 30. Beyond that, the designs may get too big to be useful for this type of challenge.
  - Be sure to get students to discuss filling strategies, and typical combinations of angle measures and side lengths.

- *Activity Sequence:*
  1. Distribute Students' Guides and materials.
  2. Define the task of *solving an outline* and give an example of an outline with more than one solution. (See Blackline Master 1, Appendix 5.)
  3. After students have finished ***Actions* 1** and **2**, post the challenge outlines; for each one, get a copy of the original solution. If time permits, let the groups work on solutions to all of the posted challenge outlines. You may want to assign design codes to the challenges, so that students don't know which outline is from which group. You may also wish to photocopy the challenge outlines for students to work on independently or for use in another lab session as a warmup activity.
  4. Give students 5-10 minutes to do ***Action* 3** and post the solutions. Discuss the similarities and differences between combinations and ask about strategies for starting and filling in.

- *Possible Responses*
  1. Possible similarities and differences: One outline may be "smoother" than the other; one or both may be symmetrical; one may be more compact and one more stretched out; one outline may show clearly which blocks were used, while the other may be harder to decipher; one or both may be generally concave or generally convex; one may have many possible solutions, or very few.
  2. Designs will vary. Possible strategies: Look at lengths of outline segments to identify short-side and long-side segments of shapes. For segments that are longer than any one PentaBlock side, students might try combinations of short-short, long-long, or short-long. Look at angles defined by the outlines and find blocks with the same angles. If students want to include the larger PentaBlocks (the star and the pentagon) in their solutions, it may be easiest to start with those shapes and build around them.
  3. Here is one possible solution for each outline.

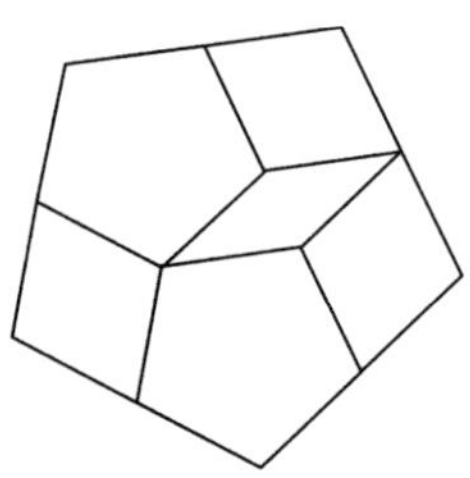

Outline 1

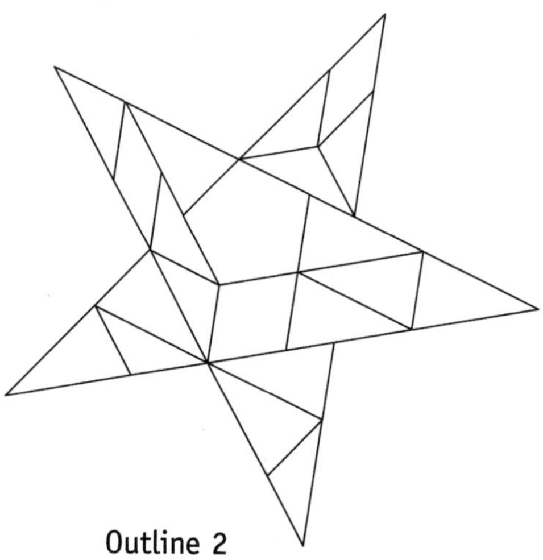

Outline 2

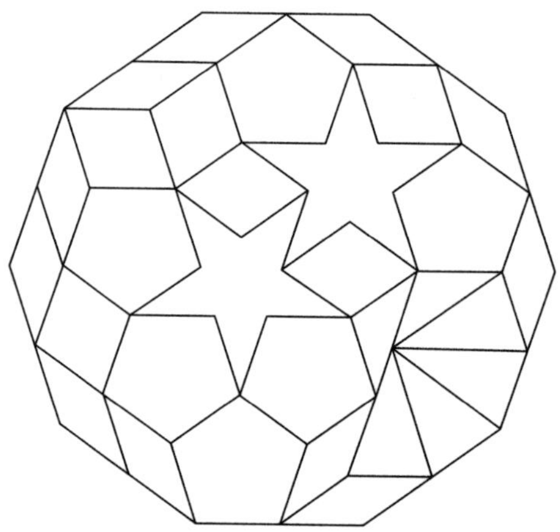

Outline 3

- *Possible Extensions*
  Try to solve pentagon, decagon, and/or star outlines of a variety of sizes. How can the concepts from Investigation 5 (similarity) help you?

Investigation 6: Spatial Reasoning: Solving Outlines

Background Information

Geometric puzzles have fascinated people for millennia. Many of the most basic (and difficult) puzzles are geometric dissections, in which a bounded area is broken up into a set of pieces. The challenge is to use all of the pieces to fill the original outline *without gaps or overlaps*. This is called *solving an outline.*

Spatial reasoning is the special type of thinking required to visualize solutions to outlines and solving related problems. The activities in this investigation are an introduction to these *fill-in* puzzles. Sometimes, solving outlines happens accidentally as you move the pieces around.

Action

Part I

1. **a.** Working individually, use 8 to 12 PentaBlocks to create a design that follows the Two Basic Rules. Record the arrangement of blocks and the number of each block type used. On a separate piece of paper, record just the outline of your design.

   b. Share your outline with a partner. Pick the one outline that you both think is more challenging to solve. Post your *challenge outline.* When all of the challenge outlines are posted, what similarities and differences, if any, can you find among them?

2. **a.** Combine pairs to make quads. Each pair in the quad should find and record one or more solutions to the challenge outline created by the other pair in the quad.

   b. In your quad, discuss the strategies you used in solving the challenge outline. Some possibilities: How did you start? For example, did you begin in the middle and work outwards, or start in a corner and work your way around the outside, or did you use some other approach? Describe how angle measures or side lengths helped you narrow down your choices of blocks. What types of outline seem easiest or hardest to solve?

   c. Using what you've learned about solving outlines, find at least one solution for each of the challenge outlines posted by the other groups. As time permits, find as many solutions as you can to each of the challenges.

3. As you may have discovered already, you can use PentaBlocks to construct pentagons, decagons, and pentacle stars in a variety of side lengths. Shown here are the outlines of a pentagon with a side of 2, a decagon with a side of 2, and a pentacle star with a side of (Φ + 1). Find at least one way (and more if possible) to fill each of these outlines. Record each arrangement you discover.

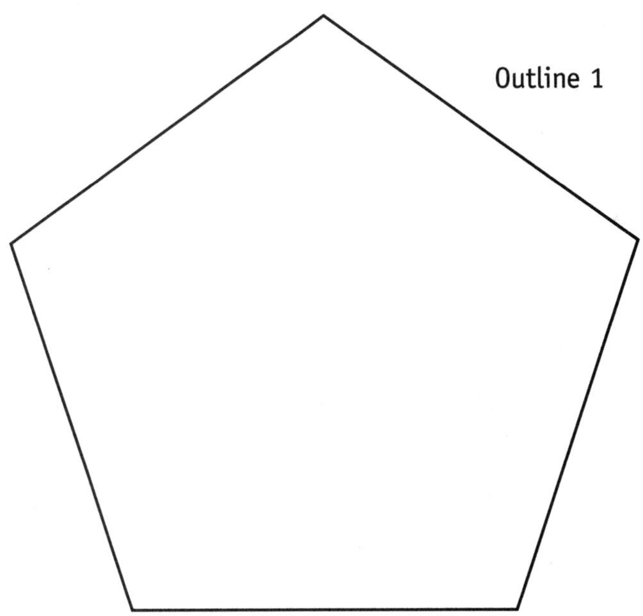

Outline 1

Treat the star and the decagon as separate outlines.

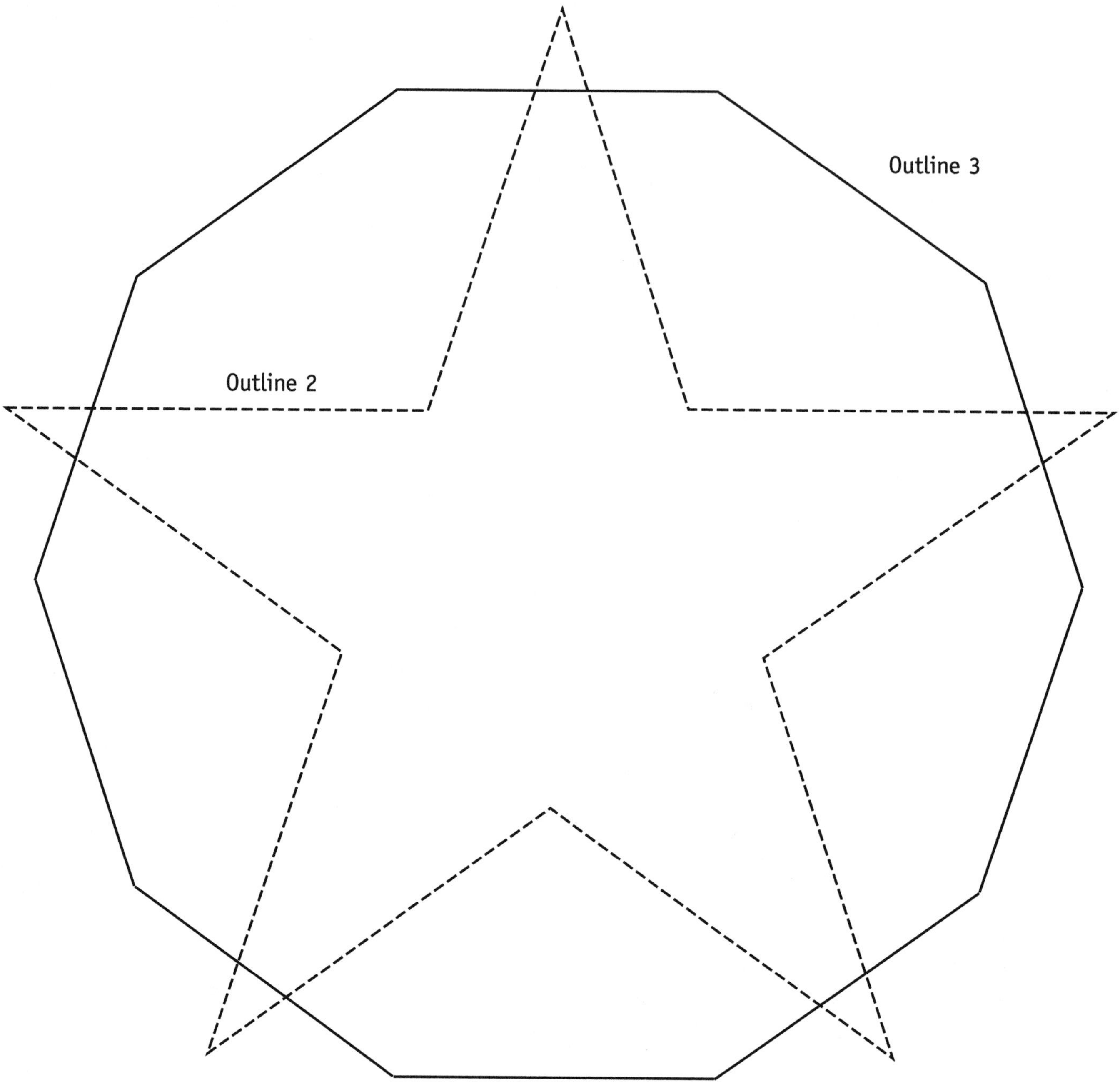

Part II

4. Write an entry in your *Investigations Journal* summarizing what this activity showed you about using PentaBlocks to fill an area or outline. Write each statement or conjecture as simply and precisely as possible.

Investigation 7: Rotational and Mirror Symmetry

ORGANIZATION

- *Mathematical Focus:*
  Figural patterns; Defining rotational and mirror symmetry
- *Special Materials:*
  Mirrors; string; transparency film; washable transparency pens; overheads showing examples of different types of symmetry
- *Approximate Time:* 50 minutes
- *Suggested Group Size:* Pairs or quads

INSTRUCTION

- *Lesson Summary:*
  - Students experience, in both a concrete and a formal way, the symmetry operations of *rotation* and *reflection*.
  - Students complete designs by using a given rotocenter or mirror.
  - Students create new designs that exhibit combinations of rotational and mirror symmetry.
  - Students describe designs with rotational or mirror symmetry.
- *Terminology:*
  - See the Students' Guide for specific descriptions and definitions of these words:

    design element (motif)
    image point, mapping a point
    N-fold rotational symmetry, degree of symmetry
    reflection, mirror, simple bilateral symmetry
    rotation, rotocenter
    symmetrical, symmetry operation
    symmetry tool
- *Specific Notes to Teachers:*
  - It is important to show examples that illustrate the essential characteristics of the symmetry types. See Blackline Masters 2 and 3, in Appendix 5, for symmetry examples.
  - You can use physical mirrors as a concrete reinforcement of the notion of mirror symmetry. Using string or a line on a transparency sheet to represent a line of symmetry helps make the transition from concrete to abstract. Students could be asked to generate additional examples.
- *Activity Sequence:*
  1. Distribute the Students' Guides, string (a piece about 12 in. long per student), and/or 3 or 4 pieces of overhead transparency film and a washable overhead pen per group.
  2. Discuss new terminology and show examples.
  3. Have students explore the use of physical mirrors and symbolic mirrors (using string or lines on transparency film) with PentaBlocks shapes or designs in Part I.

4. Have groups/pairs draw with templates (or trace blocks) to finish the incomplete designs in Part II.
5. Give groups/pairs 10 to 15 minutes for Part III.
6. You might have each group post its designs in a "gallery exhibit." Orchestrate exchange and dialogue between pairs of groups, or among groups if it seems appropriate.

- *Possible Responses:*

1. a. Both triangles are degree 1; both rhombuses are degree 2; the pentagon and star are degree 5.

b. PentaBlocks designs are possible that exhibit 1-, 2-, 5-, and 10-fold rotational symmetry.

c. In a regular polygon the degree of rotational symmetry corresponds to the number of equivalent points.

2. Responses vary.

3. a.

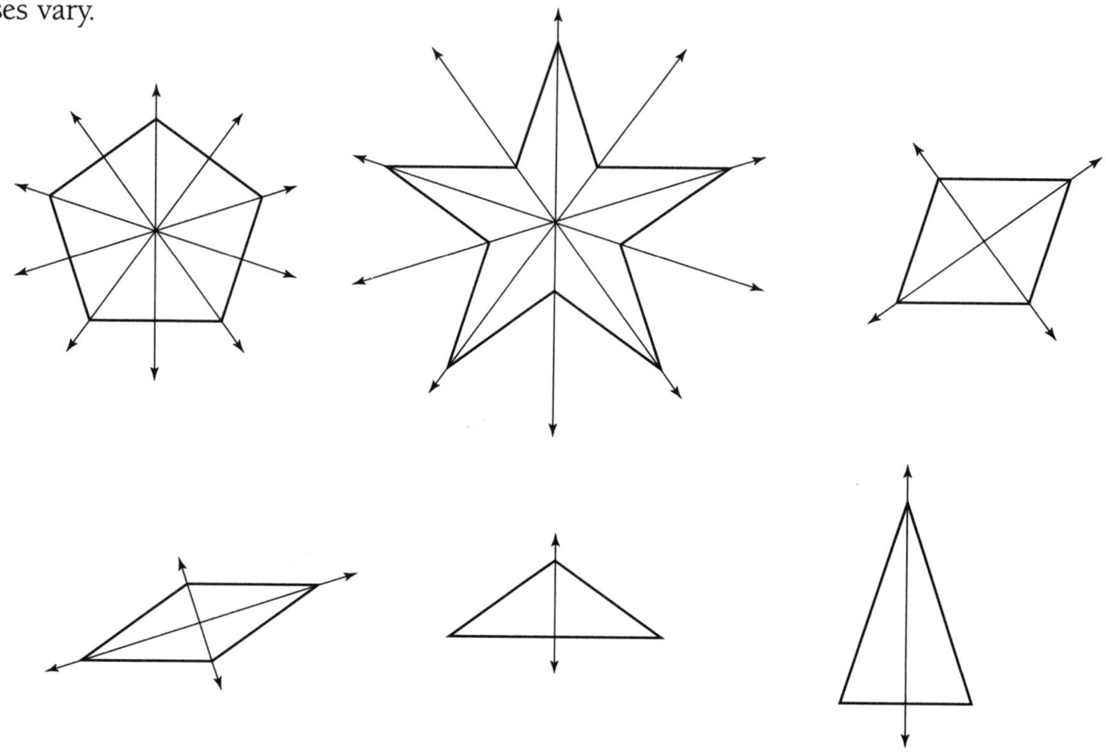

Pentagon and star: The five mirrors intersect at the rotocenter, forming 36° angles.

Rhombuses: The two mirrors intersect at the rotocenter, forming 90° angles.

Triangles: Each has a single mirror.

In all cases, the degree of rotational symmetry is the same as the number of mirrors. This is true of every shape that *has* mirrors, as long as those mirrors are not parallel to each other.

b.

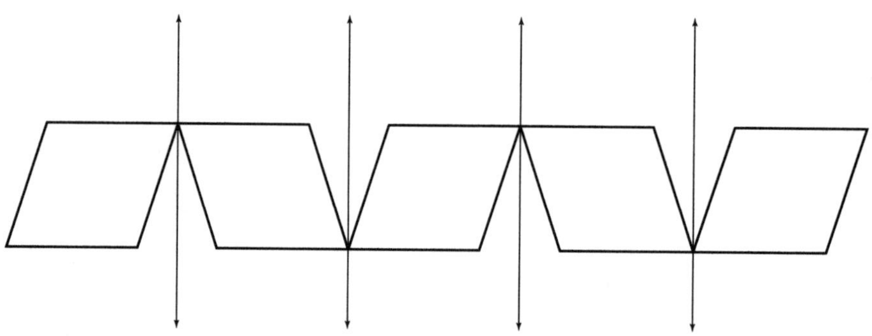

4.

a.

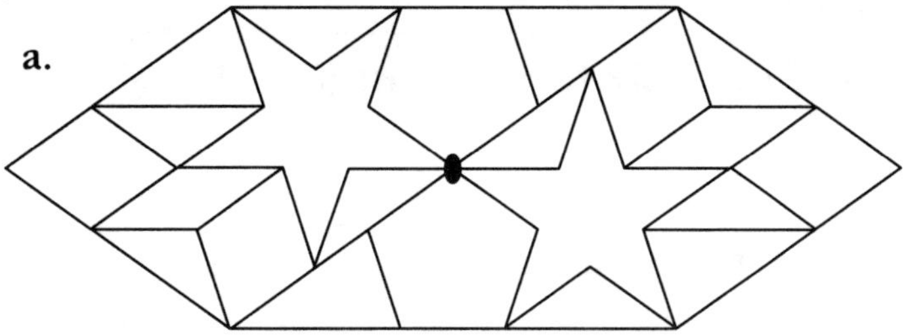

b.

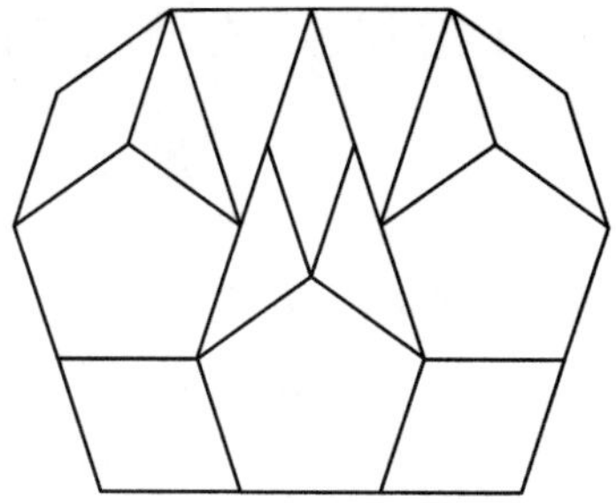

c.

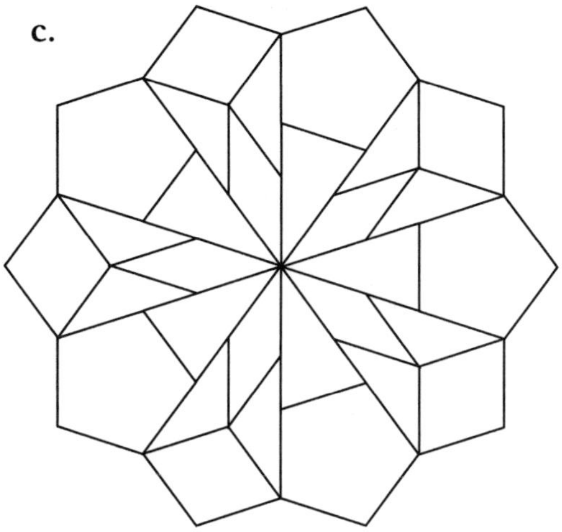

d.

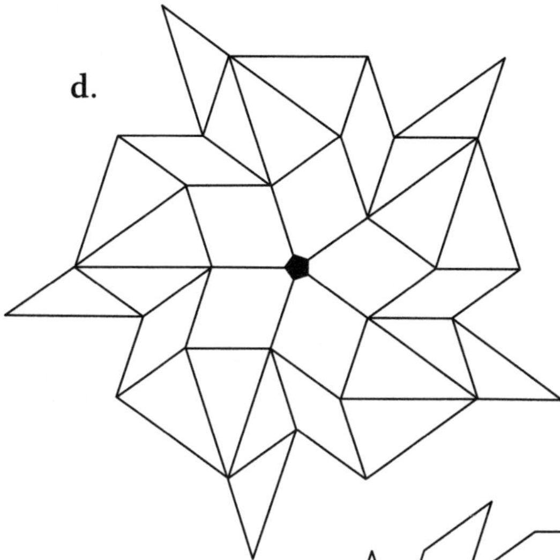

e.

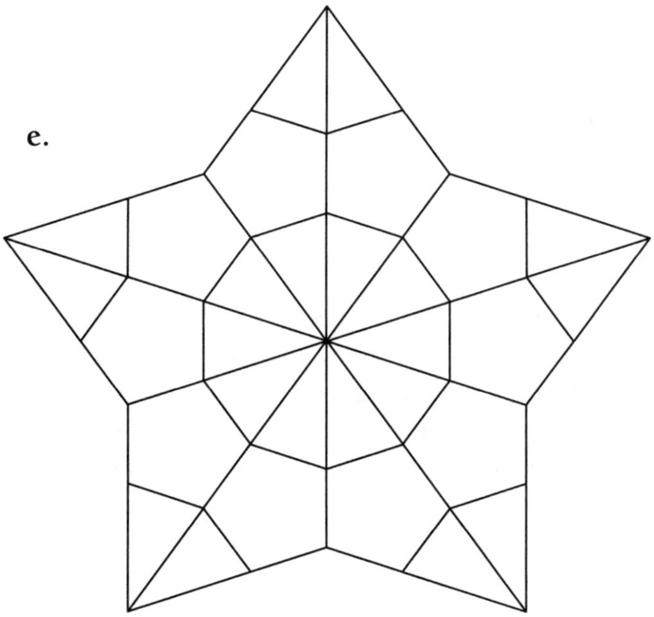

f.

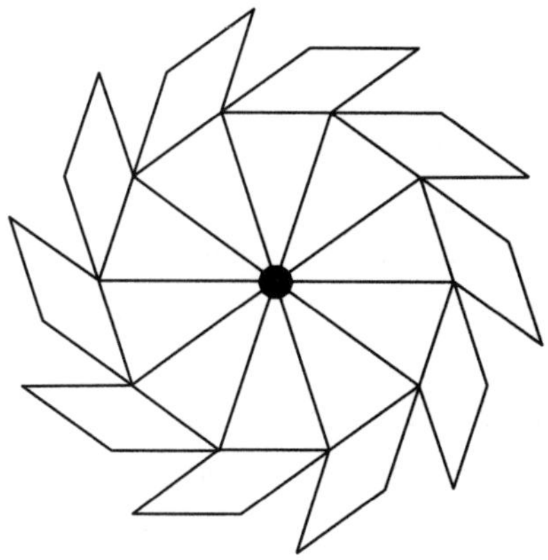

g.

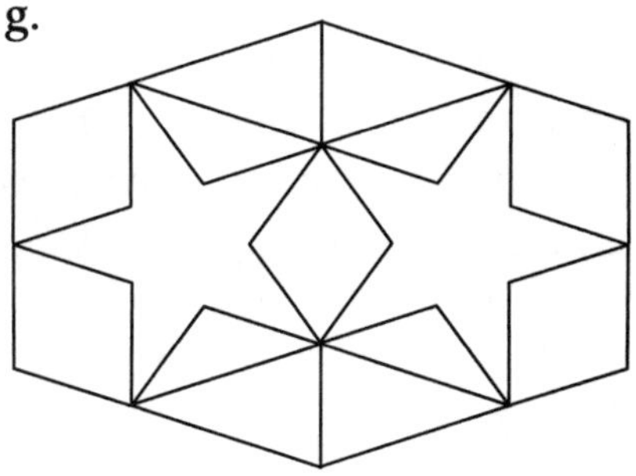

5. Designs vary.

6. Designs vary.

- *Possible Extensions:*
  1. Look for designs (for example, hub caps, corporate logos, fabric and tile designs) that have rotational and/or reflective symmetry. Copy the designs and locate the rotocenters and mirrors.
  2. Locate the mirrors and/or rotocenters for designs chosen from the appendices by the teacher.

Investigation 7: Rotational and Mirror Symmetry

Background Information

Many of you already have a sense of symmetry. You probably recognize symmetry when you see it, but you may not know just what it is that *makes* a design symmetrical. In general, a symmetrical design has some sort of regular repetition. Speaking mathematically, a design is **symmetrical** if there is a correspondence between each point and at least one other point.* Here are three symmetrical designs, with a few of their corresponding points marked. For example, point B lies in the same position on its oval as B_1, B_2, B_3, B_4, B_5, B_6, and B_7 do on theirs.

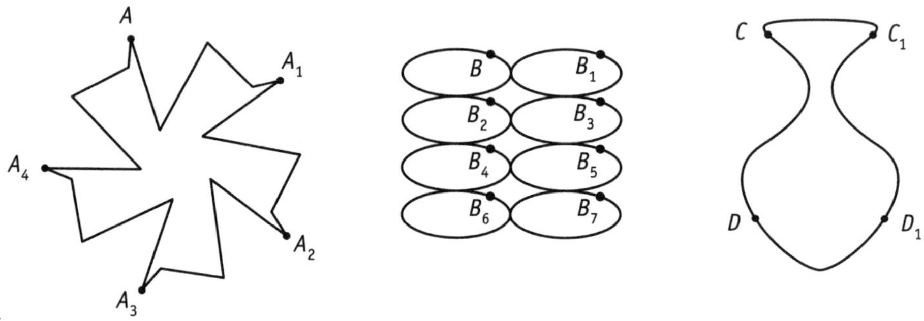

This correspondence is defined by a **symmetry operation**, which is an action that is applied to a point to locate its **image**. We say that the symmetry operation **maps** each point onto its image point(s).

There are four basic symmetry operations: *rotation, reflection, translation,* and *glide reflection*. Each of these operations has an associated symmetry **tool** that is used to create the action. Using any of the basic operations, or combinations of them, causes some sort of well-behaved and predictable repetition. The repeating part of such a design is often described as a **design element** or **motif**.

In this investigation you will explore two of the basic symmetry operations.

Rotation is the symmetry operation that rotates or "spins" a point or design element about some **rotocenter**. The rotocenter, then, is the symmetry tool for rotations. As a design is rotated a full 360° around the rotocenter, the number of times N that it coincides with its original position is described as its **N-fold rotational** symmetry, or its **degree**. For example, the first figure has $N = 1$ (or *degree 1)* rotational symmetry because it coincides with itself only once in a 360° rotation; the second figure has $N = 2$ (degree 2) rotational symmetry because it coincides twice. The third, fourth, and fifth figures coincide 3, 4, and 5 times, respectively.

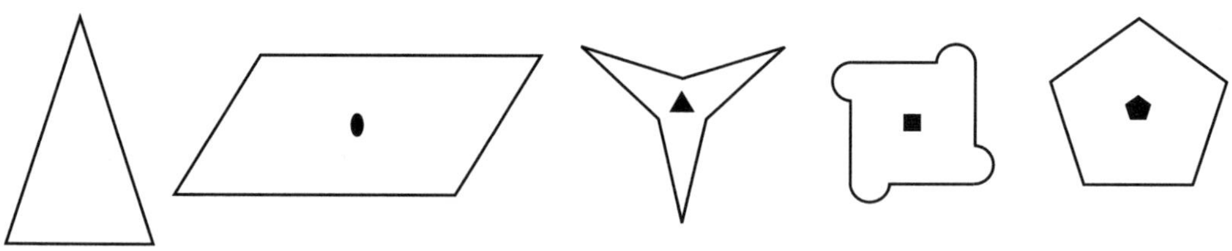

$N = 1$ $N = 2$ $N = 3$ $N = 4$ $N = 5$

* The exceptions are unique points like rotocenters and points on a mirror in a pattern with a single mirror (defined shortly). These points are unique because they have no corresponding points in the pattern.

Look at the small figures at the rotocenters of the last four designs on the previous page. In symmetry diagrams, a small *oval* is used to show a 2-fold rotocenter, a small *triangle* to symbolize a 3-fold rotocenter, a small *square* to represent a 4-fold rotocenter, and so on. A 1-fold rotocenter has no symbol, because figures with 1-fold rotational symmetry have an infinite number of rotocenters: no matter what point you choose as a rotocenter, the design coincides once and only once in 360°.

Reflection is the symmetry operation that reflects or "flips" a point or design element across a **mirror** (or **line** or **axis** of symmetry) to locate its image.

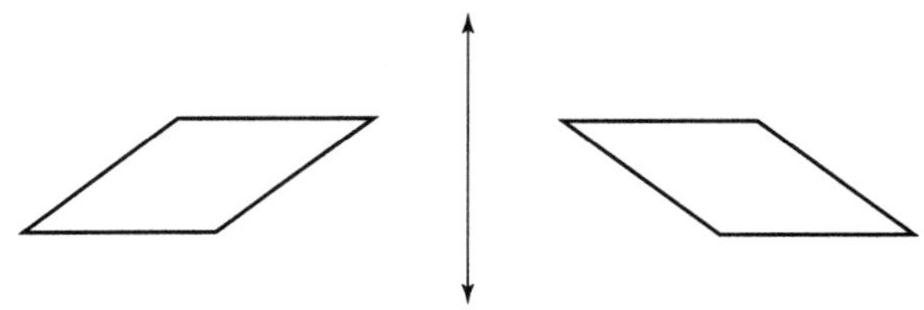

A mirror, the symmetry tool for reflection, divides a symmetrical design into two congruent halves. These halves are mirror images of each other; they would coincide if the figure were folded along the mirror line. Because a design with only one line of symmetry has exactly *two* matching parts, it is said to have **simple bilateral** symmetry. A design can have more than one mirror—even many mirrors.

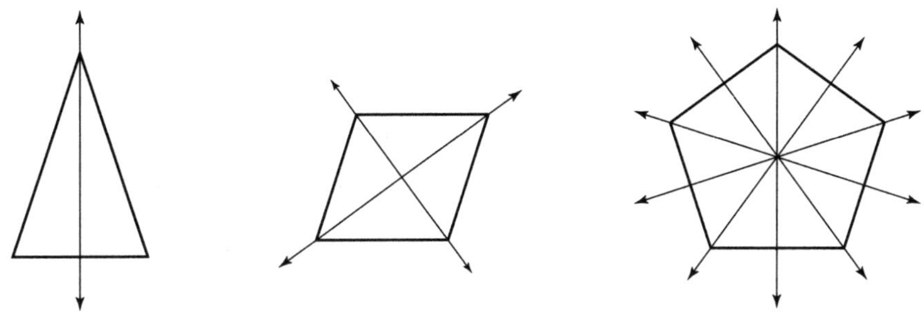

1 mirror   2 mirrors   5 mirrors

Action

Part I

1. a. Choose a PentaBlocks shape and investigate its rotational symmetry. Use the template or a block to trace the outline of the shape onto a piece of transparent film and mark the approximate position of the rotocenter on the film. Trace the shape on a piece of paper as well. Place the film on top of the paper, press down lightly on the rotocenter with a pencil or pin, and rotate the film. Does the outline coincide exactly with the shape below it the number of times you expected? Find the degree of rotational symmetry for each of the PentaBlocks shapes.

   b. Make a PentaBlocks design that you think exhibits 2-fold rotational symmetry. Trace the design and locate the rotocenter on a piece of transparent film. Then trace it on paper. As you did before, place it on top of the design and verify its rotational symmetry. What degrees of rotational symmetry can be found in designs created with PentaBlocks?

   c. Mark a single vertex of a regular pentagon and rotate the pentagon about its rotocenter. How many times in a complete rotation does that vertex coincide with a point in the original pentagon? How does the number of equivalent (original and corresponding) points seem to be related to the degree of rotation? Explore on your own and create a conjecture about this.

2. a. Place a physical mirror next to a PentaBlocks shape. Watch what happens to the mirror image as you move the mirror around. Try this with the other PentaBlocks shapes also.

   b. Make a design from PentaBlocks that has a straight line edge. Imagine what you would see if you placed a mirror along the straight edge. Use a real mirror to verify what you thought you'd see.

   c. Make a PentaBlocks design that you think exhibits mirror symmetry. Use a piece of string or a line drawn on a piece of transparent film as the mirror and place it on top of the design where the mirror should go. Verify that the two sides are reflections of each other.

3. Try exploring patterns that involve multiple mirrors.

   a. Trace the outline of each of the PentaBlocks shapes. Draw all symmetry mirrors. How many distinct mirrors does each shape have? For each shape, describe how the mirrors are related to each other. Is there any mathematical relationship between the number of mirrors and the N-fold rotational symmetry of each shape? Is this relationship always true for any shape?

   b.

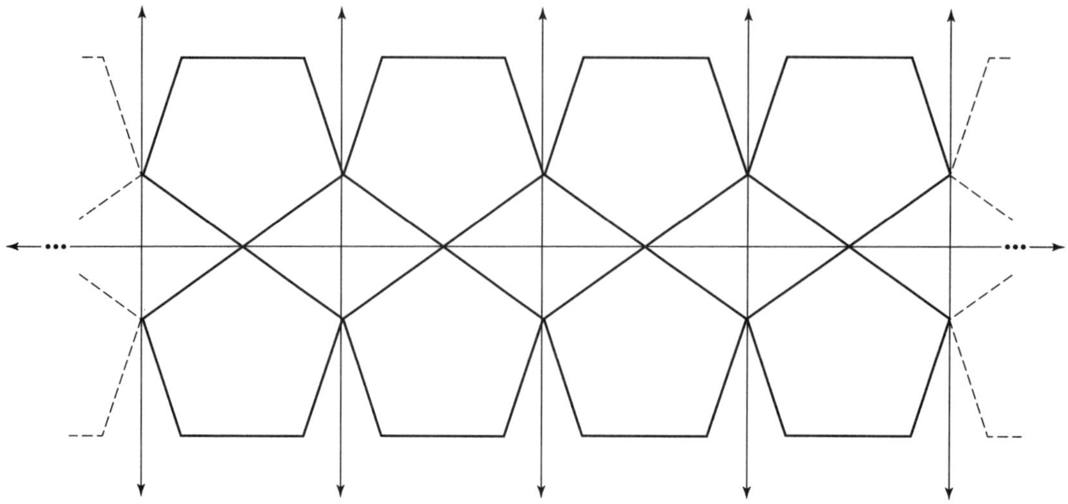

This figure illustrates a PentaBlocks pattern that has an infinite set of parallel vertical mirrors, all perpendicular to a single horizontal mirror. The ellipsis (-••••-) indicates that the mirror pattern continues. Try to create two or three additional patterns that exhibit a set of parallel mirrors. Can you create a pattern that has an infinite set of parallel mirrors but does *not* have another mirror perpendicular to the parallel mirrors?

Part II

4. Each of the following illustrations shows part of a repeating design. Each line (⟷) represents a mirror or axis of symmetry, and each small oval or filled polygon represents an N-fold rotocenter. Use a PentaBlocks template or trace blocks to continue the pattern with the symmetry as indicated.

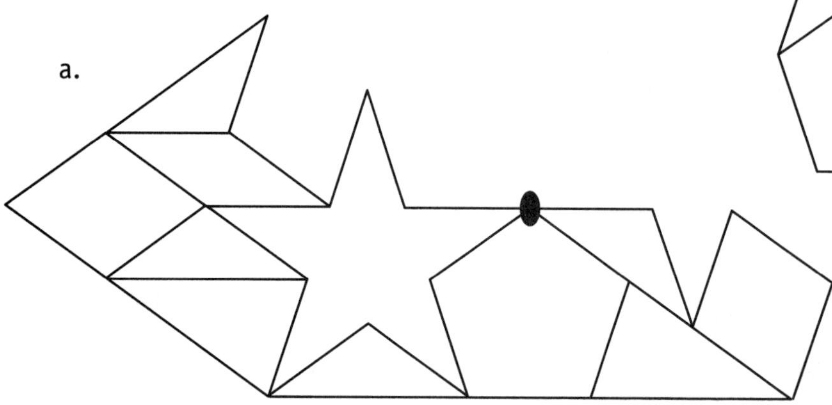

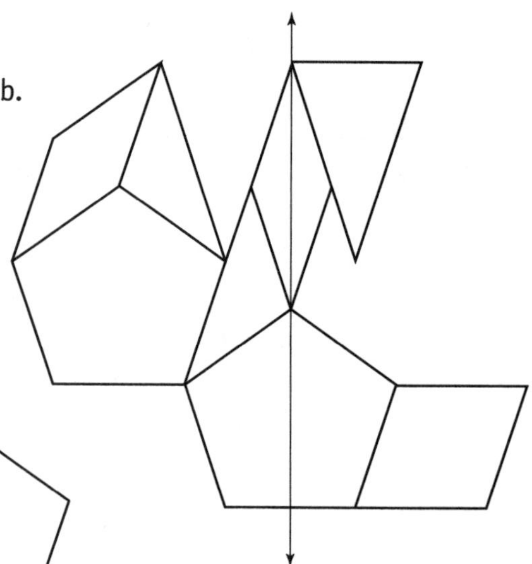

c.

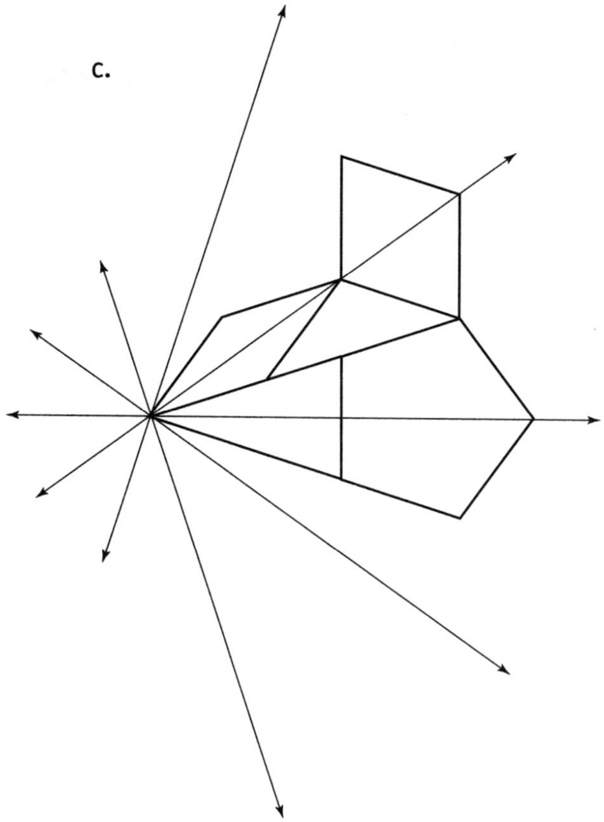

d.

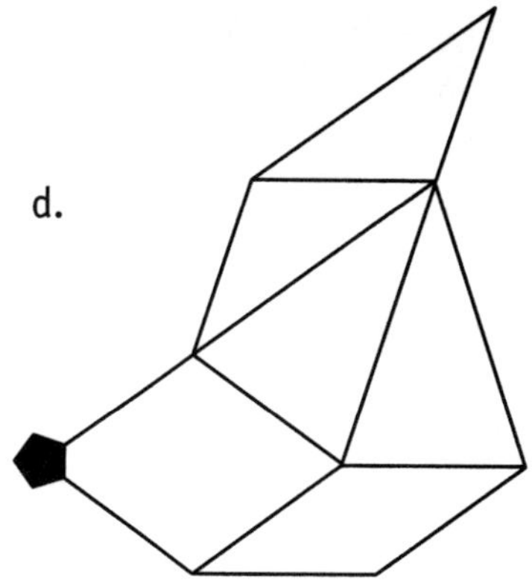

f.

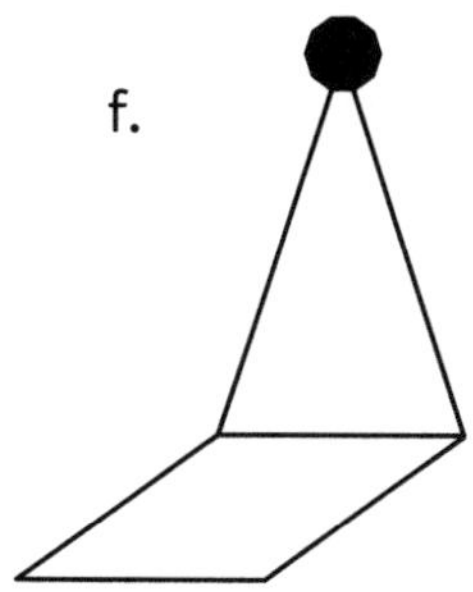

e.

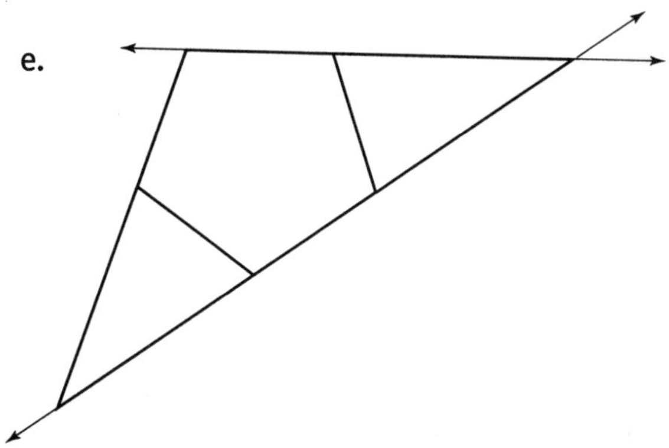

g.

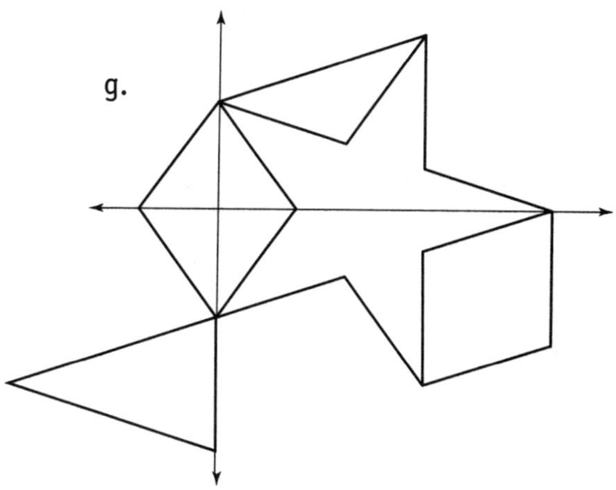

Part III

5. In your group, generate your own PentaBlocks designs, *each with a different degree of rotational symmetry*. Create as many different examples as you can in a few minutes. Show *all* rotocenters.
6. In your group, generate your own PentaBlocks designs, each with a different combination of symmetry mirror(s). Create as many different examples as you can in a few minutes. Show *all* mirrors.

Part IV

7. Write an entry in your *Investigations Journal* summarizing what you understand about reflective and rotational symmetry, as discovered in this activity. Describe any property or conjecture as simply and precisely as possible.

ORGANIZATION

- *Mathematical Focus*
  Defining and applying the translation and glide reflection symmetry operations
- *Special Materials:*
  Transparency film; washable overhead transparency pens; overhead examples
- *Approximate Time:* 50 minutes
- *Suggested Group Size:* Pairs or quads

INSTRUCTION

- *Lesson Summary:*
  - Students experience, in both a concrete and a formal way, the symmetry operations of *translation* and *glide reflection*.
  - Students complete designs by using either a translation vector or a "glide mirror/vector" or both.
  - Students create their own designs that exhibit translational or glide reflection symmetry.
  - Class discussion focuses on describing designs with these symmetries.
- *Terminology:*
  - See the Students' Guide for specific descriptions and definitions of these words:

glide mirror/vector	translation
glide reflection	translation vector

- *Specific Notes to Teachers:*
  Again, showing examples that illustrate the essential characteristics of the symmetry types is important. Using a transparency sheet to copy a design element that can be translated and/or flipped over is very helpful. Students can be asked to generate additional examples. Blackline Master 4 in Appendix 5 provides a complex design including translations and glide reflections. (The same design is also provided, without vectors, in Appendix 4.)
- *Activity Sequence:*
  1. Distribute the Student Guides, 3 or 4 pieces of overhead transparency film, and a washable overhead pen per group.
  2. Discuss new terminology, and show examples. Relate these to the previously discussed symmetry operations as completing the set needed to generate any kind of repetitive pattern in the plane.
  3. Have students use the transparency film with PentaBlocks shapes or designs in Part I.
  4. Have groups/pairs draw with templates (or trace blocks) to finish the incomplete designs in Part II.
  5. Give groups/pairs 10 to 15 minutes for Part III.
  6. You might have each group post its designs in a "gallery exhibit." Orchestrate dialogue between pairs of groups, or among groups if it seems appropriate.

- *Possible Responses:*

1. **a.** Only the rhombuses can be used to make translations with matching edges.

   b. The vector is the length of a "long" side, and it is parallel to the left leg of the triangle. Changing the distance a block is shifted (the length of the vector), or the line along which the shift occurs (the direction of the vector), or both, will change the translation.

   c. See figure. Translations will exhibit mirror symmetry if the original figure shows mirror symmetry on its own and if the translation vector is perpendicular to an axis of symmetry (mirror) for the original figure. The mirror for the complete design is a perpendicular bisector of the translation vector.

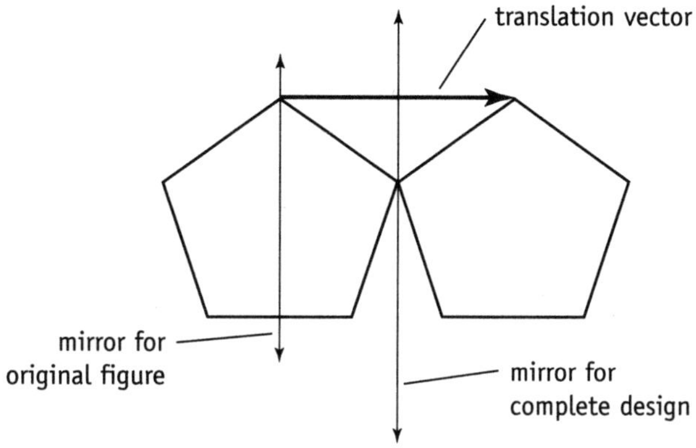

2. **a.** Answers vary.

   b. Some patterns with bilateral symmetry could be seen as also exhibiting glide reflective symmetry where the translation vector is the same length as the distance between corresponding design elements. Here is one example.

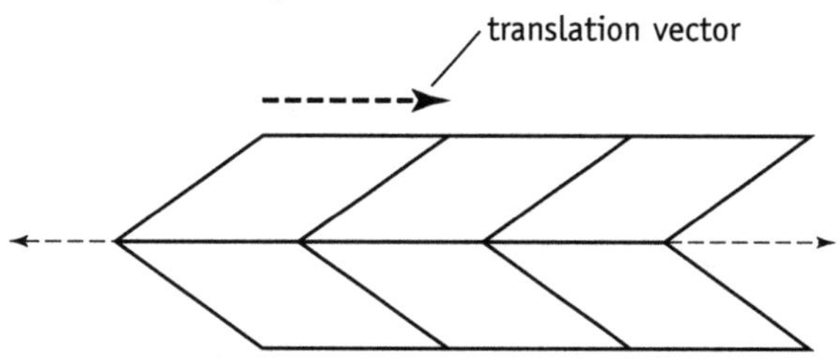

In these investigations, though, we will normally refer to such designs simply as examples of bilateral symmetry.

3.

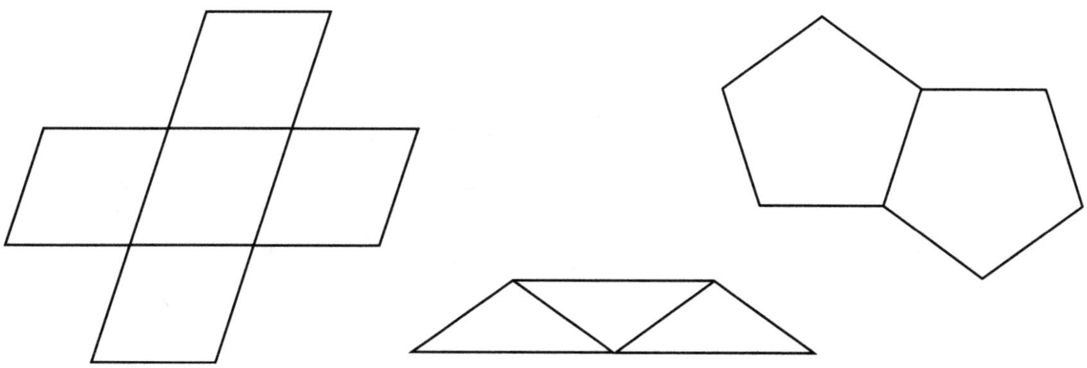

4. Designs will vary. This is a sample of what students may produce.

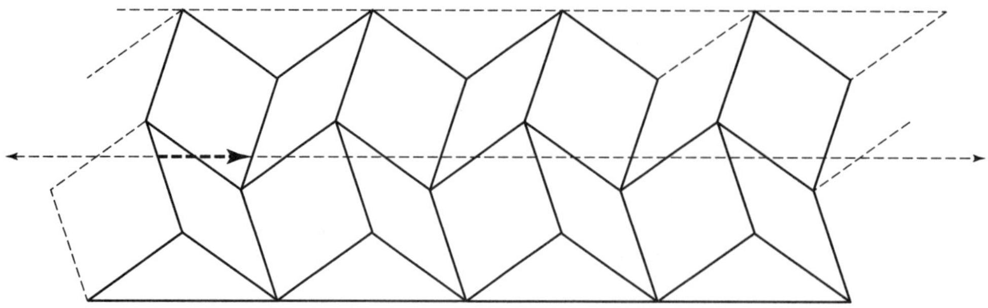

5. Designs will vary. Shown here is one four-symmetry example, showing how each symmetry type works for this one pattern.

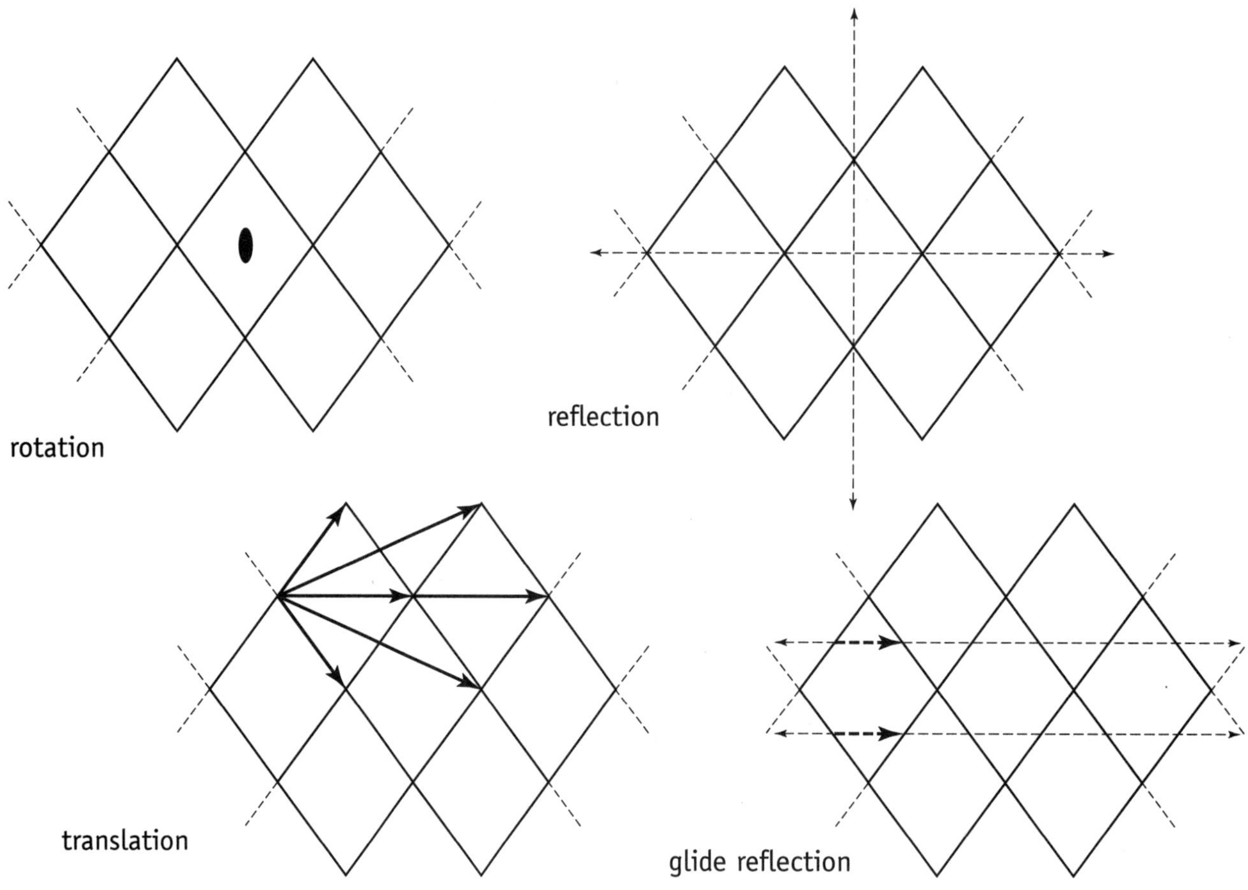

- *Possible Extensions:*

The four symmetry operations described in these last two investigations are called *isometries*. An isometry (iso = same, metry = measure) is a transformation that changes the position or orientation of a design element, but does not change the measure of any angle or length. Investigate the types of transformations that do change the measures of angles or lengths. Some types that might be investigated include dilations, point inversions, and projections. This can be carried all the way to a study of anamorphic art.

Investigation 8: Translations and Glide Reflections

Background Information

A design is often described as *symmetrical* if there is a correspondence between each point and at least one other point.* Each point or design element is mapped onto its image point by a symmetry operation. Each operation uses an associated symmetry tool to create the action.

In the previous investigation you studied rotations and reflections. In this investigation you will define and explore the other two basic symmetry operations: *translations* and *glide reflections*.

Translation is the symmetry operation that translates, "slides," or "shifts" a point or design element a certain distance along a certain line. Connecting any point to its translated image is a **translation vector** that shows the specific distance and direction that defines the particular translation. Thus, the symmetry tool for translations is the translation vector.

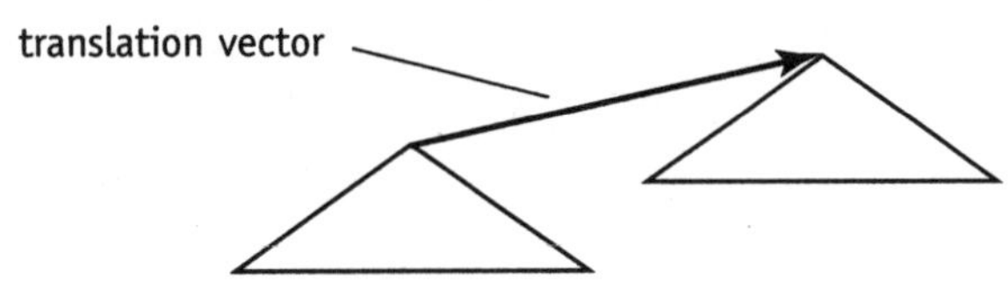

A **glide reflection** is a combination of a translation and a reflection. It doesn't matter which of the simpler operations you do first, as long as it is immediately followed by the second. The symmetry tool for glide reflections is a **glide mirror/vector**. A glide reflection reflects a point or design element across the glide mirror/vector, and it immediately translates that reflection to a new location. The design element and its image after a glide reflection, then, are mirror-images of each other but are not directly across the mirror from each other. A glide mirror/vector is shown as a dashed line with a dashed vector, to distinguish it from a normal mirror (shown as a solid line) or translation vector (shown as a solid ray).

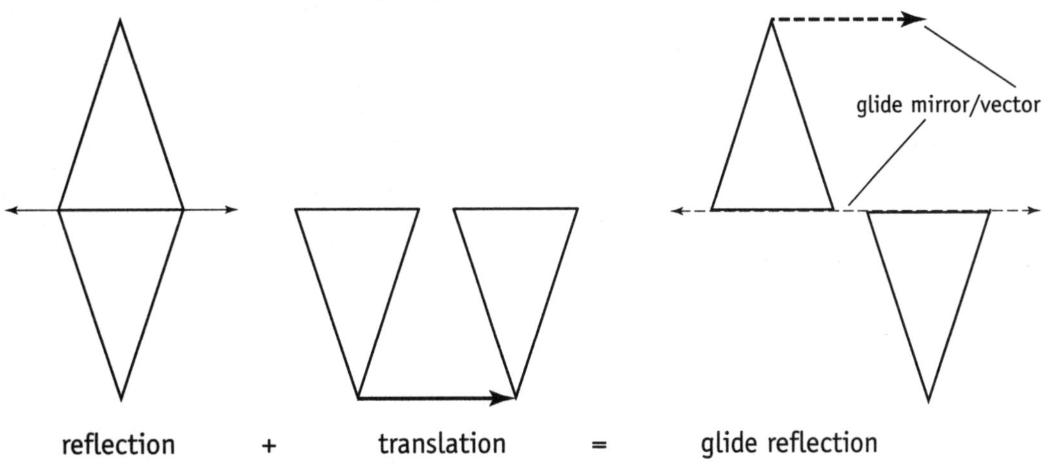

* Each point, that is, except unique rotocenters and unique mirror points.

Action

Part I.

1. **a.** Which PentaBlocks shapes can be used for a translation in which neighboring (identical) blocks fit flush?

   b. How can you describe the translation vector for the translation shown here?

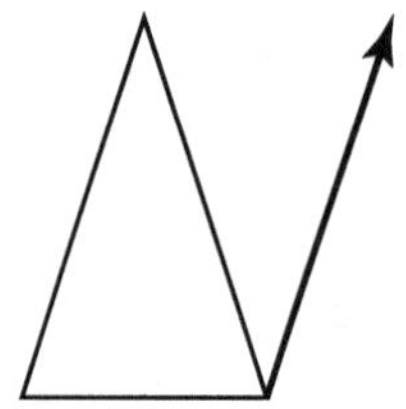

   Show and describe how to change the results by changing the translation vector.

   c. Create and illustrate a translation in which the design element and its image together exhibit mirror symmetry. Show the translation vector from one point to its corresponding point on the translated image, and show the mirror as a solid line in a distinguishable color. Looking at your drawing, can you make a conjecture that will help you predict when a translation and its original, taken as a unit, will exhibit mirror symmetry?

2. **a.** Use a PentaBlocks shape to illustrate a glide reflection. Trace the shape and show the glide mirror/vector as a dashed line and dashed ray. Use a piece of transparent film to show how to get from one design element (an individual block) to its neighboring image.

   b. Can a design that exhibits glide reflective symmetry also have simple bilateral symmetry? Explain.

Part II

3. Each of the illustrations below shows part of a repeating design. Each ray (⟶) represents a translation vector, and each dashed line (←---→) and vector (---→) represents a glide mirror/vector. Use a PentaBlocks template or trace blocks to continue the pattern with the symmetry as indicated.

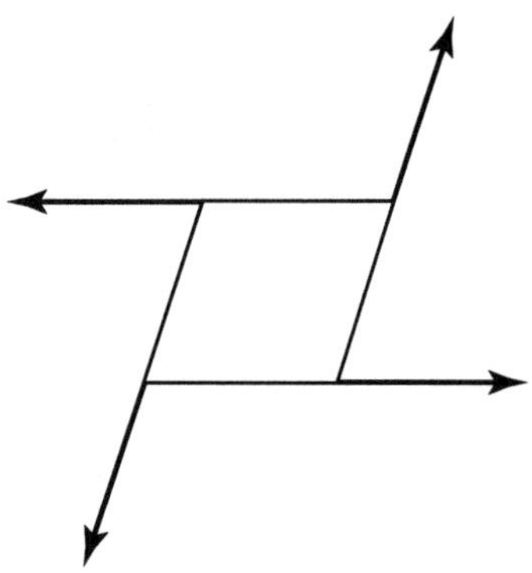

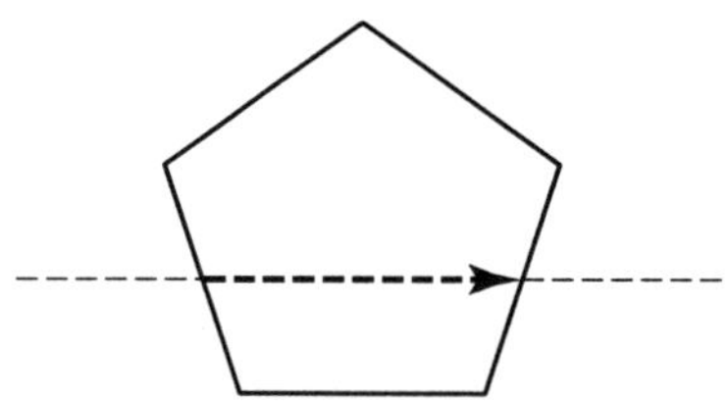

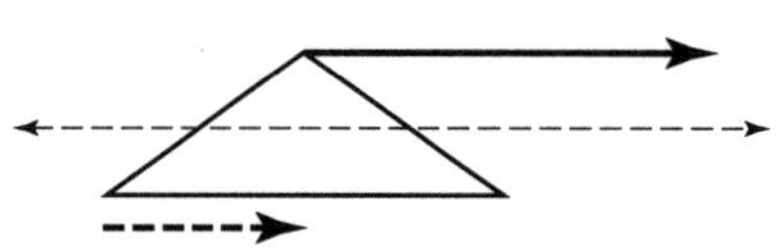

Part III

4. In your group, create an interesting glide reflective pattern that uses at least two different PentaBlocks shapes and has matching edges. In your illustration, show the glide mirror/vector clearly with a colored marker.
5. In your group, generate your own PentaBlocks designs that exhibit different combinations of at least two symmetry types; that is, try to find ways to combine rotational symmetry, mirror symmetry, translational symmetry and glide reflective symmetry. Show *all* rotocenters, translation vectors and mirrors of either type. Can you find at least one design that exhibits all four types of symmetry?

Part IV

6. Write an entry in your *Investigations Journal* summarizing what you understand about translations and glide reflections as discovered in this activity. Describe any property or conjecture as simply and precisely as possible.

Teacher's Guide

ORGANIZATION

- *Mathematical Focus:*
  Defining and investigating *centered* and *linear* patterns
- *Special Materials:* Transparency film and pens for each group; PentaBlocks templates for recording designs
- *Approximate Time:* One or two 50-minute sessions
- *Suggested Group Size:* Quads

INSTRUCTION

- *Lesson Summary:*
  - Students create centered designs that exhibit rotational and/or mirror symmetry. Students investigate the relationship between unique points and segments joining a point and its image.
  - Students create a variety of linear designs, including both bands and meanders. Students investigate the properties of translation vectors, and how they relate to the boundary lines.
- *Terminology:*
  - Please refer to the Students' Guide for specific descriptions and definitions of these words:

    centered pattern; point group
    equivalence set
    linear pattern; line group
    linear band; meander; boundary line
    unique point
- *Specific Notes to Teachers:*
  - A key issue for a repetitive pattern is its *predictability*. That is, can you know what pieces to add and where to add them in order to continue the pattern?
  - This investigation introduces all three types of predictable patterns but explores only the centered and linear patterns. The basic vocabulary introduced here is essential for more fully understanding planar patterns and tessellations, which are explored in Investigation 10 (page 10).
  - It is important to show examples of every type of design in the beginning, so that the subtle differences between types is clear. You might have a "Gallery Exhibit" of student-generated designs with each one labeled by type. Posting examples or showing transparencies clearly identifying centers, translation vectors, corresponding points, and boundary lines would be helpful.
- *Activity Sequence:*
  1. Hand out Students' Guides, and give the students enough time to try several designs each for ***Actions*** **1**, **2**, and **3**.
  2. Encourage students to share their ***Action*** **4** designs with other groups. Because these designs can be complex, you may want students to move from group to group rather than spend time recording these designs.

3. Be sure each group has transparencies and pens for ***Action* 5**. Encourage groups to share their conjectures from ***Action* 5c**, or else display and discuss conjectures as a class.

- *Possible Responses:*

1. **a.** Here is one possibility:

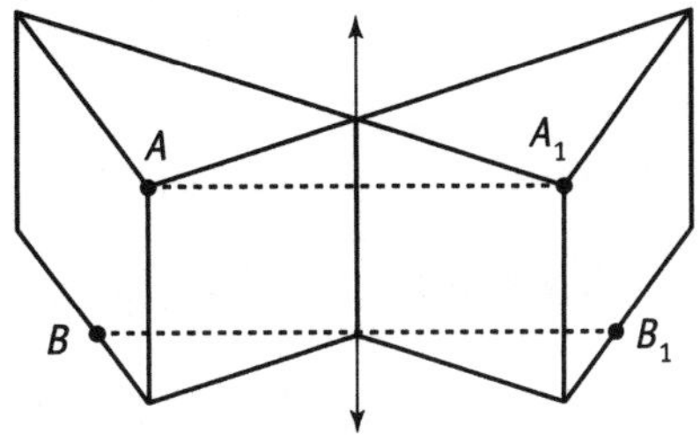

The mirror is the perpendicular bisector of segment AA_1.

b. Yes.

c. Yes: that a point and its image are equidistant from the mirror, and the mirror is always a perpendicular bisector of the segment connecting a point and its image.

2. **a.** Here is one possibility:

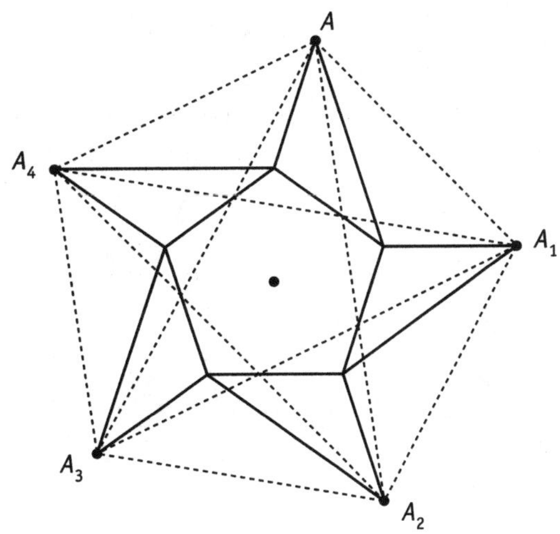

b. The rotocenter is the center of the regular pentagon formed by connecting the equivalent points consecutively.

c. The segments outline a much smaller regular pentagon within the original one, and the center point is once again the rotocenter.

d. Here is one possibility with degree 6.

Results are similar, with the additional consequence that some of the segments pass through the center.

e. When a figure has N-degree rotational symmetry, equivalent points can be connected to form a regular N-gon.

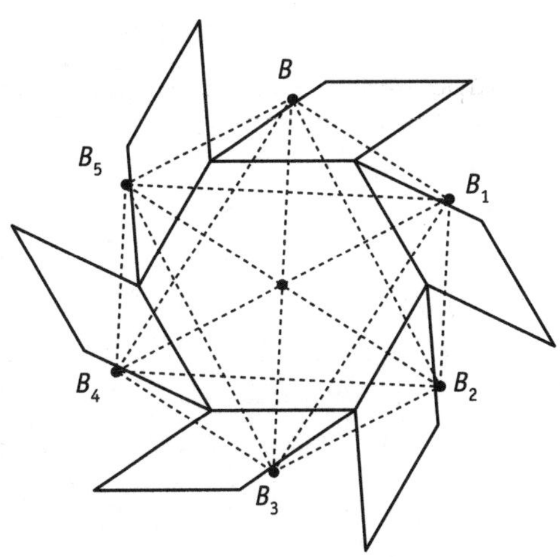

3. Here is one possibility (at right):

   Using a design that exhibits both 5-fold rotational and mirror symmetries seems to confirm the conclusions from ***Actions* 1c** and **2e**.

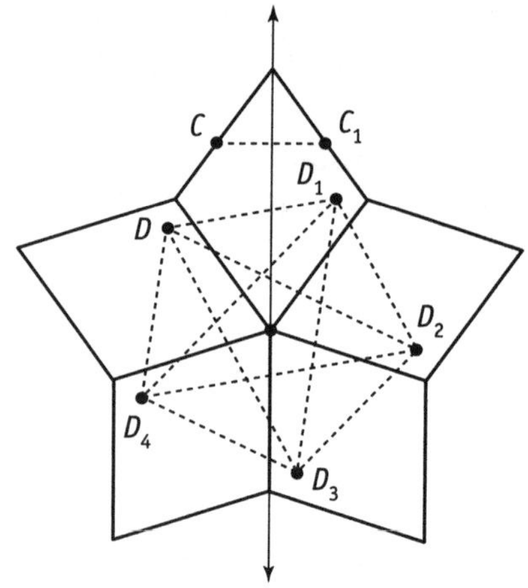

4. **a.** Every thin rhombus does have at least one corresponding block. Descriptions will vary but should include something about rotational symmetry.

   b.

c. Designs will vary.

d.

5. **a.** The boundary line is the extension of this translation vector. In fact, any two such boundary points determine one of the boundary lines.
   b. This same translation vector will connect any point of the design to a corresponding point.
   c. There is no difference if the boundary lines are or are not included in the design.

- *Possible Extensions:*
  1. Centered designs and mandalas have been used for millennia in many cultures to focus concentration or to enhance spirituality. Find examples of mandalas from religious and artistic sources and from a variety of cultures. Comment on their similarities and differences.
  2. Find examples of different types of centered or linear patterns from wallpaper, flooring, and fabric samples. Create a display or exhibit that describes the mathematics in each example.
  3. Trace a segment of a linear band design onto paper. Make copies of this strip with a photocopier and cut them into strips along the boundary lines. Can you place these strips next to each other so that they create a planar patterns? Is there only one way to do this, or are there several? Describe how this could lead to studying one class of planar patterns.
  4. The three basic types of patterns are described in terms of *point* groups, *line* groups, and *plane* groups. In fact, the concept of a *group* is of great importance in the study of advanced mathematical structures. Investigate the definition and properties related to groups. Explore why it is useful in applying abstract mathematics to real-world phenomena.

Investigation 9: Centered and Linear Patterns

Background Information:

The PentaBlocks let you explore designs that continue in some regular, predictable way on the plane. There are three basic types of predictable, two-dimensional patterns that you will study in some depth. Each type has its own special features. You will explore the features of two types of patterns in this investigation: centered patterns and linear patterns.

Centered Patterns

The key feature of a **centered** pattern, or **point** group, is that it has one or more unique points, which act as a center of the pattern. When you investigated rotations and reflections, you saw that rotocenters and points on the single mirror (in simple bilateral symmetry) are unique because they have no corresponding points; that is, no other point fits into the design in exactly the same way. Centered patterns can be finite or infinite. In fact, many centered patterns can be extended outward from some center figure in a variety of ways.

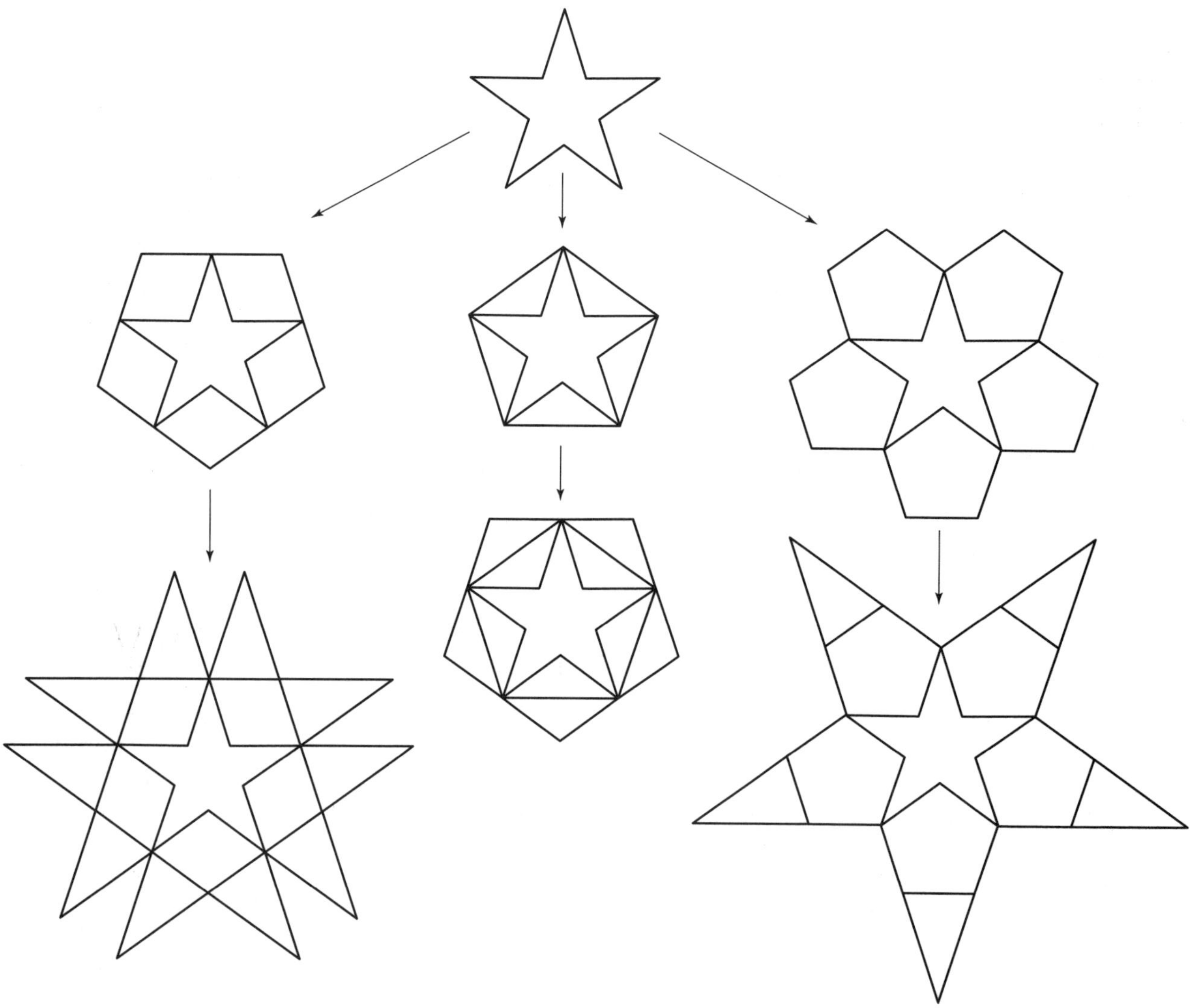

The examples below show **a**, a pattern centered about a unique point; **b**, a design centered about a pentagon (with its unique center point); and **c**, another design that has simple bilateral symmetry and is centered on a mirror.

a.

b.

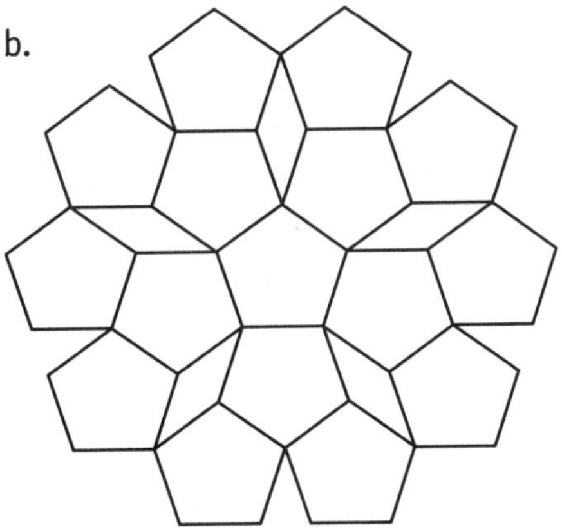

c.

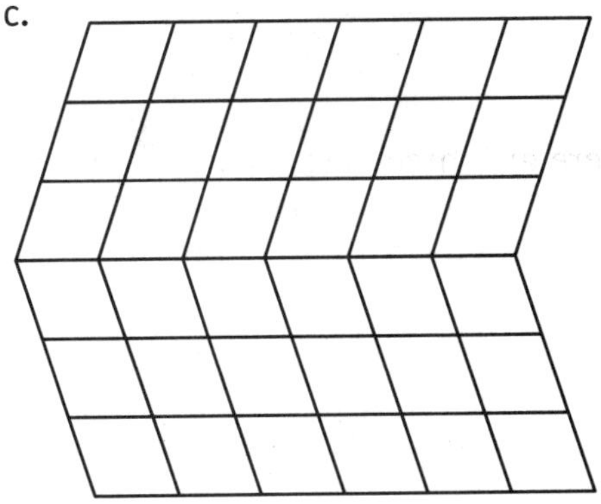

Linear Patterns

A **linear** pattern, or **line group**, is confined within a pair of parallel **boundary lines**. These boundary lines are not necessarily part of the design itself. When the boundary lines *are* part of the design, it is called a **linear band** design; the first two designs in the illustrations below are examples of linear band designs. When the boundary lines are *not* part of the design, the pattern is described as a **meander**, as in the bottom two examples shown below. They are called meanders because the outer edge of the design meanders instead of lying on a line.

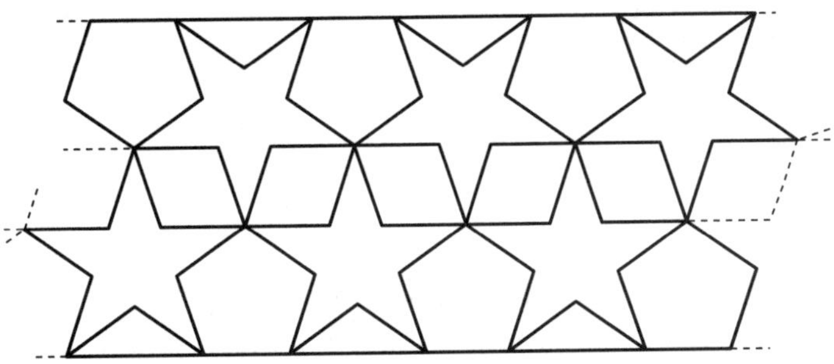

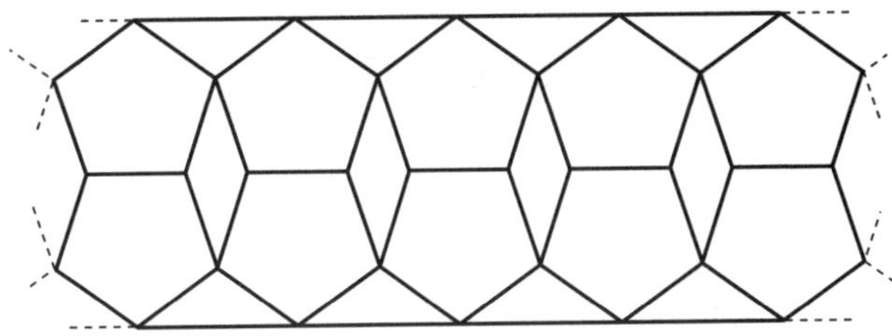

Two linear band designs

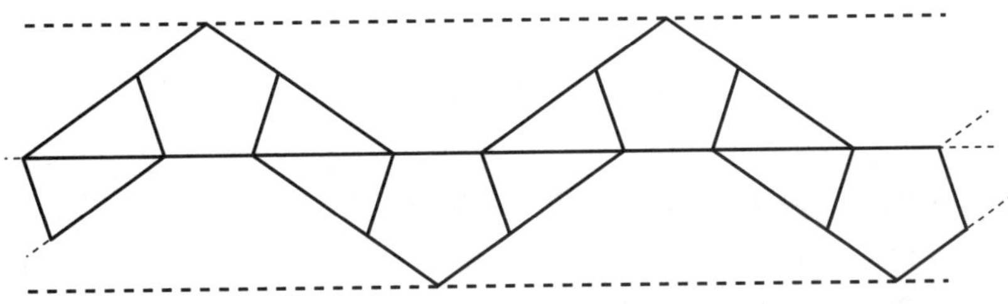

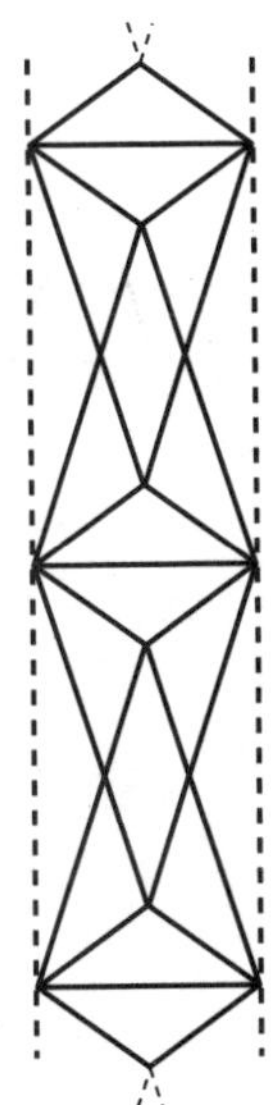

Two meanders with boundary lines shown as dashed segments

You can create a linear design by repeating a simple translation of a design element.

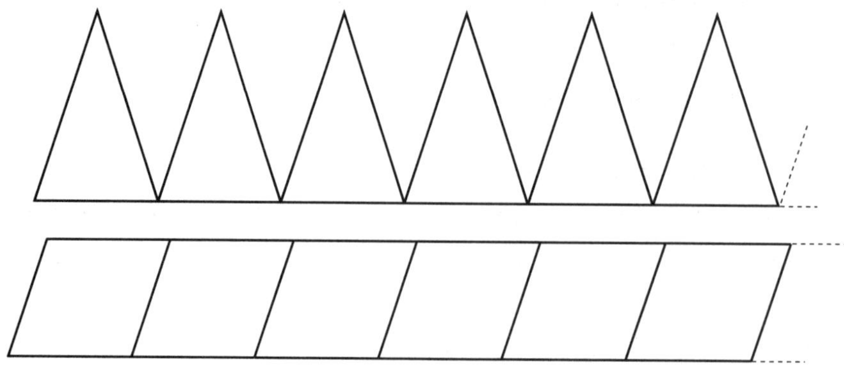

Every point in a linear design is part of an infinite **equivalence set** of corresponding points. Each corresponding point fits into the overall pattern in exactly the same way. This means that *a linear design has NO unique points*; instead, every point has an infinite number of corresponding points. Connecting any two corresponding points in an equivalence set is a translation vector, which shows the direction and distance to get from the first point to the second. In this meander, two points (A and B) are chosen at random and shown along with two of their respective corresponding points, and the translation vectors that define them.

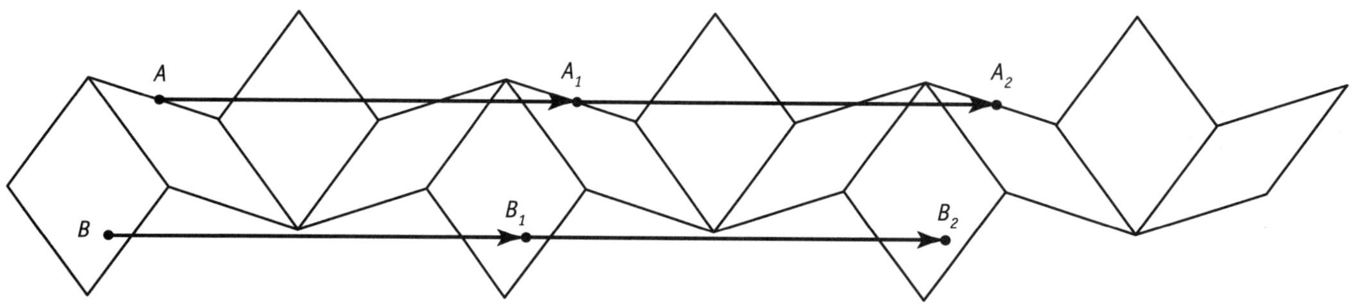

Planar Patterns

A planar pattern, or plane group, covers the infinite plane in a continuous and predictable way. As with linear patterns, there are no unique points, and every point in a repeating planar pattern is part of an infinite equivalence set. You will explore planar patterns in the next investigation.

Action:

Part I

1. **a.** Create and trace onto paper a centered PentaBlocks design that exhibits *only simple bilateral* symmetry. Highlight, in color, one specific point A in the design that is *not* on the mirror. Highlight, in the same color, its image A_1 in the reflection across the mirror. How does the mirror relate to segment AA_1?

   b. In a different color, highlight some other point B and its image B_1. Does the mirror relate to segment BB_1 in the same way?

   c. Follow this procedure with a variety of points. Does this suggest some conjecture?

2. **a.** Create and trace onto paper a centered design that exhibits *only rotational symmetry,* of an *odd* degree. Identify and mark the center in black. Highlight some other point and all of its equivalent points in color. Connect the original highlighted point and its images in clockwise order.

b. Describe the relationship between the center point and the figure made in ***Action* 2a**.

c. Draw segments connecting each pair of equivalent points above. How does the center point relate to this set of segments?

d. Repeat ***Actions* 2a**, **2b**, and **2c** using a centered design with only rotational symmetry of an even degree of 4 or greater. You can use PentaBlocks to create a design of degree 10 or simply sketch a design of another even degree.

e. What conjectures does this investigation suggest? Try to be as general as possible.

3. Repeat the preceding processes with a design that exhibits *both* rotational and mirror symmetry. Does this confirm you conjectures or suggest any changes?

4. a. This figure shows a centered design of thin rhombuses surrounding a regular pentagon. Does every thin rhombus have at least one corresponding block? How would you describe the pattern made by the rhombuses?

b. There are other designs using a pentagon-based "centerpiece" surrounded by thin rhombuses that are somewhat like this. One such pattern has a centerpiece of two pentagons; another is centered about a figure made up of six pentagons. Can you discover these?

c. Try to create another predictable design with a pentagon-based center, using only one type of rhombus.

d. Try to create a design that works like this with a centerpiece based on the star and using only one type of rhombus.

Part II

5. a. Create and record at least two different linear designs with the PentaBlocks in which the boundary lines are *not* part of the designs themselves (that is, they are meanders). Connect two consecutive corresponding points on the outermost edge of your design with a translation vector. Record the vector on a transparency. How does this translation vector relate to the boundary line? What conjecture does this suggest?

b. Use the transparency to investigate whether the same translation vector would connect any other point of the design to one of its equivalent points. What happens?

c. How do you think your answers would be different if the boundary lines were included in the design (that is, if it were a linear band design)? Check this out by creating two different band designs and repeating ***Actions* 5a** and **5b** for them. Decide which conjectures are true for all linear designs, only meanders, or only linear bands.

Part III

6. Write an entry in your *Investigations Journal* summarizing what this activity has shown you about the properties of centered and linear designs. Write each statement or conjecture as simply and precisely as possible.

ORGANIZATION

- *Mathematical Focus:*
  Planar patterns or plane group designs; periodicity (period parallelograms and translation vectors) and uniformity (including communicating vertex information); tessellations
- *Special Materials:* Transparency film and pens; colored pencils or markers
- *Approximate Time:* One to three 50-minute sessions
- *Suggested Group Size:* Quads or pairs

INSTRUCTION

- *Lesson Summary:*
  - Students explore the periodicity of planar patterns through lattices of corresponding points and period parallelograms.
  - Students explore the uniformity of planar patterns by examining vertex information; students create their own symbol system to communicate vertex information.
  - Students create their own planar designs and investigate their periodicity and uniformity.
- *Terminology:*
  - Please refer to the Students' Guide for specific descriptions and definitions of these words:
    dihedral tiling, monohedral tiling, polyhedral tiling
    lattice, grid, period parallelogram
    matching edges, edge-to-edge tessellation
    open pattern, periodic open pattern, spaces
    periodic tiling, aperiodic tiling, fundamental region
    planar pattern
    tiling, tessellation
    uniform tiling, *k*-uniform tiling, nonuniform tiling
    vertex of a tiling, identical vertices, corner
    vertex type, valence of a vertex
- *Specific Notes to Teachers:*
  - This investigation explores both tessellations ("closed" or continuous planar patterns) and open planar patterns.
  - The more deeply students explore tessellations, the more helpful precise language becomes (especially words such as *periodic, vertex, types,* and so forth). Help students clarify what you or they specifically mean if there is the possibility of confusion. Be wary, though, of spending too much time on precision of language too soon; this can disrupt the flow of creativity.
  - While the basic concepts of periodicity and uniformity are relatively easy for most students to understand, some of the details and subtleties can be confusing and difficult for students. Decide beforehand how deeply you expect students to understand the distinctions and clarify which differences you want them to know or simply "appreciate."
  - Communicating vertex information is important when students are trying to describe tessellations fully. See below for a suggested symbol system to communicate vertices of the PentaBlocks.

- A student exhibition is a powerful learning tool. To generate more student ideas, consider giving special recognition for the most original pattern, or best use of stars, or other motivating categories.
- Historical Note: The term *tessellation* comes from the Greek and Latin for square tile. The interest in tiling designs was stimulated by advances in glazing technology, which created a water-impervious surface on clay. This, in turn, allowed for the development of systems of running water and standing pools.
- If you run this investigation over more than one day, have students make a journal entry for each lab session.

- *Activity Sequence:*
  1. Distribute the Student Guides, colored pencils, three or four pieces of overhead transparency film, and a washable overhead pen per group.
  2. Discuss new terminology and ask for examples.
  3. Have students familiarize themselves with tessellations in ***Action* 1**, and then use the transparencies to explore period parallelograms in ***Action* 2**.
  4. If time permits, have groups exchange their recorded patterns from ***Action* 3** and verify the existence of period parallelograms in the patterns.
  5. Give students 10–15 minutes to go through ***Action* 4**, and then discuss the results as a class.

- *Possible Responses:*

1. a. The triangles and rhombuses tile by themselves in several ways. (Four are shown below.) The pentagon and star do not tile by themselves.

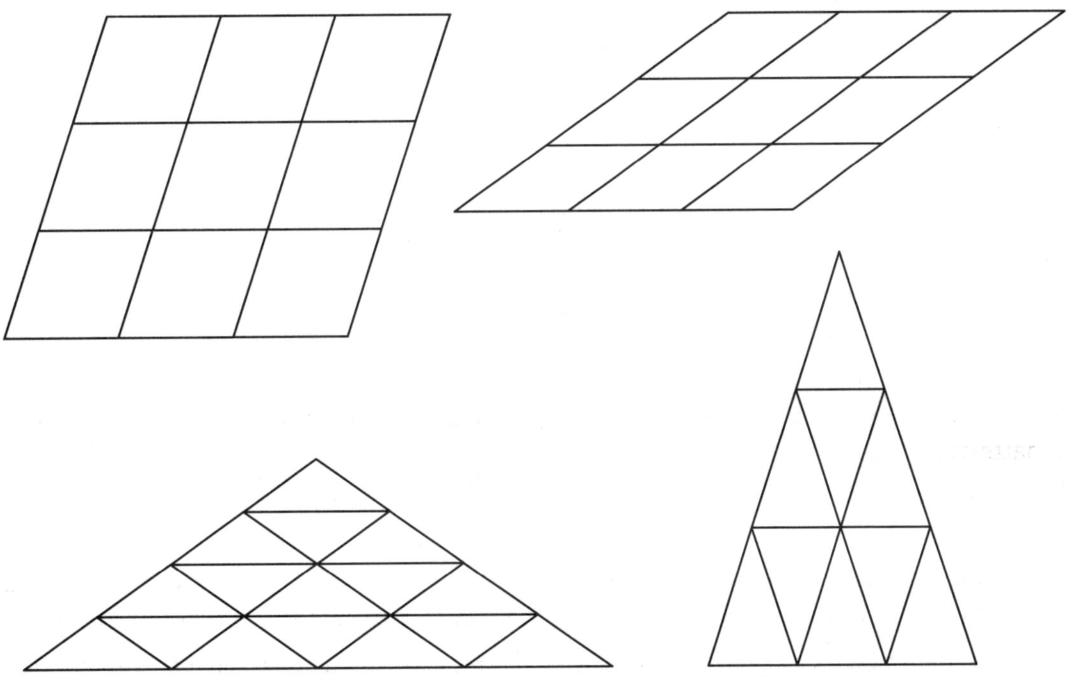

b. For a polygon to tessellate, its vertices must have angles that will combine to form multiples of 180°. Rhombuses always tessellate, because consecutive angles add up to 180°. Triangles always tessellate, because their angles add up to 180°.

c. Answers will vary. Here are possible responses for the four figures shown on the previous page: The top two are simple translations. The bottom two can be seen as translations and glide reflections.

d. All monohedral planar patterns can be seen as extensions of either a centered or a linear pattern. Because of this, they can all be described as a combination of symmetry operations acting on a single block shape.

2. a. The areas are equal. Intuitively, this can be explained by splitting the parallelograms into triangles and rearranging them to form other parallelograms. In this figure, the first parallelogram can be rearranged to form the second, and the third to form the fourth.

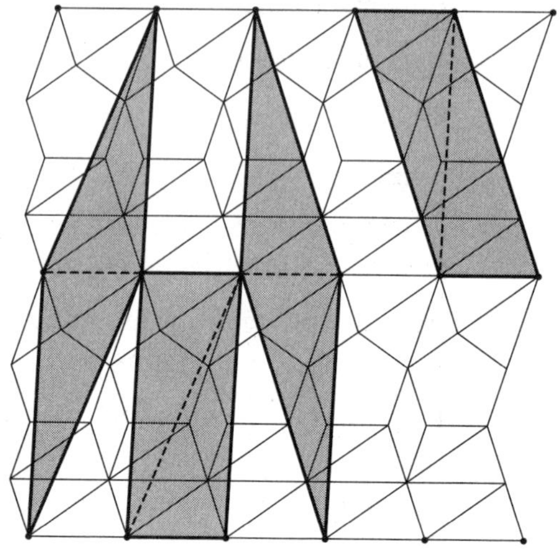

b. They all match, indicating that the parallelogram's contents represent a fundamental region for the pattern.

3. a. Responses vary. (See appendices for possibilities.)

b. Some possibilities:

1.

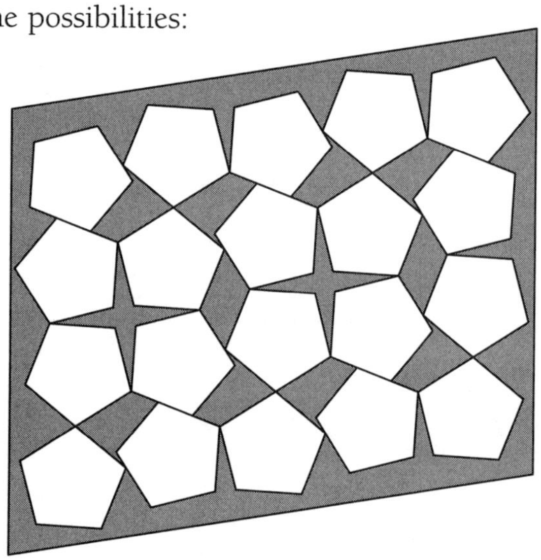

2.

3.

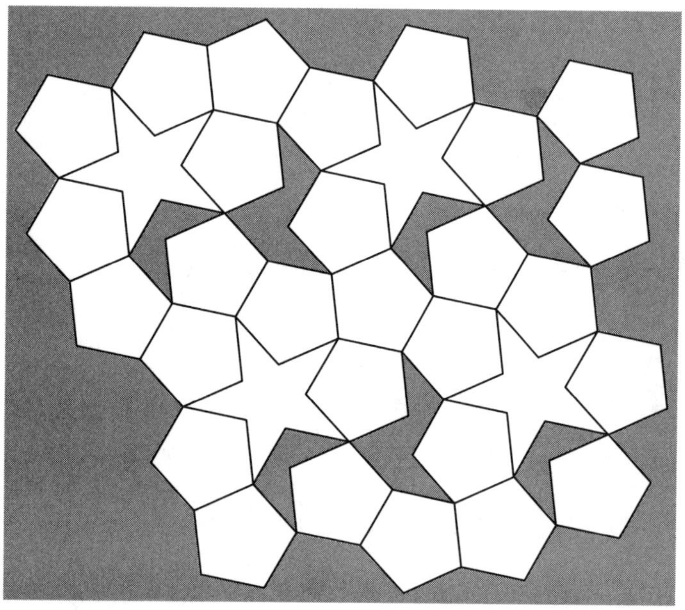

c. Responses vary.

4. **A.** Open, periodic, monohedral, uniform
   B. Edge-to-edge tessellation, periodic, dihedral, 2-uniform (vertices 4-valent and 8-valent). Can be seen as a linear band translated horizontally.
   C. Open, periodic, monohedral, 4-uniform. Can be seen as a linear band translated downward.
   D. Centered, monohedral, 3-uniform (vertices 4-valent and 5-valent)
   E. Simple bilateral symmetry, single mirror, polyhedral, nonuniform
5. **a.** Responses vary.
   b.

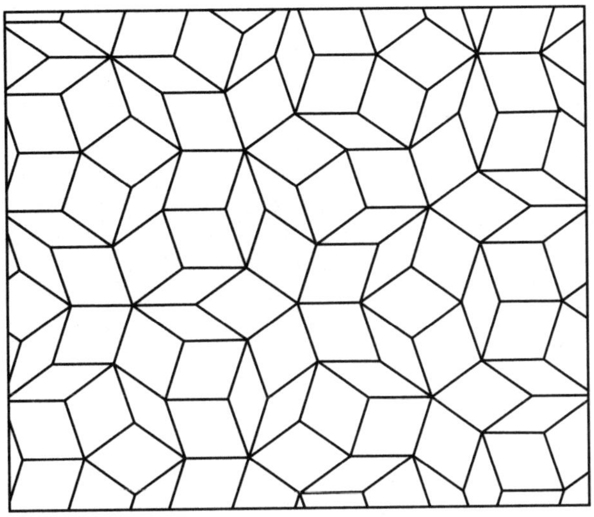

   c.

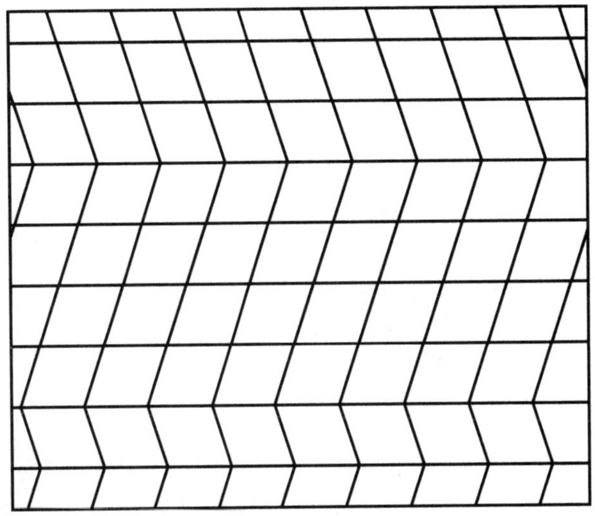

6. One possible system would abbreviate the PentaBlocks in this way:

S (star)	P (pentagon)
TT (tall triangle)	sT (short triangle)
FR (fat rhombus)	tR (thin rhombus)

You could place a subscript beside the abbreviation to indicate whether the larger or the smaller angle is the one being described (1 for smaller, 2 for larger). Because the pentagon is equiangular, no subscript would be needed for P.

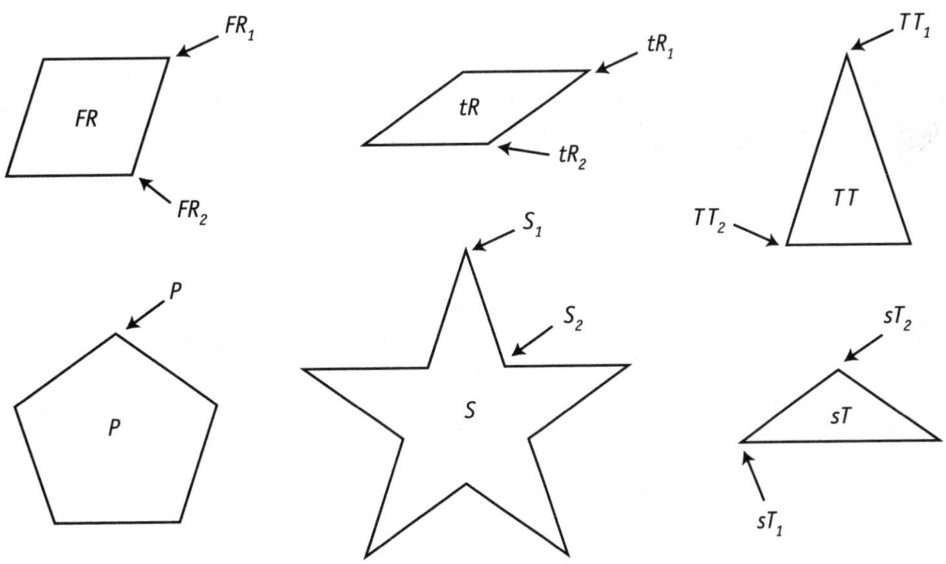

You could describe vertices clockwise and use the convention of starting with the block that has the fewest sides. If there are two blocks that both have the fewest sides, start with the smaller angle measure.

According to this scheme, the vertices shown would be described in this way:

A: sT_1, sT_1, sT_2, sT_1, sT_1 sT_2

B: FR_2, FR_2, tR_2

C: tR_1, FR_1, FR_1, tR_1, FR_1, FR_1

7. A. Not uniform, because it has 6 different vertices:

1. FR_1, tR_2, P, S_1
2. tR_1, FR_2, P, FR_2
3. FR_2, S_2
4. tR_1, P, FR_1, S_1, P
5. P, S_2
6. FR_1, S_1, P, tR_2

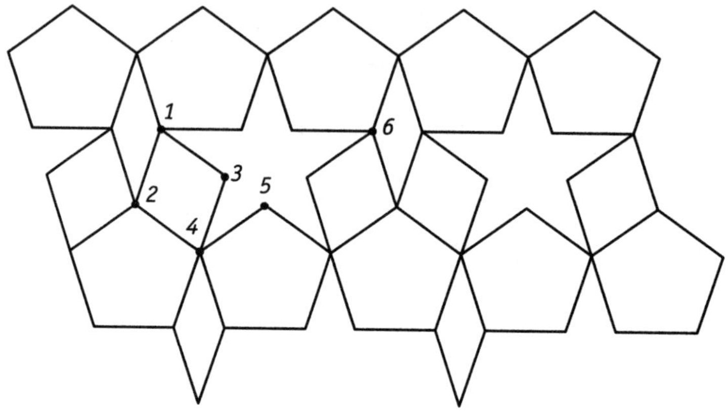

B. Not uniform, because it has 3 different vertices. Shown here is one possible notation for corners and for vertices involving "blank tiles."

7. TT_2, Open 108°, TT side
8. TT_2, TT side, Open 108°
9. TT_1, TT_2, Open 180°, TT_2

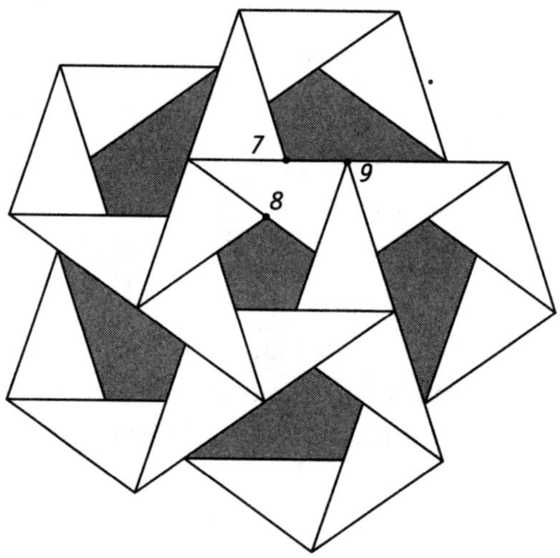

C. Uniform, because vertices are all identical.

10. TT_1, TT_2, FR_2, FR_1, TT_2

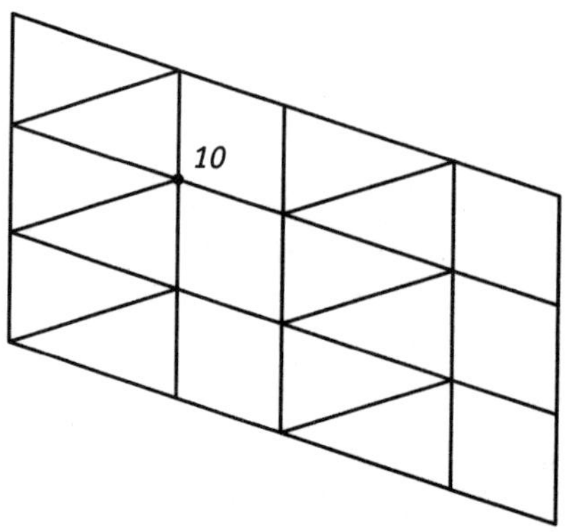

8. a.

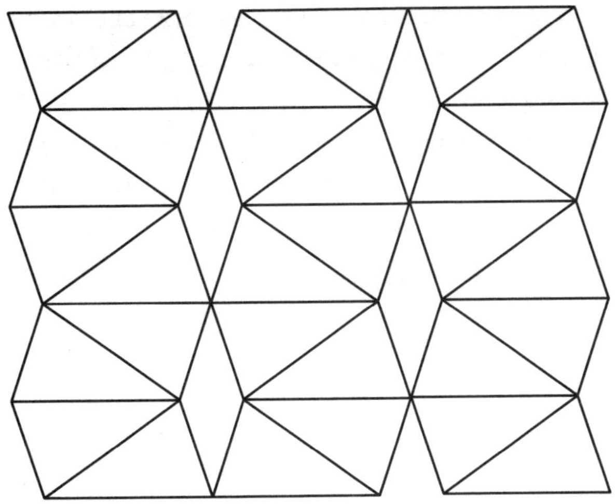

b. Yes, several different patterns could use the same types of vertex if they used them in different positions or frequencies. For example:

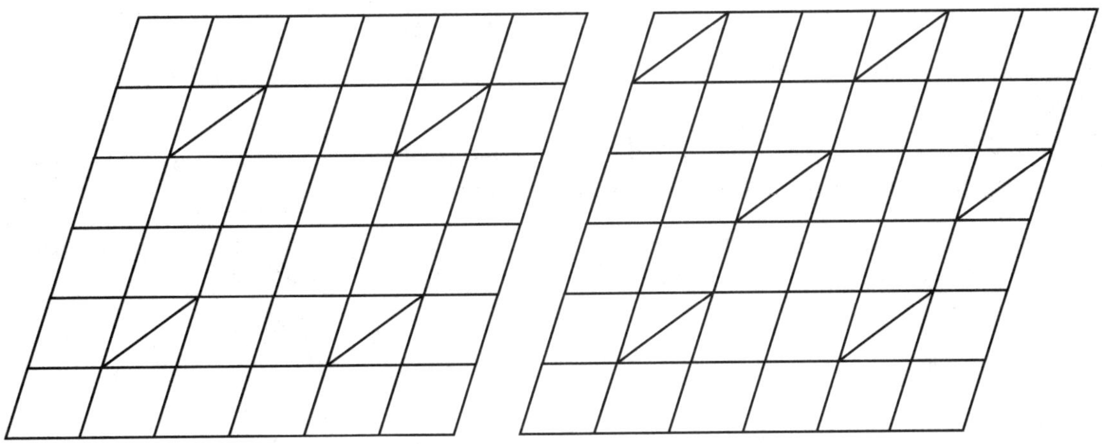

9. A likely result is two overlapping but otherwise identical sets of parallelograms.

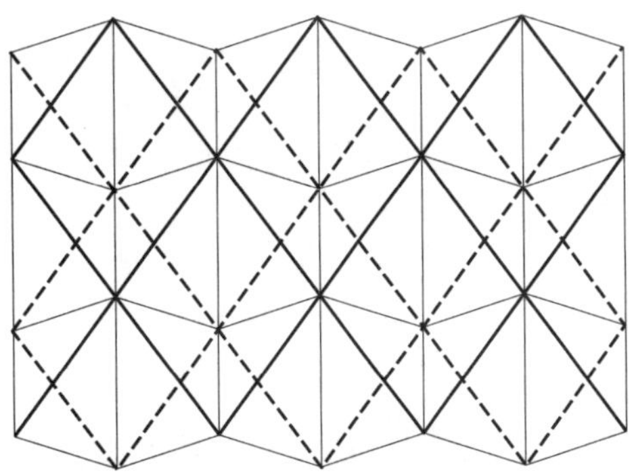

- *Possible Extensions:*

1. a. The assumption behind using a period parallelogram is that all parallelograms tile the plane by themselves. How could you prove this?

   b. How can you relate this idea to centered patterns or linear patterns?

2. Investigate the early history and use of tiling by the ancient Greeks and Romans as well as in early Islamic cultures.
3. Leonhard Euler was one of the most prolific mathematicians of all time. Among his accomplishments is the Euler formula for tilings, which relates the number of polygons to the number of *sides* of polygons meeting at a vertex of a periodic tiling. Research this formula and verify its correctness with periodic patterns you've created. What other formulas are credited to Euler?
4. The English mathematician Roger Penrose was fascinated with periodicity and created what have come to be called the Penrose Aperiodic Tilings. Research his work. How are his "darts" and "kites" or his rhombuses related to the PentaBlocks?
5. The notion of a fundamental region is important in the textile sciences and industries. How is it used in the design of fabric, floor and wall coverings, etc? How are fundamental regions related to period parallelograms? How has computer technology used the mathematics of patterns to assist in textile design?
6. It was suggested that all you need to prove periodicity in a tiling is to find a period parallelogram that is determined by equivalent points. Describe how this notion is related to finding two distinct translation vectors connecting equivalent points in the lattice.
   a. Illustrate and describe how this notion is related to finding two distinct translation vectors connecting a specific vertex to two distinct equivalent points in the lattice.
   b. How can you express this result in terms of linear combinations of the two vectors? Would the combinations require integral coefficients? Could these be expressed in terms of matrices?
   c. How is this process related to resolving vectors in physics? What physical phenomena might be studied with this type of integrated analysis?
7. Pick's Theorem is a simple rule for finding the area of a polygon outlined on a lattice. It assumes that all vertices are lattice points, and it works like this:

$$\text{Area} = \frac{\text{Number of points on boundary}}{2} + \text{Number of points enclosed by boundary} - 1$$

   Investigate this theorem, using a variety of lattices and outlines, and relate it to the parallelogram lattices for periodic planar patterns. Report on your results.

Background Information:

You have already explored two of the three basic types of predictable patterns on the plane. For a **centered** design you know to look for unique points, like the points on a single mirror or some obvious center point or figure. A **linear** design is identified by being confined within a pair of parallel boundary lines.

In this investigation you will focus on the third type of predictable pattern: **planar** patterns, which extend throughout the entire plane, in any direction, in a predictable and describable way. There are two basic types of planar patterns involving polygons:

1. If the polygons of a pattern cover the plane without gaps or overlaps, the pattern is called a **tessellation** or **tiling**, and each polygon is a **tile**.

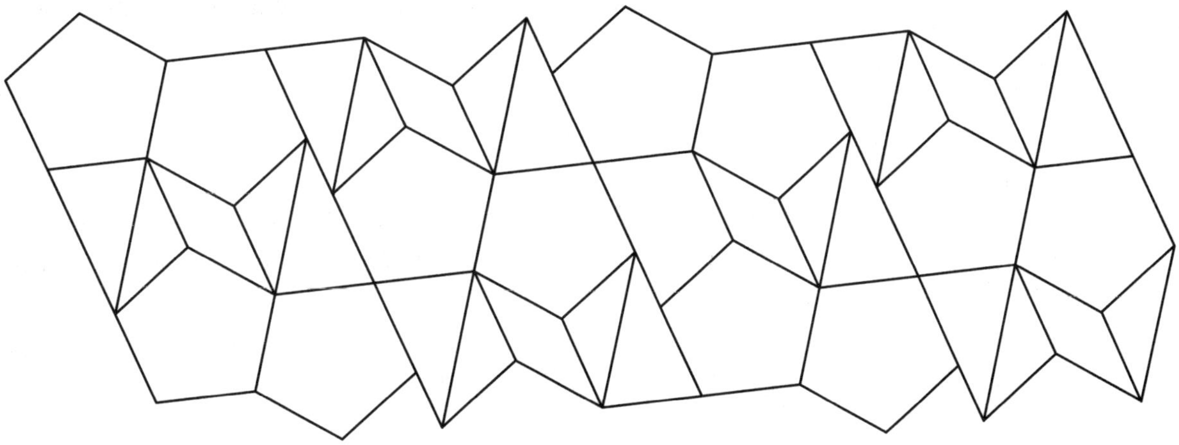

2. If the polygons do not completely cover the plane but leave gaps, the pattern is an **open pattern**, with **spaces** between polygons.

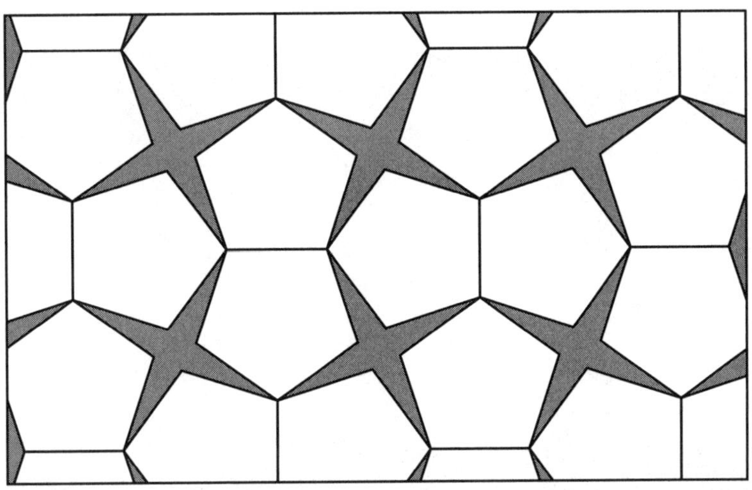

You will explore the two key features of repetitive planar patterns that describe their predictability: **periodicity** and **uniformity**.

Periodicity

The basic idea of periodicity is that you could take a small piece of a pattern and use it to predict how to cover the entire plane. Stated more precisely, a tiling is **periodic** if you can repeatedly translate some **fundamental region** to recreate the infinite plane.

Because all parallelograms tile the plane periodically by themselves, a planar pattern is periodic as long as equivalent points can form a **period parallelogram**. This is most easily understood by highlighting a set of equivalent points in a planar pattern to create a **lattice**. In this tiling of fat rhombuses (Figure A), the upper-left corners of the rhombuses are taken as equivalent points for forming a lattice.

Figure A

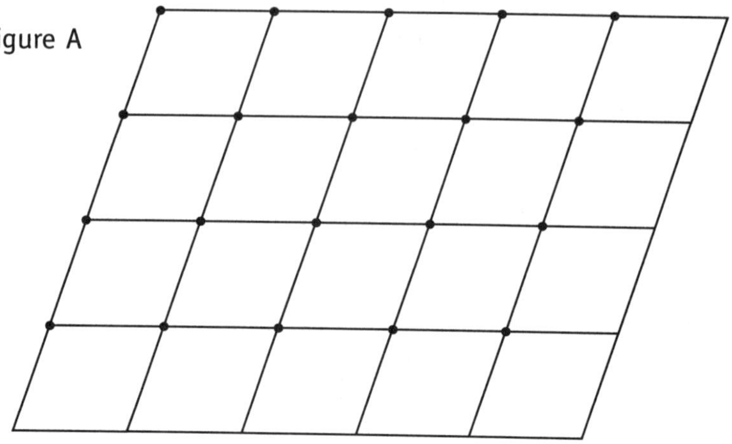

You can use the lattice points to create a **grid** of two distinct families of equally spaced parallel lines whose intersections define one possible period parallelogram. Figure B is one possible grid (and period parallelogram) created from the lattice of Figure A. As you can see, one lattice of points can be used to make different grids.

Figure B

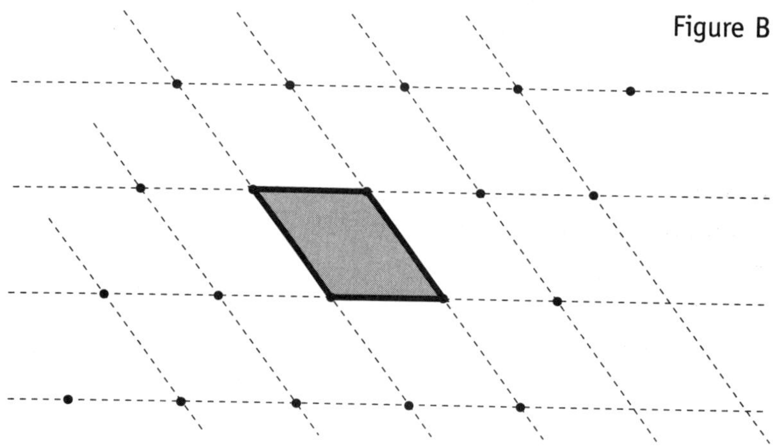

Because a lattice can determine many grids, every periodic pattern has many possible period parallelograms.

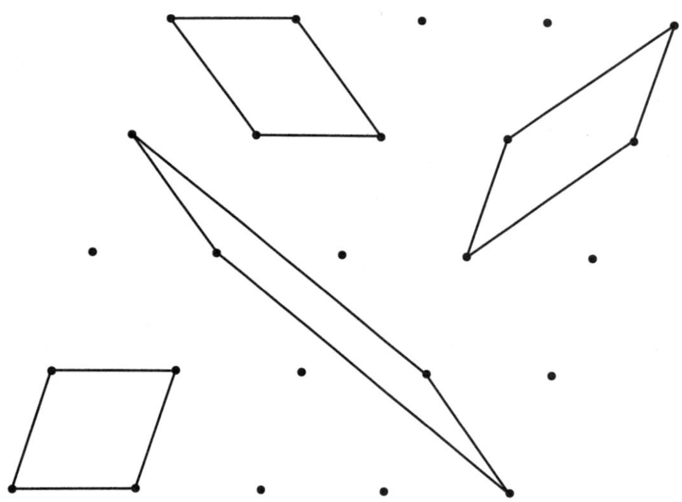

This figure shows one of many lattices and period parallelograms that could be created from a more complex periodic pattern. Often, as in this case, a period parallelogram "cuts" through one or more shapes.

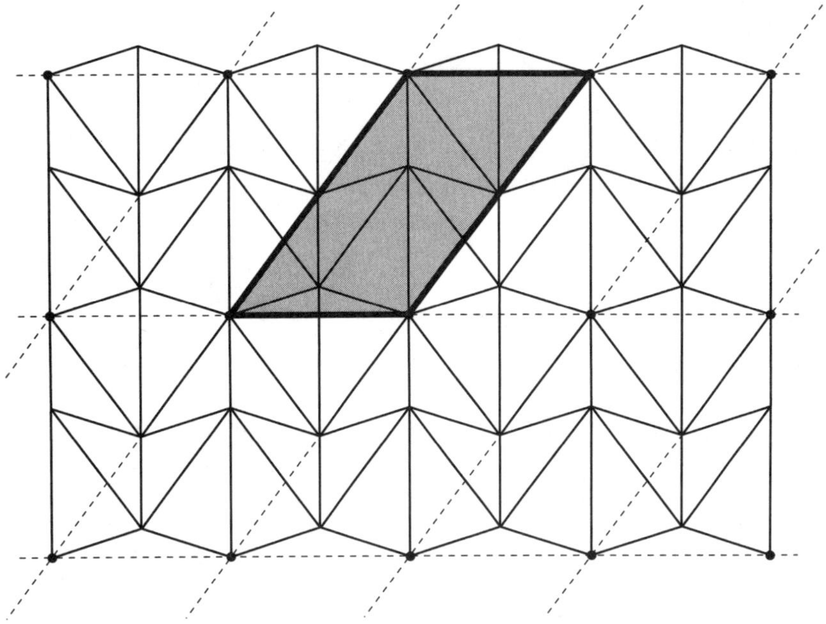

Uniformity

Uniformity describes how the polygons of a tiling meet at the vertices. A tiling is **uniform** if every vertex is **identical**, meaning they have *exactly* the same set of angles of the same set of polygons in the same clockwise order.

Two vertex distinctions need to be made:

- A tessellation is said to be **edge to edge**, or to have **matching edges**, if all adjacent tiles share common vertices and complete sides. In such a case, the common vertex is called a **vertex of a tiling**.
- In some tessellations, the vertex of one tile is found somewhere along the edge of an adjacent tile. Because the vertices don't match, this is not considered edge-to-edge. A point like this is called a **corner**, rather than *vertex of a tiling*. Point *C* is a corner in the illustration below. Point *V* is a vertex of the tiling.

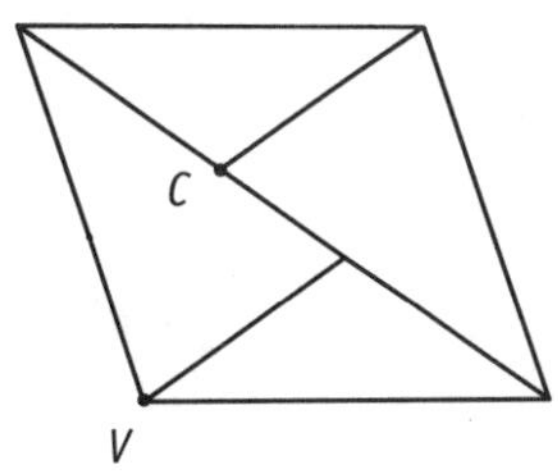

Vertices in open patterns can also be described as corners or as vertices of an "open tiling" (even though an open pattern isn't a true tessellation), depending on the shape and position of the "blank tile" (the space between tiles).

The more completely you study planar patterns, the more ways you need to describe or distinguish differences. For example:

- You can describe how many different types of tiles a tiling contains: a **monohedral** tiling has only one type of tile, a **dihedral** tiling has two types, and so on. The general term for a tiling with more than one type of tile is **polyhedral**.

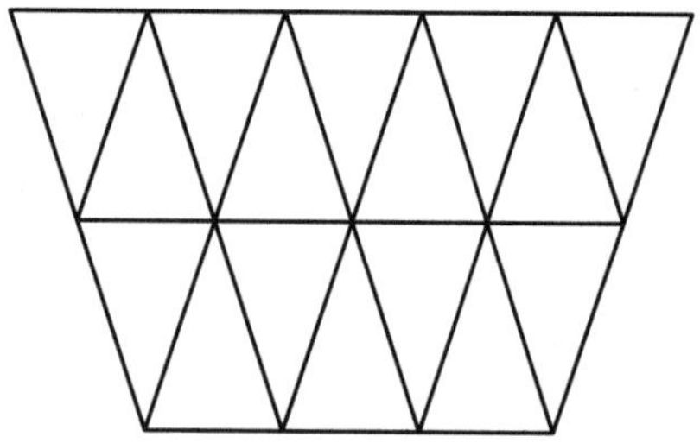

Monohedral tiling

Dihedral tiling

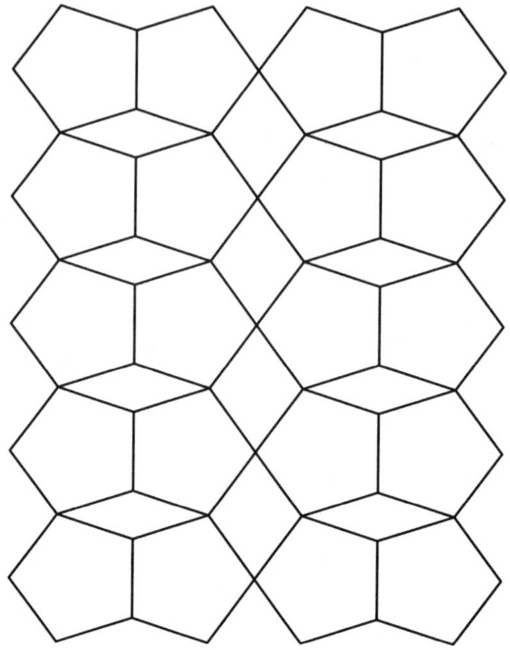

Trihedral tiling

- The *valence* of a vertex is the number of polygons that meet at that vertex.

The valence of vertex *A* is 3.

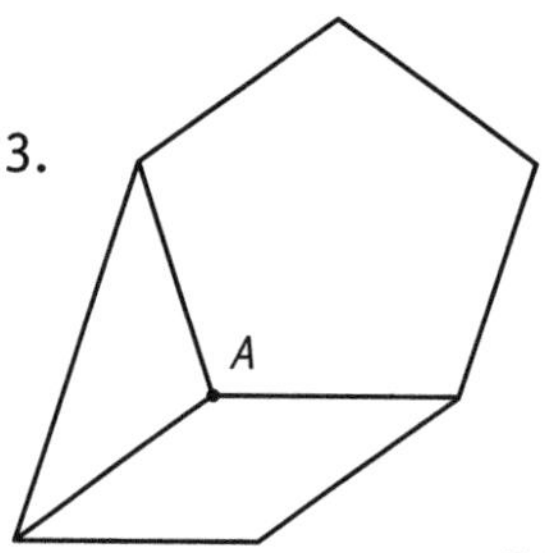

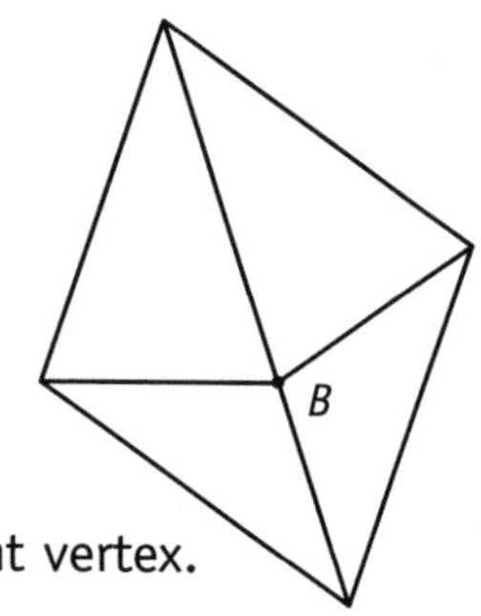

B is a 4-valent vertex.

- Vertices of a tiling can be described as different **types** if they differ in their valence or differ by which specific angles of which specific polygons meet there, and in what clockwise order they meet. Many planar patterns have more than one type of vertex, so they would be considered **nonuniform**, or ***k*-uniform**, where *k* is the number of different types of vertices in the pattern.

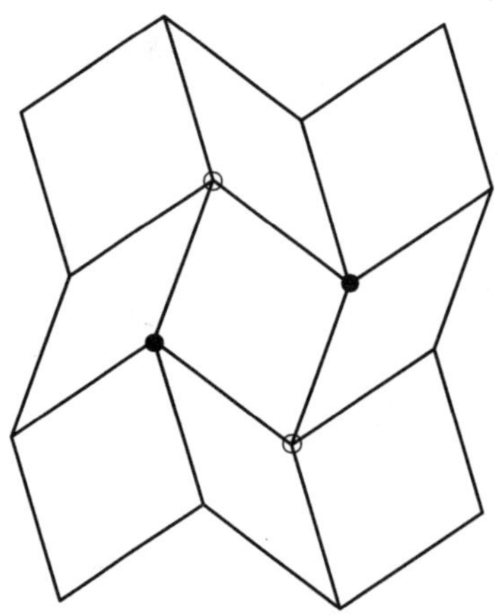

This is a dihedral 2-uniform tiling with the two vertex types distinguished by open or closed circles. All four vertices use the same angles; but they use them in two different clockwise orders. All vertices are vertices of the tiling.

Action:

Part I

1. **a.** Try to "force" each of the PentaBlocks shapes to tile the plane by itself. Some shapes do this in more than one way; others cannot tile alone. Record your results.
   b. Develop or confirm conjectures about which specific features of shapes allow them to tessellate by themselves or not.
   c. Try to describe each of the planar patterns you discovered in ***Action* 1a** in terms of the basic symmetry operations acting on some starting block.
   d. Which, if any, of these planar patterns could be thought of as extensions of a centered or linear pattern? Does this lead to any conjectures about forming planar patterns?
2. **a.** The figure below shows a periodic tiling. Isolate a convenient point and color-code the lattice of its equivalent points. Show a number of different period parallelograms that use these lattice points as vertices and that have no lattice points in their interiors. What is your conjecture about the areas of these parallelograms? How might you explain your reasoning?
   b. Use a sheet of transparency film to copy the details of the pattern within one of the period parallelograms. Translate the transparency image so that it is superimposed upon another of the parallelograms. Do the details match? What mathematical concepts about periodic tilings does this illustrate?

3. **a.** Create at least five periodic tilings, each of which uses at least three different PentaBlocks shapes. Record each pattern. Color-code one equivalence set in each pattern to confirm that you could find at least one period parallelogram.

   b. The figure shown here is an open pattern made from pentagons alone. The open spaces are all congruent and are equivalent in that they are all in the same position and orientation within the pattern.

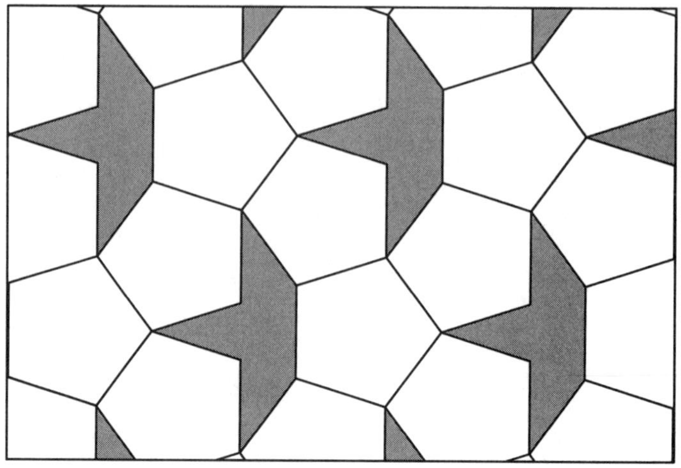

   If you consider each open space as an "open space block," or blank tile, then the pattern created by the pentagons and spaces forms what could be considered a *periodic open pattern*.

   1) Create at least one more periodic open pattern involving only pentagons.

   2) Create at least one periodic open pattern that uses only stars.

   3) Create at least one periodic open pattern that uses a combination of pentagons and stars.

   c. Color-code an equivalence set in one of the open patterns you created in ***Action* 3b** above. Identify at least one period parallelogram for this open pattern.

4. Describe each of the following patterns using as many terms as apply from among the following: centered; linear band or meander; simple bilateral symmetry (single mirror); tessellation or open pattern; number of different types of tiles (*k*-hedral); uniform (or not); valence; edge-to-edge (or not).

A.

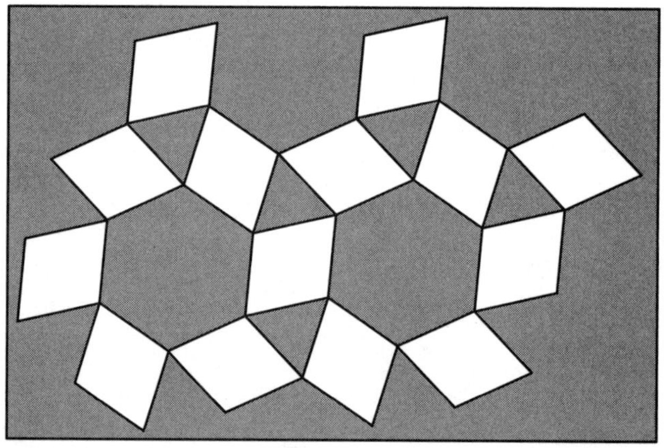

B.

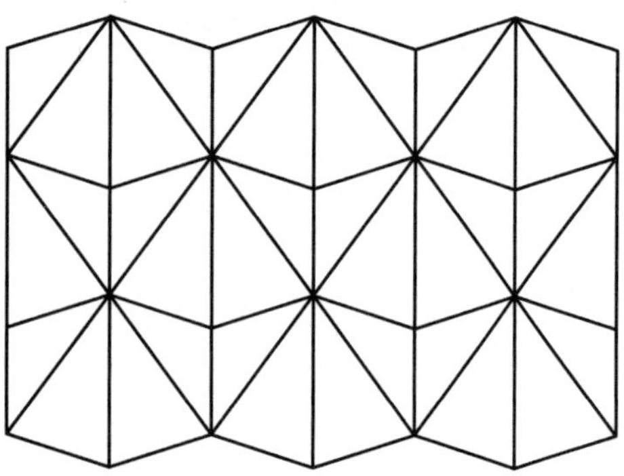

C.

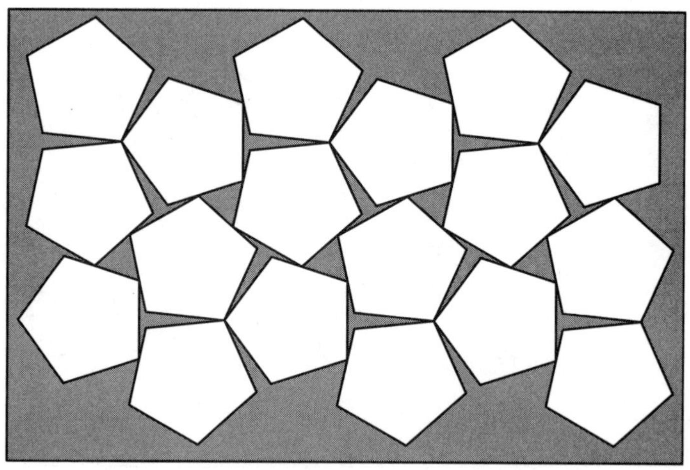

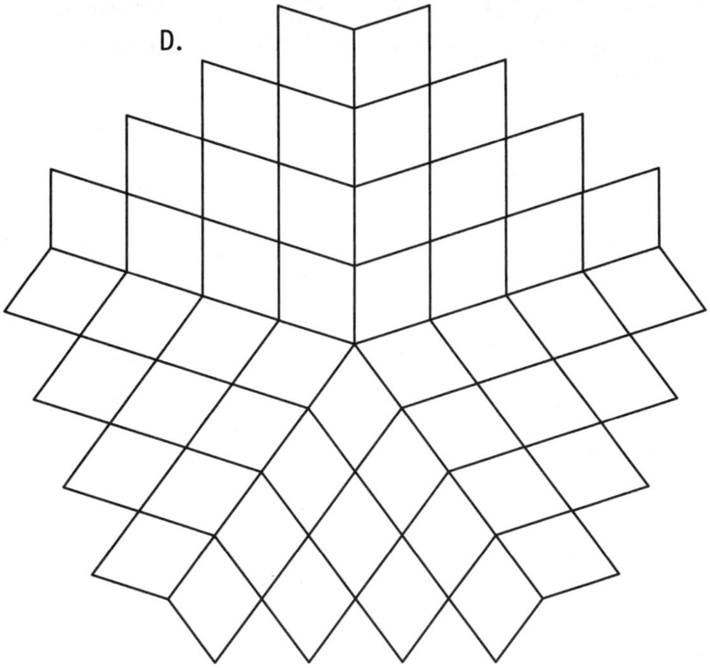

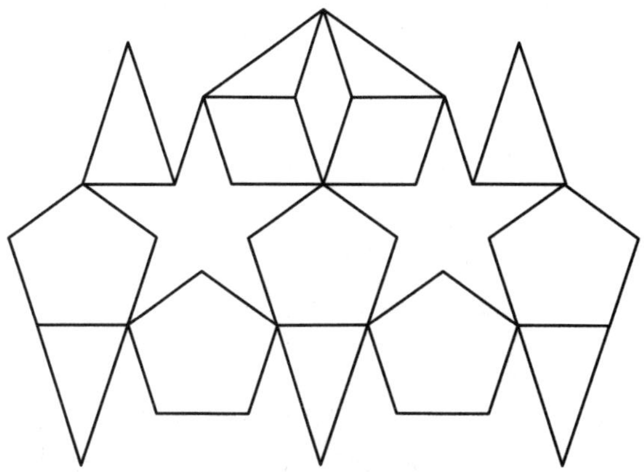

5. **a.** You can also cover the plane with polygons in an *aperiodic* or (*nonperiodic*) way. Use a variety of PentaBlocks shapes to create an aperiodic tessellation.
   b. Try to find a combination that uses only *two* shapes and still covers the plane without repetition.
   c. Try to create an aperiodic tessellation that uses only *one* shape.
6. Communicating vertex information is crucial in evaluating uniformity. Develop a PentaBlocks symbol system and use it to describe each vertex indicated below.

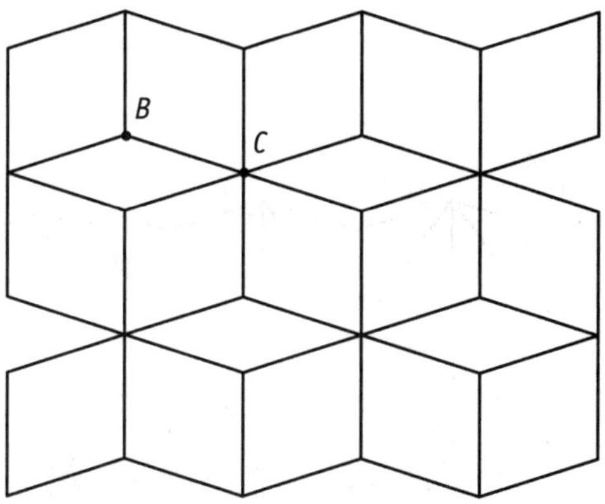

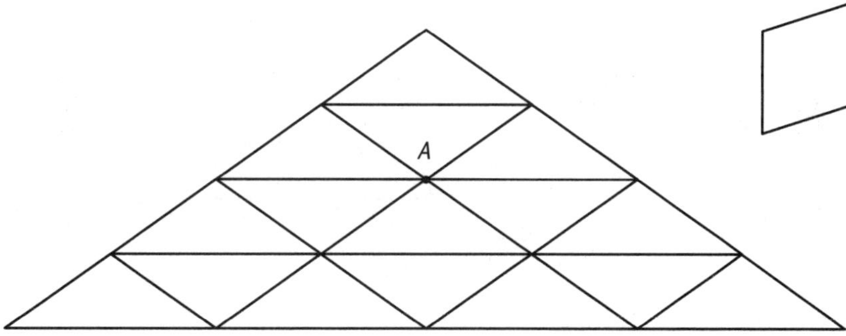

7. For each of the PentaBlocks patterns shown below, explain whether or not it is uniform. If it is *not* uniform, highlight each type of vertex with its own color. Describe each type of vertex.

A.

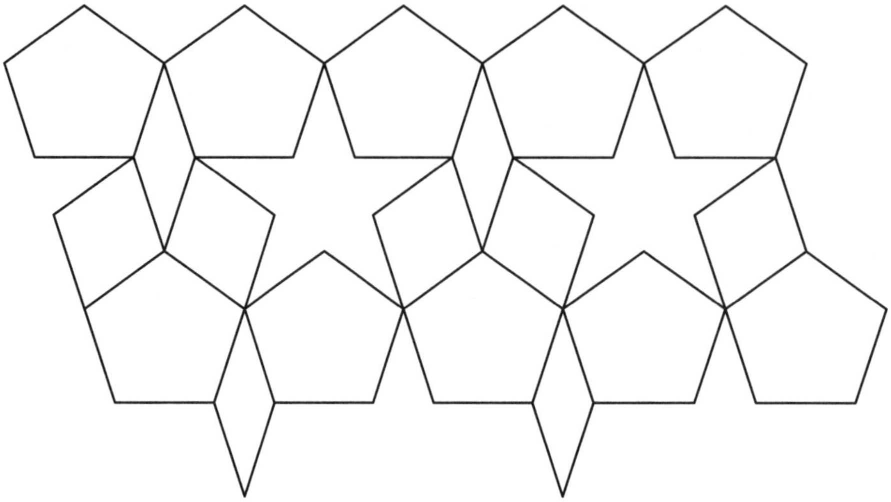

B.

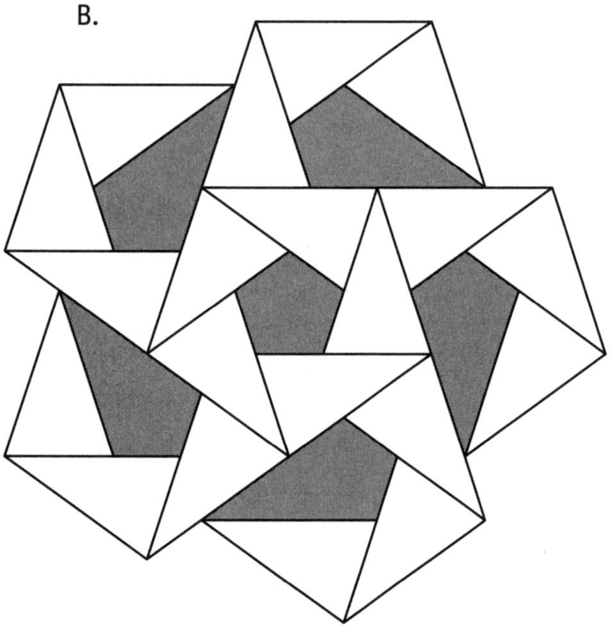

C.

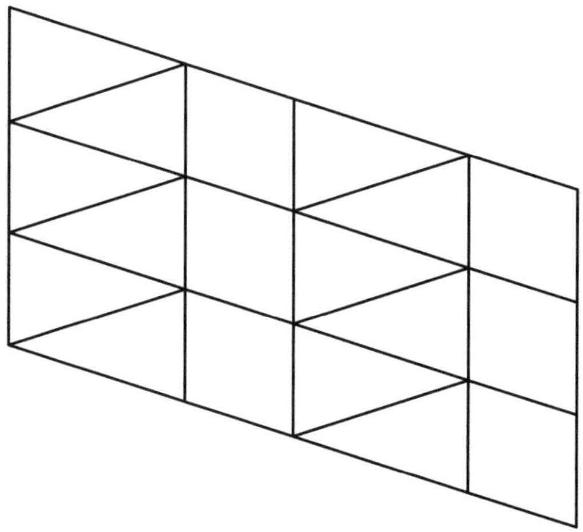

8. **a.** A certain 2-uniform planar pattern contains vertices of the following two types: TT_2, TT_2, tR_1, TT_2, TT_2, tR_1 and TT_1, TT_2, tR_2, TT_2, TT_1, where the symbols represent these shapes and vertices.

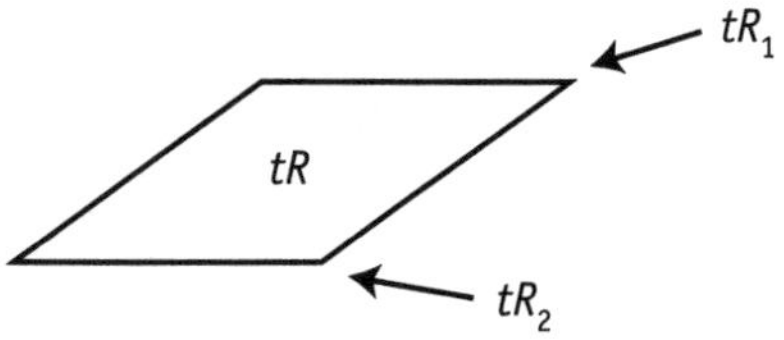

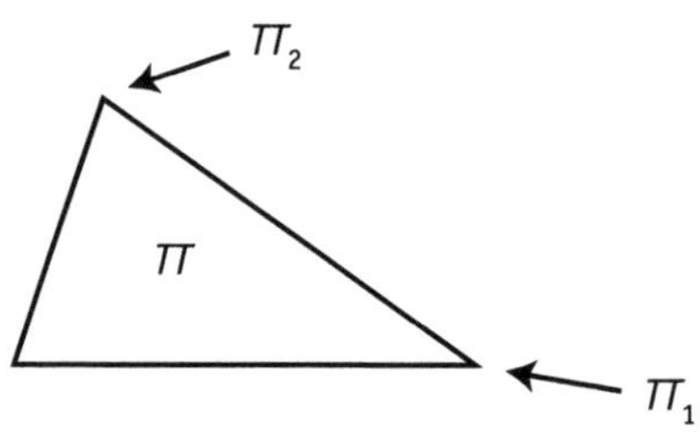

Build and record the design.

b. Pick out a design you've already examined or create a new one. Identify and describe each type of vertex. Challenge another group to build the design from PentaBlocks, given only its vertex information. Is it possible that two different designs could have the same vertex descriptions?

9. Nonuniform planar patterns have different types of vertices. Take one of the patterns from ***Action* 4** that has exactly two different types of vertex, and color-code vertices of the same type with the same color. Can you connect these to form a parallelogram grid? How does this relate to what you did with other equivalence sets?

Part II

Write an entry in your *Investigations Journal* summarizing what this activity has helped you discover about planar patterns. Write each statement or conjecture as simply and precisely as possible.

Teacher's Guide

Investigation 11: Connections Between the PentaBlocks and the Classics

ORGANIZATION

- *Mathematical Focus*
  Organizing search strategies; problem solving
- *Special Materials:*
  "Classic" Pattern Blocks (one set per group)
- *Approximate Time:* 50 minutes
- *Suggested Group Size:* Quads or pairs

INSTRUCTION

- *Lesson Summary:*
  - Students are prompted to make an organized search for connections between the PentaBlocks and the classic pattern blocks, using physical manipulation as well as an analytical approach.
- *Specific Notes to Teachers:*
  - This investigation requires students to analyze geometric patterns as well as create them.
  - There are a variety of problem-solving skills that are exercised in this investigation, including making organized lists, using guess-and-check, working backwards, making tables of data, and analyzing numerical data.
  - Look for surprises and opportunities to make or break generalizations. There are likely to be many such opportunities.
  - You may want to adapt the activities you used to explore PentaBlocks attributes and set relationships (Investigation 4), so that they can be used to explore the classic blocks.
- *Activity Sequence:*
  1. Distribute the classic pattern blocks and have students do ***Action* 1**.
  2. Distribute the PentaBlocks for ***Action* 2**, and invite different groups to compare their results.
  3. Have students continue with ***Action* 3**, **4**, and **5**. If your time is limited, you may consider assigning these three tasks to separate groups and having them share their results.
  4. For ***Action* 7**, be sure each group completes **a**, **b**, and **c**. Then, if time is limited, you may want to assign the remaining subsections to separate groups and have them share their results.
- *Possible Responses:*

  1. a. Hexagon: all 120°; square: all 90°; triangle: all 60°; trapezoid: 120° and 60° (nonalternating); blue rhombus: alternating 120° and 60°; tan rhombus: alternating 30° and 150°. The fundamental angle is 30°. Because the fundamental angle is a factor of 90°, the classic shapes can be arranged in combinations to form measures of 90°, 180°, or 360°.

  The PentaBlocks are based on a fundamental angle of 36°, which is a factor of 180° but not of 90°. The PentaBlocks, therefore, can be arranged in combinations to form measures of 180° or 360°, but not 90°.

  b. The classic pattern blocks also have only two distinct side lengths: 1 and 2.

c. The triangle, square, and hexagon are all regular (and therefore equilateral and equiangular as well). The trapezoid is isosceles. All the pattern blocks are convex. Three are rhombuses: the square and the blue and tan rhombuses. These three are therefore also parallelograms. Quadrilaterals include these three as well as the trapezoid. All the pattern blocks have diagonals except for the triangle; but only the three rhombuses have diagonals that are perpendicular. The trapezoid's diagonals are both the same length, as are those of the square. The hexagon has nine diagonals, three of one length and six of another. The hexagon and the blue rhombus are the only blocks with any diagonals of rational length.

2. On the one hand, consecutive angles of every rhombus are supplementary, so rhombus combinations between the families of blocks can have remarkable and pleasing symmetry. On the other hand, though, the angles and side lengths of the PentaBlocks triangles yield asymmetrical forms, or forms with 5- or 10-fold symmetry; the same is true with combinations involving the pentagon or star. Five-fold symmetry does not work well with the 2-, 4-, or 6-fold symmetries found within combinations of the classics.

3. Here is one version involving regular triangles:

4. Here is one possibility with the regular triangle as a center:

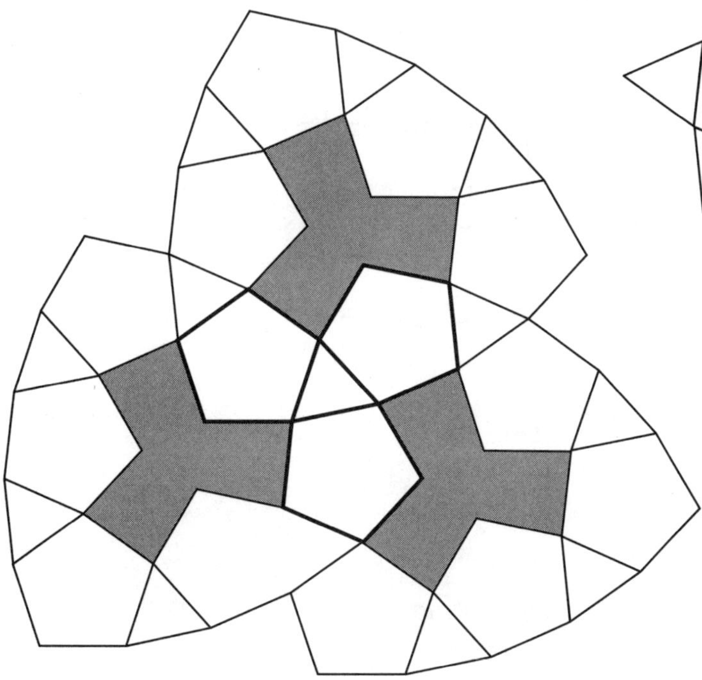

5. There are six shapes in each set, so there are 12 x 6 = 72 possible combinations to explore. Because the Φ side length doesn't relate to the classics, PentaBlocks triangles may require different strategies. One possible strategy involves using the Φ side as part of a "blank tile," as in this design of short triangles and regular triangles:

For interactions between classic blocks and rhombuses, refer to ***Action 7***. The star, because it is a concave polygon, is very difficult to combine by these methods.

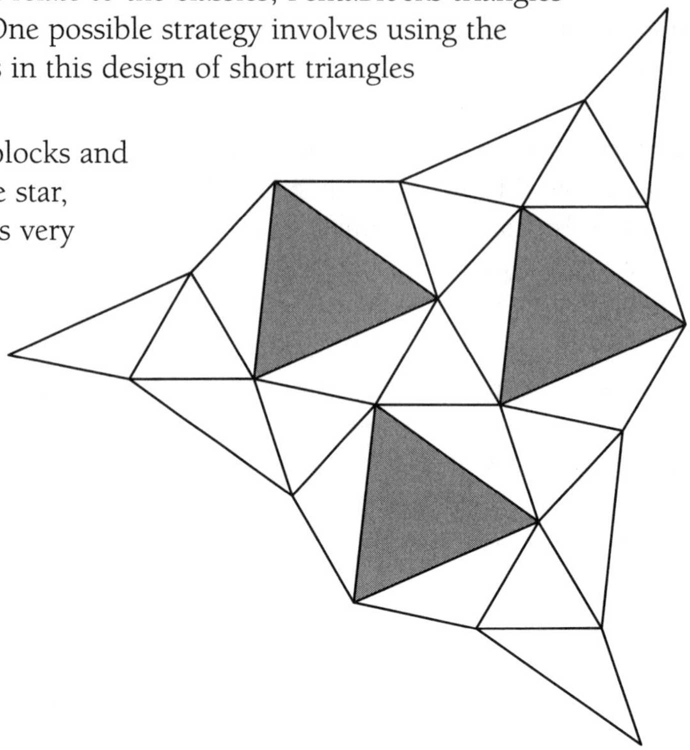

6. **a.** Responses will vary.

   b. This combination will remain a meander. Because opposite sides of a rhombus are parallel, the rhombuses don't affect the orientations of the triangles. The triangles appear in a 2-triangle sequence, with every other triangle appearing in the same orientation. Therefore the design is a linear meander. (You can test this idea by eliminating the rhombuses altogether.) Note that there is a fairly sophisticated set of angle relationships involved here, which would be difficult for even experienced geometers to communicate succinctly.

7. **a.**

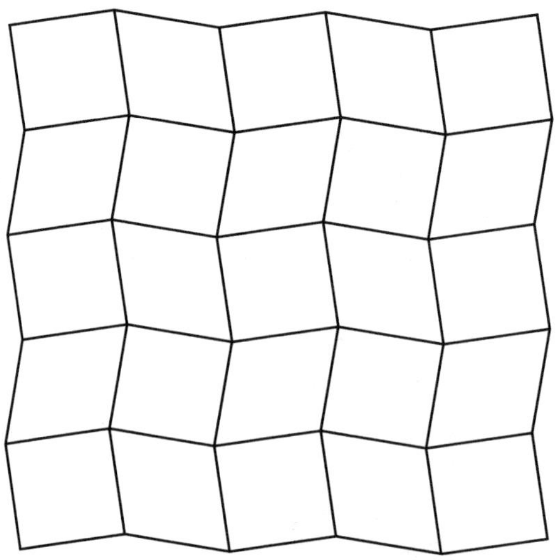

   b. Spins are the same within a row and reverse on alternating rows.

   c. Yes

d. Yes

e. Yes. Because consecutive angles of a rhombus add up to 180°, any two kinds of rhombuses can combine in this way to add up to 360°, surrounding each vertex. And because all sides of a rhombus are the same length, any side will match any other side.

f. The results are the same in terms of spin and general configuration, but there is one big difference: Because the nonrhombic parallelogram has sides that are too long to match with the square, the figure is an open pattern.

The "blank tiles" are squares that measure Φ on each side. If instead of a parallelogram and a square you used *two* parallelograms, each 1 by Φ, the figure would tessellate as well.

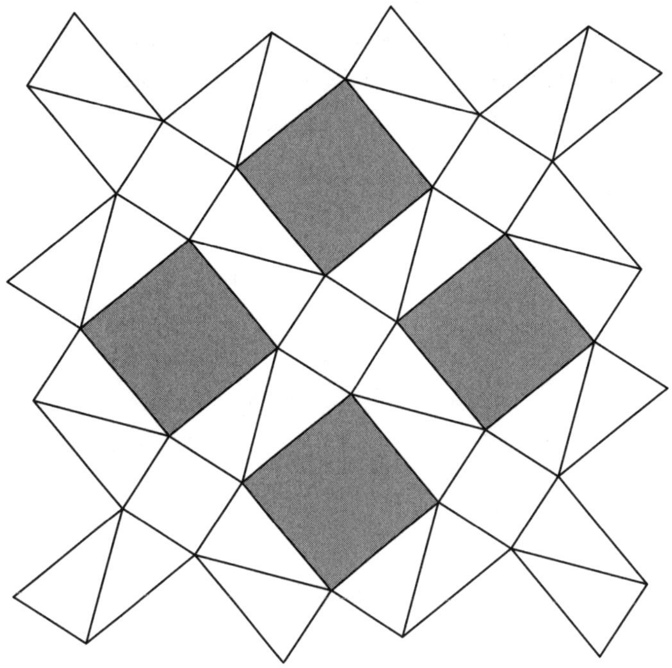

g. There will always be ten pentagons, regardless of the size of the parallelogram. One explanation can be seen by first creating a ring of ten pentagons with no rhombuses. The pentagons outline a regular decagon. When the pentagons are alternated with congruent parallelograms (rhombic or not), the pentagons spread apart, but they don't change orientation. You could think of the parallelograms as a sequence of translation vectors connecting the adjoining pentagon sides. This is why: because opposite sides of a parallelogram are parallel, the orientations of the individual pentagons are the same as with the pentagon ring, and the fact that the parallelograms are the same size assures that the distance between pentagons is uniform.

- ***Possible Extensions:***

Think about the set of shapes that make up each of the two different families of pattern blocks. Each family has enough different shapes that each shape "works" or interacts particularly well with one or more of the other shapes to create many patterns. Notice also there are not too many shapes, five or six in each set.

- Suppose you were to create an additional pattern block set based on a fundamental angle of 45°. What set of shapes would you choose?
- Suppose you wanted to create a set of regular stars to use with the pattern blocks. What stars would you recommend that might be particularly compatible with the 36° family of PentaBlocks? with the 30° family of classic pattern blocks? or with the new 45° family you created?

Investigation 11: Connections Between the PentaBlocks and the Classics

Background Information

The PentaBlocks shapes readily combine with one another because of their compatible angle measures: They are all based on a 36° angle. What happens when they are combined with shapes based on a different angle measure? The "classic" pattern blocks, which you may have seen in earlier grades, are a case in point. These shapes include the regular triangle, square, and hexagon, as well as an isosceles trapezoid (half a hexagon) and two rhombuses.

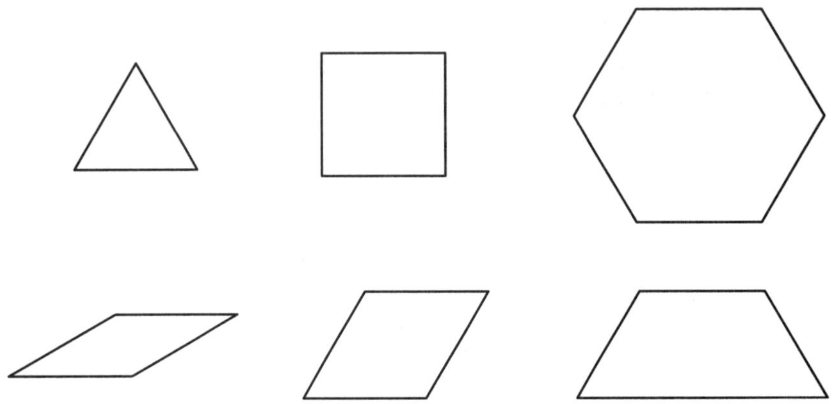

In this investigation you will be asked to search for relationships between the two families of pattern blocks in an organized and analytical way.

Action

Part I

1. **a.** In Investigation 1, you discovered that the angles of the PentaBlocks shapes are all multiples of the fundamental 36° angle. Discover by manipulation and logic (rather than by direct measurement) the angle measures and fundamental angle for the classic pattern blocks. How do the PentaBlocks angle measures compare with the angle measures found in the classics?

   b. In the first investigation, you also discovered that the PentaBlocks shapes have only two distinct side lengths, 1 and Φ. How does this compare with the classics?

   c. In another investigation you explored set relationships based on the attributes of the PentaBlocks shapes. What set and subset relationships exist among the classics? Use what you learned in Investigation 4 about attributes involving sides, angles, diagonals, and other mathematical relationships.

Part II

While the questions above consider the two different families of blocks *separately*, those that follow are designed to investigate the way the two families *interact* to form geometric patterns.

2. A strategy for exploring ways to surround a point might be to think about combinations written in each family that add up to 180°. For example, any three of the 60° angles chosen from the

classic blocks will have a combined total of 180°, and any five of the 36° angles from the PentaBlocks shapes also add up to 180°. Because 180 + 180 = 360, these eight shapes can combine in any order to surround a point.

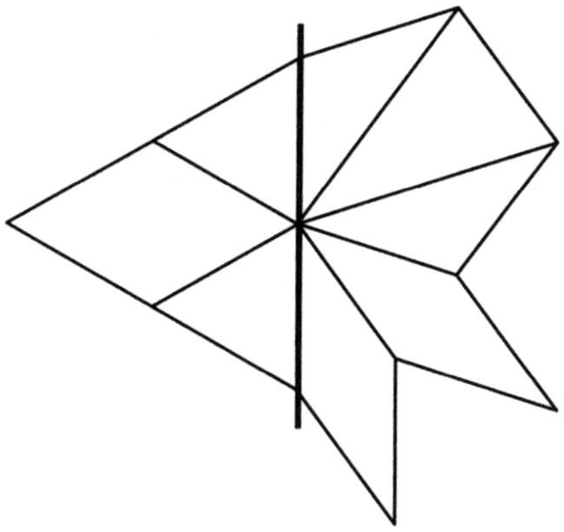

60° + 60° + 60° = 180°   36° + 36° + 36° + 36° + 36° = 180°

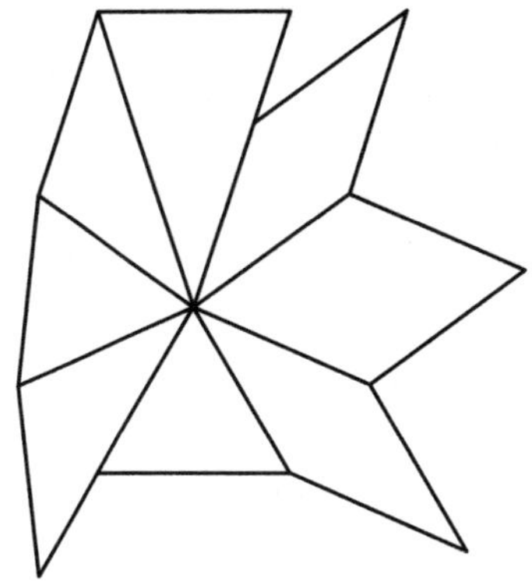

The same shapes in a different order

Despite the apparent ease with which you can surround a point using both families, there are relatively few combination of blocks between families that combine to make aesthetically pleasing patterns about a vertex. Why might this be true?

3. One strategy for organizing a search for geometric patterns is to begin with a center pentagon. As a first move out from the center, surround the pentagon on each side with the same classic block shape. Systematically explore secondary placements of the same classic shape and/or pentagons, radiating out from the center in a variety of ways. For example, the design to the right began with a pentagon surrounded by squares, with more pentagons and squares added in succession to create the pattern shown. Some beginnings like this will suggest additional shapes to be used to complete a symmetrical or periodic pattern.

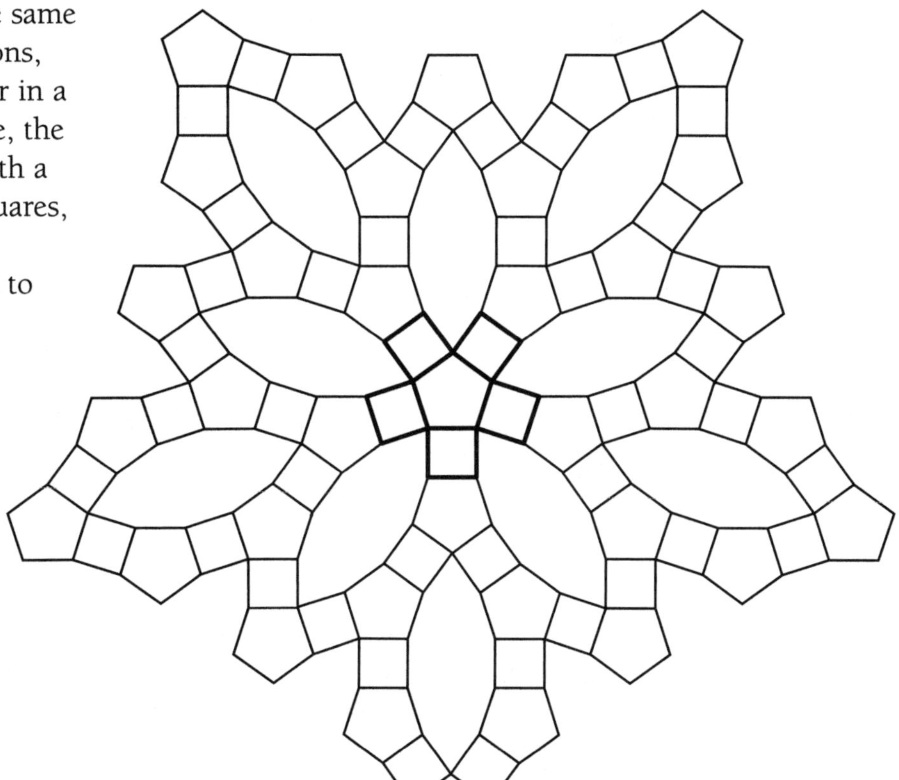

The "spinner" on the right was begun by surrounding a pentagon with red trapezoids in rotational symmetry. This left gaps of 72°, which were filled by the base angles of the tall PentaBlocks triangle.

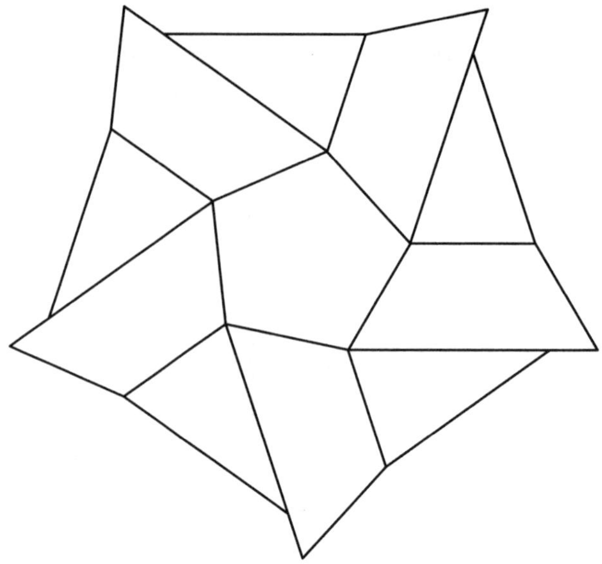

In an organized fashion, begin by surrounding a pentagon first by the regular (green) triangle and create a pattern with these two shapes. Then try surrounding the pentagon with squares, and so on. Record all patterns that are interesting by virtue of their symmetry, periodicity, or some other feature that you find compelling.

4. As a counterpoint to the pattern strategy introduced in ***Action* 2**, begin with a classic block shape surrounded by pentagons. As before, explore secondary placements of the same classic shape and pentagons to yield patterns of interest. Record all compelling patterns.

5. The two major strategies suggested in ***Actions* 3** and **4** began by combining pentagons with the various classic shapes. How would the results of each experiment differ if you used a different PentaBlocks shape? In fact, how many combinations of two blocks are possible, using one from each family?

6. **a.** Another strategy for studying the interaction of the two families is to pick one shape from each family and alternate placing them next to each other, trying to create a closed ring or a meander. For example, alternately placing pentagons and regular triangles creates a ring partially illustrated here, and alternately placing short triangles and classic {60°, 120°} rhombuses creates the meander below it. Try a variety of combinations of blocks from each family to find patterns of interest.

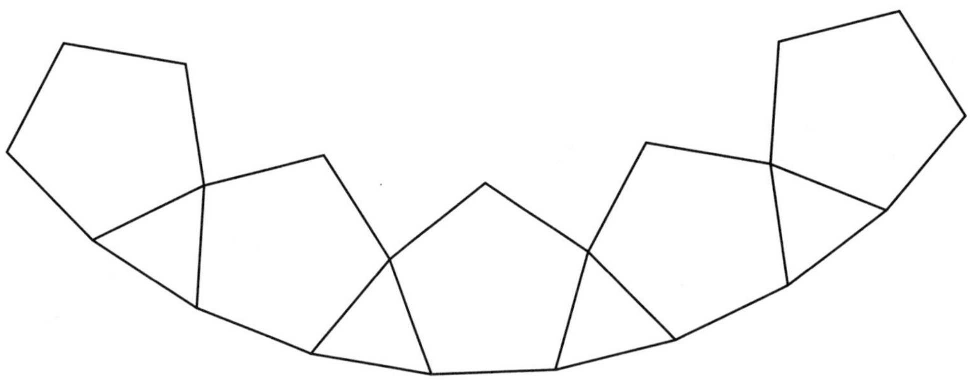

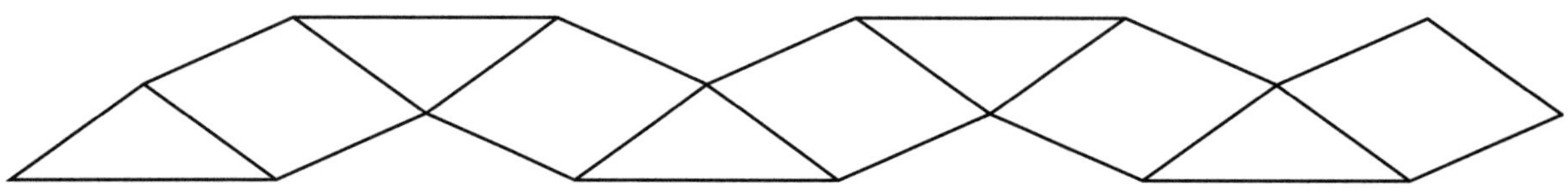

b. Examine this combination of tall triangles and classic {60°, 120°} rhombuses.

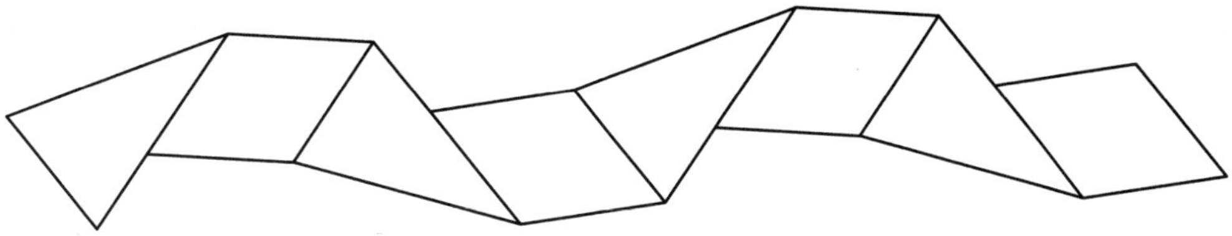

Will it remain a meander, or will it eventually become a ring? Try to create a conjecture that will predict when alternate placements will create rings or meanders.

7. a. Rhombuses have special characteristics that lend themselves to other interesting connections. Pick any of the classic rhombuses (the square, the {30°, 150°}, or the {60°, 120°}) to combine with either of the PentaBlocks rhombuses (the {36°, 144°} or the {72°, 108°}). Use one of classics as the starting block and surround it by PentaBlocks rhombuses to form a spinner with four-fold rotational symmetry. In these illustrations, the square and the {72°, 108°} rhombus are used.

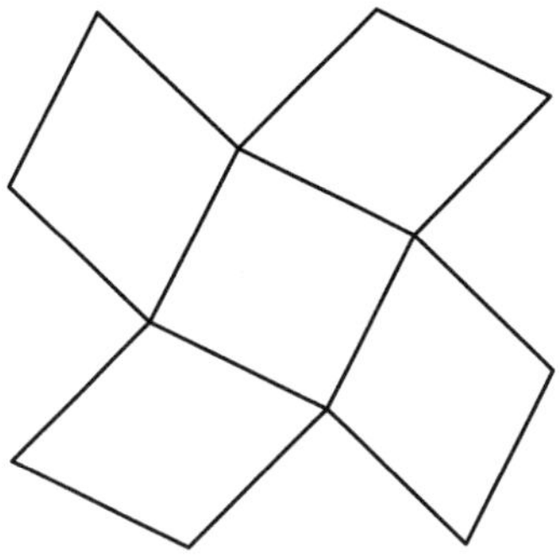

Counterclockwise

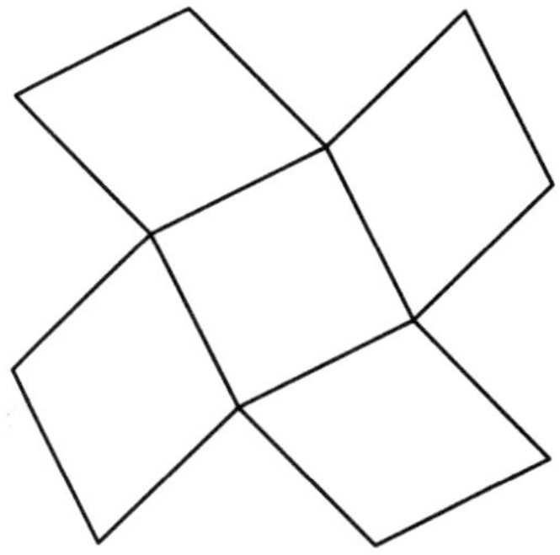

Clockwise

Note that the spinner can spin clockwise or counterclockwise. Add additional squares and green rhombuses to continue the pattern outwardly in all directions, making a tessellation.

b. Describe what happens to the direction of the spin for either rhombus.

c. Can the pattern be continued infinitely in the plane?

d. Would this be true of any combination of one rhombus from the classics and one rhombus from the PentaBlocks?

e. What essential characteristics of these rhombuses makes this work this way? Would this be true of *any* combination of rhombuses?

f. Join two of the same PentaBlocks triangles to form a nonrhombic parallelogram. Use multiples of this parallelogram and the square to create a pattern like the one you did above. How are the results different? What conjectures arise from this exploration?

g. Make a "ring" using pentagons and any of the classic rhombuses—the square, the {30°, 150°}, or the {60°, 120°}. To do this, place pentagons edge-to-edge on the parallel sides of the rhombuses, and place the rhombuses in the same position relative to the pentagon.

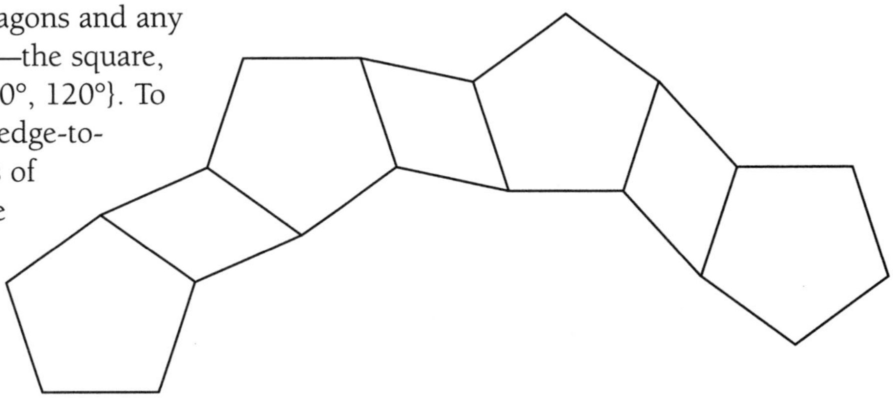

How many pentagons will be in the ring? Does this work for all rhombuses in the classics? Does it work for the rhombuses in the PentaBlocks? Will this work for any rhombus? . . . any parallelogram? (You can test this by using a nonrhombic parallelogram as in question **f** above.) Give an intuitive or an analytical explanation.

Part III

Write an entry in your *Investigations Journal* summarizing what this activity has helped you understand about doing organized searches. Comment on the part that creativity and imagination play in this type of exploration. Write any statement or conjecture as simply and precisely as possible.

Appendix 1

Annotated Bibliography

Beard, Col. R. S., ***Patterns in Space***, Creative Publications, 1973
This is an amazing exposition of meticulous (pre-computer graphics) mathematics. Polygons, stars, ellipsoids, spirals, and polyhedra all undergo Col. Beard's masterful construction and dimensional analysis. The visuals are great and the scholarship is outstanding.

Boles, M. & Newman, R., ***The Golden Relationship — Book 1: Universal Patterns***, Pythagorean Press, 1990
This fine text offers a wealth of information on Φ, the Fibonacci numbers, all types of special triangles and relationships, dynamic rectangles, spirals, and more. Even the appendices are outstanding.

Boles, M. & Newman, R., ***The Golden Relationship — Book 2: The Surface Plane***, Pythagorean Press, 1992
Consistent in format with Book 1, the usefulness and stimulation density are set on "max". This volume focuses on grids that subdivide the plane, symmetry, the circle in the plane, tiling the plane, fractals, and manipulating the "pliable" plane.

Coxford, A., et al, ***Geometry From Multiple Perspectives***, NCTM, 1991
This is the NCTM Addenda Series secondary level book on geometry. It offers problems, sample dialogues, and special notes to teachers and is an excellent resource in every way.

Devlin, K., ***Mathematics: The Science of Patterns***, Scientific American Library, 1994
Attractive and engaging, Devlin takes us on a tour from the ancients and historical characters through to modern knot theory, toying with Conway's convex solid that fills space aperiodically, Wiles's probably valid proof of Fermat's Last Theorem, and quasicrystals with their unexpected natural pentagonal symmetry. All of these are presented as ways to reveal the beauty and powerful utility of pattern.

Gardner, M., ***Penrose Tiles to Trapdoor Ciphers***, W. H. Freeman & Co., 1989
This classic is but one of the collections of problems, puzzles, and paradoxes that appeared in Gardner's popular *Scientific American* column, "Mathematical Games". Here, Gardner juggles Penrose's Tilings, Conway's Surreal Numbers, Mandelbrot's Fractals, and much more to remind us why he has the reputation as a master mathematical magician.

Ghyka, M., ***The Geometry of Art and Life***, Dover Publications, 1977
Is there order, harmony, and proportion in life? In this classic, Professor Ghyka presents views from the mathematical and mystical ancient Greeks up through the Renaissance artists on this question. The Golden Ratio reverberates throughout the ages.

Grümbaum, B. and Shepard, G., ***Tilings and Patterns: An Introduction***, W. H. Freeman & Co., 1989
This is sure to become the classic mathematical reference on regular patterns in the plane. Examples from thousands of years and countless cultures are combined with purposefully provocative mathematical oddities to provide a backdrop for the most comprehensive study of two-dimensional patterns to date.

Hargittai, István & Magdolna, ***Symmetry: A Unifying Concept***, Shelter Publications (Bolinas, CA), 1994
Dense with black and white photos and illustrations from art, nature and science, this is a sensitivity

training manual for symmetry. Amplified by clear and simple text, the images include corporate logos, art from around the world, quasicystals and much, much more.

Huntley, H. E., ***The Divine Proportion***, Dover, 1970
This is yet another classic that explores the relationship between geometry and aesthetics and leads us to expanded views of the connections to and from the Golden Section.

Kappraff, J., ***Connections: The Geometric Bridge Between Art and Science***, McGraw-Hill, 1991
Drawing on the work of Pythagoreas, Escher, Penrose, Fuller, and others, Kappraff explores many of the mathematical threads that are intricately woven into Design Science. Hundreds of illustrations and problems entertain and enlighten.

Lawlor, R., ***Sacred Geometry: Philosophy and Practice***, Norton Publishing Co., 1982.
This fascinating collection of understanding about systems of numbers, shape, and proportion is presented as taught and used by the ancient geometers in Egypt, Greece, India, and China to describe forms in nature and to determine forms in art, architecture, and design.

Schneider, M., ***A Beginner's Guide to Constructing the Universe***, HarperCollins, 1994
Modern science seems to be reaffirming the ancient belief that a consistent language underpins every level of the universe, from atoms to galaxies. Schneider translates that eloquent language into lyrical prose documented by hundreds of eye-opening photos and images. Each of the numbers 1 through 10 has its own chapter, and each is a cornucopia crammed with an abundance of that number's historic, mythological, arithmetic, geometric, and philosophic aspects. The pentagonal chapter is positively profound. Throughout the book, sidebar quotes, illustrations and factoids keep the reader as stimulated as MTV (M = "math"). This book is a hearty feast for the eyes, mind and soul.

Seymour, D. and Britton, J., ***Introduction to Tessellations***, Dale Seymour Publications, 1985
Another excellent Dale Seymour resource book that develops many concepts related to tessellations through activities and thoughtful dialog. I think this is the best book on the topic at the secondary level.

Stevens, P., ***Handbook of Regular Patterns: An Introduction to Symmetry in Two Dimensions***, MIT Press, 1981
Nearly a thousand designs from cultures throughout history and around the globe are offered as examples in an analysis defining a scheme of a mere 36 generalized categories into which all designs can be classified. Imagine, just 36 archetypes! Though less comprehensive, the text is very much more accessible than Grümbaum & Shepard for secondary level study.

Appendix 2: Glossary

Definitions and Descriptions

Aperiodic pattern (Inv. 10): A planar pattern that is not periodic

Area (Inv. 3): The area of a bounded region on a surface is a measure that tells how much surface is enclosed within that region.

Area Addition Postulate (Inv. 3): If a bounded region on a surface is subdivided into a set a of smaller bounded regions, the sum of the areas of the separate regions is equal to the area of the original region.

Axis of symmetry (Inv. 7): See *Mirror*.

Band design (Inv. 9): A linear design in which the parallel boundary lines are part of the design

Basic Rules for making PentaBlocks designs (Inv. 1): See *Lie Flat Rule* and *Fit Flush Rule*.

Boundary lines (Inv. 9): Parallel lines within which there is a linear design

Centered pattern (Inv. 9): A pattern in which one or more unique points act as the center of the pattern; also called *a point group*

Complementary angles (Inv. 1): When two angles add up to 90 degrees they are complementary, or *complements* of each other.

Concave polygon (Inv. 1): A polygon is concave if any diagonal is outside the polygon.

Congruent polygons (Inv. 1): Polygons that have exactly the same shape and size

Convex polygon (Inv. 1): A polygon is convex if all diagonals are within the interior.

Corner (Inv. 10): A point in a tessellation where the vertex of one tile is found along the edge of an adjacent tile

Degree of rotation (Inv. 7): The number of times that a design coincides with itself or its original position in the course of a 360 degree rotation

Dents of a star (Inv. 1): The vertices of a star with interior angles more than 180 degrees

Design element (Inv. 7): The repeating part of a design

Diagonal (Inv. 1): A segment that joins nonconsecutive vertices of a polygon

Dihedral tiling (Inv. 10): A tessellation or tiling that uses two types of tiles

Edge-to-edge tessellation (Inv. 10): A tessellation is said to be edge to edge, or to have *matching edges*, if all adjacent tiles share common vertices and complete sides.

Equiangular polygon (Inv. 1): A polygon with all angles equal

Equilateral polygon (Inv. 1): A polygon with all sides equal

Equivalence set (Inv. 9): In any repeating design, the infinite set of corresponding points in which each point fits into the overall pattern in exactly the same way

Fit Flush Rule (Inv. 1): Adjacent blocks fit flush, with at least one vertex in common

Fundamental region (Inv. 10): A part of a planar design that can be repeatedly translated to recreate the infinite plane

Glide reflection (Inv. 8): A combination of a translation and a reflection, a glide reflection reflects a point or design element across a glide-mirror/vector and immediately translates that reflection to a new location.

Glide-mirror/vector (Inv. 8): The symmetry tool for glide reflections. A glide-mirror/vector is a combination of a mirror and a vector that reflects a point or design element and immediately translates that reflection.

Image (Inv. 7): The point or design element that results from applying a symmetry tool to a given point or design element

Interior angle (Inv. 1): An angle of the polygon formed by two of its sides

Isosceles polygon (Inv. 1): A polygon with at least two sides equal

***k*-uniform patterns** (Inv. 10): Planar patterns where *k* is the number of different kinds of vertices in the pattern

Lattice (Inv. 10): A lattice is formed when a set of equivalent points in a planar pattern is highlighted; the points can be used to create a grid of two distinct families of equally spaced parallel lines whose intersections define possible period parallelograms.

Lie Flat Rule (Inv. 1): Blocks are placed flat on the table, not standing up on their edges.

Line group (Inv. 9): See *Linear pattern*.

Line of symmetry (Inv. 7): See *Mirror*.

Linear pattern (Inv. 9): A pattern confined within a pair of parallel boundary lines which may or may not be part of the design itself; also called a *line group*

Matching sides (Inv. 10): See *Edge-to-edge tessellation*.

Meander (Inv. 9): A linear design in which the parallel boundary lines are not part of the design

Mirror (Inv. 7): The mirror is the symmetry tool for reflections and divides a symmetrical design into two congruent halves. It is also known as the line (or axis) of symmetry in a design.

Monohedral tiling (Inv. 10): A tessellation or tiling that uses only one type of tile

Motif (Inv. 7): See *design element*.

Multiplier (Inv. 5): For a given pair of similar figures, the ratio of corresponding sides defines a dilation factor or multiplier.

N-fold rotational symmetry (Inv. 7): The number of times (*N*) that a design coincides with itself or its original position in the course of a 360 degree rotation

Nonuniform patterns (Inv. 10): Planar patterns with more than one type of vertex

Open pattern (Inv. 10): A planar pattern in which the polygons do not completely cover the plane but leave gaps or spaces

Period parallelogram (Inv. 10): A parallelogram formed by connecting equivalent points in a planar pattern; a planar pattern is periodic as long as equivalent points can form a period parallelogram.

Periodicity (Inv. 10): In planar patterns, periodicity describes how to use a small section of the design to reconstruct the entire plane.

Planar pattern (Inv. 10): A design that covers the plane in a continuous and predictable way; also called a plane group

Plane group (Inv. 10): See *Planar pattern*.

Point group (Inv. 9): See *Centered pattern*.

Points of a star (Inv. 1): The vertices of a star with interior angles less than 180 degrees

Polygon (Inv. 1): A polygon is a closed path of connected line segments that lie in a plane and do not cross each other.

Polyhedral tiling (Inv. 10): A tessellation or tiling that uses more than one type of tile

Rectangle (Inv. 1): An equiangular quadrilateral

Reflection (Inv. 7): The symmetry operation that reflects or flips a point or design element across a mirror to locate its image

Regular convex polygon (Inv. 1): A polygon that is both equilateral and equiangular

Rhombus (Inv. 1): An equilateral quadrilateral

Rotation (Inv. 7): The symmetry operation that rotates or spins a point or design element about some point called the rotocenter.

Rotocenter (Inv. 7): The symmetry tool for rotations, a rotocenter is the point about which a point or design is rotated.

Sides of a polygon (Inv. 1): The segments that form a polygon

Similar figures (Inv. 5): Figures with exactly the same shape.

Similar polygons (Inv. 1): Polygons that have exactly the same shape

Simple bilateral symmetry (Inv. 7): A design with only one mirror has exactly two matching sides and so is said to have simple bilateral symmetry.

Square (Inv. 1): A regular quadrilateral

Star (Inv. 1): A concave polygon whose vertices alternate between points (with interior angles less than 180 degrees) and dents (with interior angles more than 180 degrees)

Super-supplementary angles (Inv. 1): When two angles add up to 360 degrees they are super-supplementary, or *super-supplements* of each other.

Supplementary angles (Inv. 1): When two angles add up to 180 degrees they are supplementary, or *supplements* of each other.

Symmetrical design (Inv. 7): A design is symmetrical if there is a correspondence between each point and at least one other point. Points of a symmetrical design that are rotocenters or those on a single mirror are exceptions in that they may have no corresponding points in the design.

Symmetry operation (Inv. 7): An action that is applied to a point or design element to locate its image point; a symmetry operation maps each point onto its image point

Symmetry tool (Inv. 7): The rotocenter, mirror and/or vector used in performing a symmetry operation

Tessellation (Inv. 10): A planar pattern in which the design elements cover the plane without gaps or overlaps; also called a *tiling*

Tile (Inv. 10): Each design element in a tessellation or tiling

Tiling (Inv. 10): See *Tessellation.*

Translation (Inv. 8): The symmetry operation that slides or shifts a point or design element a certain distance in a certain direction

Translation vector (Inv. 8): The symmetry tool for translations. A translations vector is a vector that connects any point to its translated image and shows the specific distance and direction that defines the particular translation.

Types of vertices (Inv. 10): Vertices in a pattern can be distinguished as different types, as determined by their valence, or by which specific angles of which specific polygons meet there, and in what clockwise order they meet.

Uniform tiling (Inv. 10): A tiling is uniform if every vertex is identical, meaning that they all have exactly the same set of angles of the same set of polygons in the same clockwise order.

Uniformity (Inv. 10): In planar patterns, uniformity describes how the design elements meet at the vertices.

Valence of a vertex (Inv. 10): The number of polygons that meet at a vertex in a planar pattern

Vertex of a polygon (Inv. 1): The point at which two sides of a polygon meet

Vertex of a tiling (Inv. 10): The common vertex in an edge-to-edge tessellation

Appendix 3

Theory and Research Support the Use of Manipulatives

Describing School Geometry

School geometry may be considered to be a collection of skills and ideas concerning relationships and changes in shape, size, and location. It integrates and unifies the mathematical skills of arithmetic, algebra and statistics, along with reasoning, logic, and proof. The visual and analytical aspects of school geometry help us understand and appreciate the forms and structures that pervade the natural and designed universe, including pattern and aesthetics.

More than most other branches of mathematics, school geometry lends itself to a laboratory approach. Investigations with manipulatives yield data to analyze, interpret, and use to form or validate conclusions. Just the opportunity to "play" in a safe, stimulating, and creative environment encourages dealing with complexity, tolerating ambiguity, and accepting uncertainty.

Goals of a contemporary geometry curriculum for grades 7–12 should include

- development of thinking that involves making reasonable conjectures and reasoned conclusions
- development of generalizations about spatial patterns and relationships involving bisection, parallelism, perpendicularity, intersection, and (congruence as a special case of) similarity
- development of communication skills to read, speak, and write about (as well as to comprehend and to apply) the concepts and procedures of school geometry
- development of technology skills (appropriately using geometric construction tools, models, or calculator and computer applications) that will help generate or validate conclusions about the fundamental spatial relationships

Performance Skill Areas

"Doing" school geometry engages the learner with the content, and the results of that interaction on the student's understanding need to be assessed by teachers. To help think about the connections between geometric content and what students *do*, Alan Hoffer (1981) provides a set of five action-skill areas for doing school geometry:

AREA	PERFORMANCE EXAMPLES
Visual	Exploring objects, models, and pictures to understand how figures and their parts are related
Verbal	Developing a language and symbols which must be read, written, spoken and translated into visual images effectively and precisely
Drawing	Making simple sketches and using the classic Euclidean construction tools (drawing compass and straight-edge), various grids and projections, and the software power of such dynamic interactive applications as *The Geometer's SketchPad*™ or *Cabri*™ *Geometry*
Logical	Developing and testing the truth of statements or validity of arguments to form conjectures, support conclusions, and describe geometric relationships
Applied	Using counting, measuring, calculations and geometric principles to model mathematical relationships; and using resources efficiently, including space, time, energy and materials, to solve real problems (for example, problems in design, engineering, the arts, and practical constructions)

Hoffer's model of action-skills areas is complemented by another important research-based model about the developmental learning of geometry. In the late 1950's Dina van Heile-Geldof and Pierre van Heile proposed that there were five distinct learning levels for doing geometry. The levels are sequential. To function effectively at a particular level, the learner must have successfully passed through the preceding levels. A learner progresses from level to level as a result of experiences rather than chronological age. Schooling provides purposefully designed and sequenced instructional activities. If an instructional activity is at one level and the learner is operating at a lower level, then the learner is usually unable to perform as required and, therefore, is not likely to "get it" at anything more than a superficial level. The result is that little meaningful learning takes place, and frustration is experienced by both the teacher and learner.

Evidence shows that an individual's developmental level of geometric understanding can be quantified (P.H. van Heile 1959, 1973, Wirszup 1976). These developmental levels should be considered in planning for appropriate geometric instruction. Each of the van Heile levels is described below in terms of the kinds of performances that are reasonable to expect by the learner who has reached that level.

- *Level 1: Visualization*

  The learner views geometric elements in terms of their physical appearance, not in terms of their individual parts. For example, a learner might recognize and differentiate a square from a collection of others shapes, but will be unable to tell why it is a square, or what differentiates a square from other four-sided shapes.

- *Level 2: Analysis*

  The learner becomes aware of characteristics and attributes of geometric shape, size, and location, but is unable to understand a) the significance of clear definitions, or b) the impact of the relationships between those attributes and ideas of bisection, parallelism, perpendicularity, intersection, and similarity.

  For example, the learner can identify the pair of parallel and congruent sides of a parallelogram, but is unable to tell why this implies that its opposite angle pairs are congruent.

- *Level 3: Ordering*

  The learner becomes aware of the five basic relationships (bisection, parallelism, perpendicularity, intersection, and similarity), their impact on properties of figures, their use in classifying shapes, and the significance of changes in shape, size, and location of elements. Informal and intuitive conjecturing are possible, but the significance of a "deductive" system is not fully understood.

  For example, the learner is able to classify a collection of shapes based on relationship criteria, but is unable to prove formally that certain characteristics or attributes are a result of others (that is, the height of an rhombus is directly related to the angle and side measurements of the rhombus).

- *Level 4: Deduction*

  The learner has developed meaningful connections among critical aspects of a geometric situations and has started to master the skills of creating formal deductive proofs.

  For example, a learner can draw the shape of the region where two congruent cylinders intersect if they are mutually perpendicular, but is unable to explain whether it is possible to construct, with only a compass and straightedge, a rectangle with the same area as a specific circle.

- *Level 5: Rigor*

  The learner has developed an understanding of the formal, abstract principles, definitions, and postulates that distinguish different geometric contexts based on the notions of shape, size and location, the five basic relationships equivalent in stature to bisect, parallel, perpendicular, intersect and similar and the systems used to measure or quantify locations.

  For example, a learner is able to characterize and distinguish various nonEuclidean geometries and apply their principles.

  This last level traditionally *has not* been included in a typical course of school geometry, despite the desire by some teachers to present a rigorous course.

Research suggests that explorations cannot happen at advanced levels until large chunks of content, skills, and communication are mastered at earlier levels. Writing formal proofs requires the student to recognize, analyze, and order information about a figure (or geometric idea, or construction), or induce patterns and communicate them effectively. Therefore, emphasizing the writing of formal proofs before the students are ready will not only frustrate the students, but will waste precious time they need to really prepare for generating or confirming conclusions. An awareness of the developmental levels of our students, as well as the performance skills necessary for the content and activities, should influence instructional planning.

As a manipulative, pattern blocks in general provide a controlled geometric context. Their basic unalterable geometric properties generate a finite variety of interactions and interrelationships among specific blocks. Because of this, the different families of pattern blocks might be considered separately or jointly to represent a geometric system constrained by the properties of the shapes involved.

Pattern blocks are engaging and fascinating, with a natural appeal that compels nearly everyone to explore and create attractive designs that have order, symmetry, composition, balance, and form. Behind this natural appeal can be found the principles of school geometry. Hoffer's performance skills and van Heile's levels can be combined to suggest explorations that guide the development of geometric understanding. The list below highlights some examples of activities designed for exploring pattern blocks to provide opportunities for deeper geometric learning.

- *Visual*

  Visualization
  - Within a tiling can you find particular shapes in their original size and in expanded versions? (That is, are there larger but similar versions of a particular shape?)

  Analysis
  - Within a tiling can you find shapes that replicate themselves at different sizes, while others seem not to do this? Can you identify the angles of each of these figures?

  Ordering
  - If you use only one shape, what types of tiling patterns are possible? Can you sketch them on an appropriate grid?
  - If you use exactly two different (exactly three different, exactly four...) shapes, can you show all their different possible tilings?

  Deduction
  - Can you use geometric data (concerning angles, sides, diagonals ...) about any block or combination of blocks to generate any conjectures or conclusions about resulting tiling behaviors?

Rigor

- Given a family set of the pattern block shapes, can you suggest some other blocks that might be added to the set to enhance its tiling potential?
- Given the different pattern block families, why are some blocks 'compatible' as tiling pieces and others are not?
- Which of the relationships and "rules" for creating patterns that hold true in one family also hold true for other pattern block families? What are the *basic requirements* of a family for which these rules hold true?

In playing with pattern blocks, the ability to actually manipulate the blocks as design elements allows feedback and provides an open-ended, nonthreatening opportunity for trial and error.

- ***Drawing***

Visualization

- Can you make sketches of tilings and identify the shapes used?

Analysis

- Can you use given properties of a block or a tiling to draw a continuation of it given only a small fundamental region?

Ordering

- Given particular blocks, can you draw a tiling pattern defined from properties of the blocks or their combinations?

Deduction

- From given information about a tiling pattern (or blocks) can you draw it (or a tiling based on them)?

With the pattern blocks and their templates available, as well as instruction in standard Euclidean constructions or dynamic geometry computer applications, it would be relatively easy to transfer visual images with real pattern blocks to available grids, plain paper or blank computer sketches. With the addition of colors, these designs motivate students to extend or modify their designs and develop a sense of continuity about their explorations.

- ***Applied***

Visualization

- Can you identify block elements within natural phenomena, tiling designs in art, quilting patterns, and physical constructions?

Analysis

- Can you represent physical phenomena or relationships through the use of the pattern blocks?

Ordering

- Can you represent the "fixed" geometric relationships between the pattern blocks within one family or between the families?

Deduction

- Can you deduce properties of the blocks or of specific tiling patterns by manipulating the blocks in ways related to location or changes in location?
- Can you solve a tiling problem, given some specific constraints, using deductions from the properties of the blocks involved?

The pattern blocks provide an interactive environment in which teachers can orchestrate critical experiences to expand students' visual, drawing, and applied skills based on real objects, while engaging a real need for effective communication and logical reasoning. Learners, armed with language related to the blocks, can:

- translate between block manipulations;
- describe tiling patterns in term of location or changes of location;
- classify blocks or tiling patterns based on a variety of attributes such as symmetries, angle types, diagonal properties, and side relationships.

Working with manipulatives, and especially patterns blocks, gives students experiences in a visual/tactile environment that allows them access to what Howard Gardner refers to as their *multiple intelligences*. While the manipulations operate at van Heile Level 1, they nourish access to deeper mathematical understandings at Level 2 and beyond. Learners who have explored manipulatives generally have better spatial reasoning and problem solving skills.

Perhaps the real beauty of pattern blocks is an inherent presence of mathematical and aesthetic principles which seems to mesmerize everyone who plays with them. Van Heile would have loved them.

Bibliography

Caine, Renate & Caine, Geoffrey. *Making Connections: Teaching and the Human Brain*. Menlo Park: Addison-Wesley Innovative Learning Publ., 1994

Gardner, Howard. Frames of Mind: *The Theory of Multiple Intelligences*. New York: Basic Books, 1985

Hoffer, Alan. *Geometry, A Model for the Universe*. Menlo Park: Addison-Wesley Publishing Co., 1979

Hoffer, Alan. "Geometry is More Than Proof.", *Mathematics Teacher* 74, (January 1981): pp.11–18

Hoffer, Alan. "van Heile-Based Research." Acquisition of Mathematical Concepts and Processes, edited by Beth Southwell, et al., Academic Press, NY, 1983: pp. 205–27

Lindquist, Mary Montgomery, editor; *Learning and Teaching Geometry, K–12, 1987 Yearbook*. The National Council of Teachers of Mathematics, Inc. Reston, VA 1987.

Piaget, Jean; Inhelder, Barbel; and Szeminska, Alina. *The Child's Conception of Geometry*. Translated by E. A. Lunzar. New York: Harper and Row, 1964.

Rising, Gerald R., editor; *Didactics and Mathematics*. Creative Publications, Palo Alto, CA 1978.

Usiskin, Zalman. "van Heile Levels and Achievement in Secondary School Geometry." Final Report, Cognitive Development and Achievement in Secondary School Geometry Project. Chicago: Univ. of Chicago, 1982.

Wirszup, Izaak. "Breakthroughs in the Psychology of Learning and Teaching Geometry." *Space and Geometry*. Columbus, Ohio: ERIC Center, August 1976

Woodward, Ernest and Hamel, Thomas. *Visualizing Geometry, A van Heile Level Approach*. J. Weston Walch Publishing, Portland, MA 1990.

A Sampler of PentaBlocks Designs

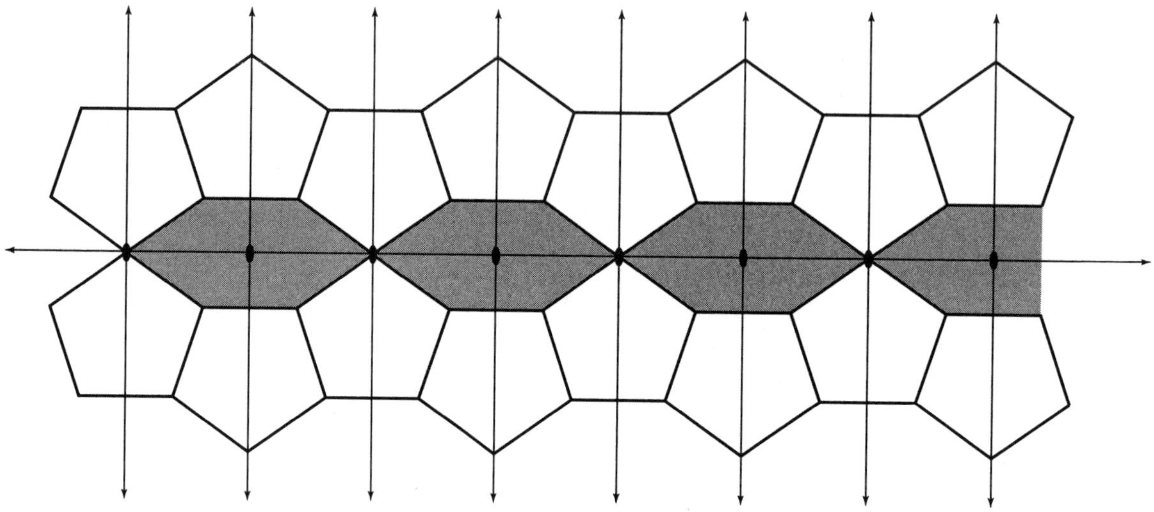

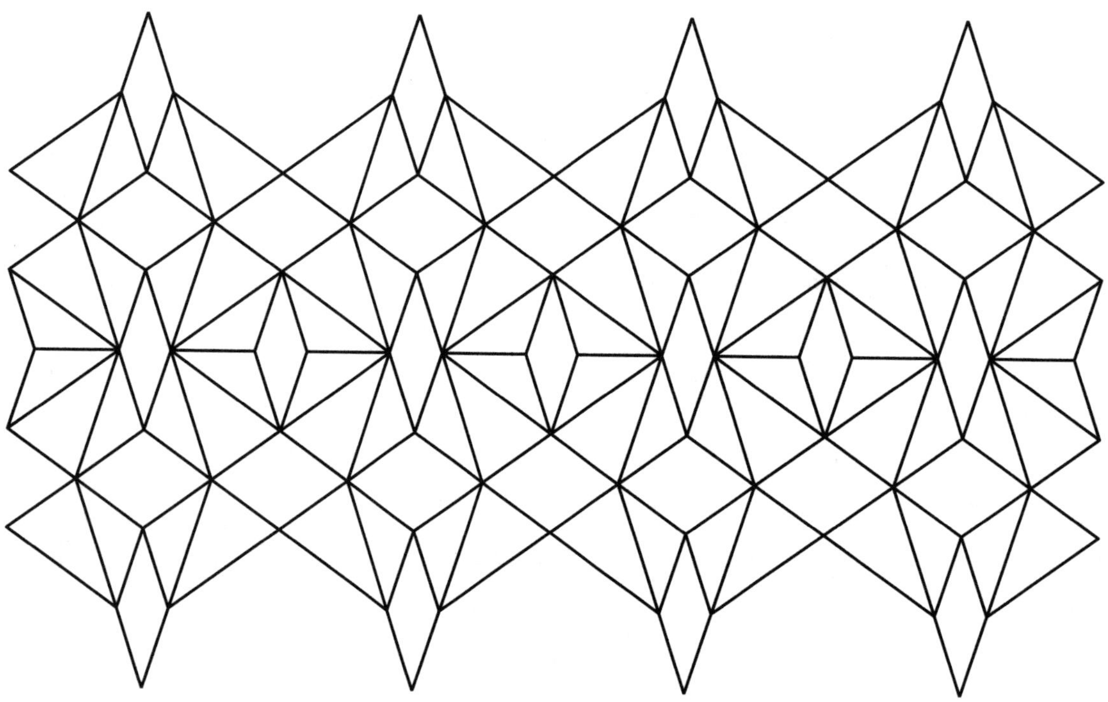

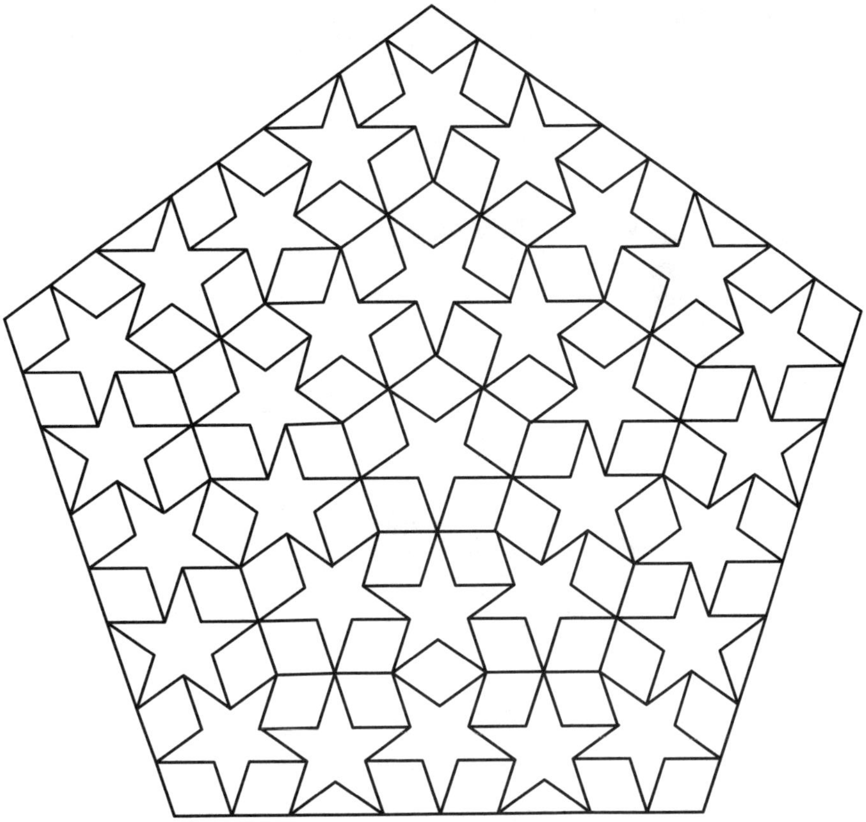

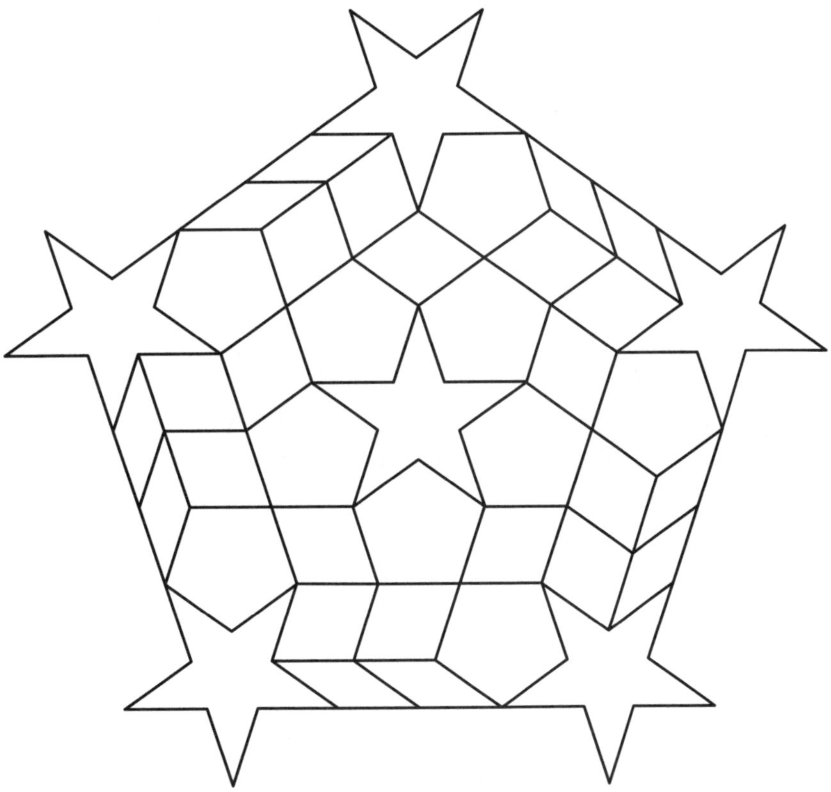

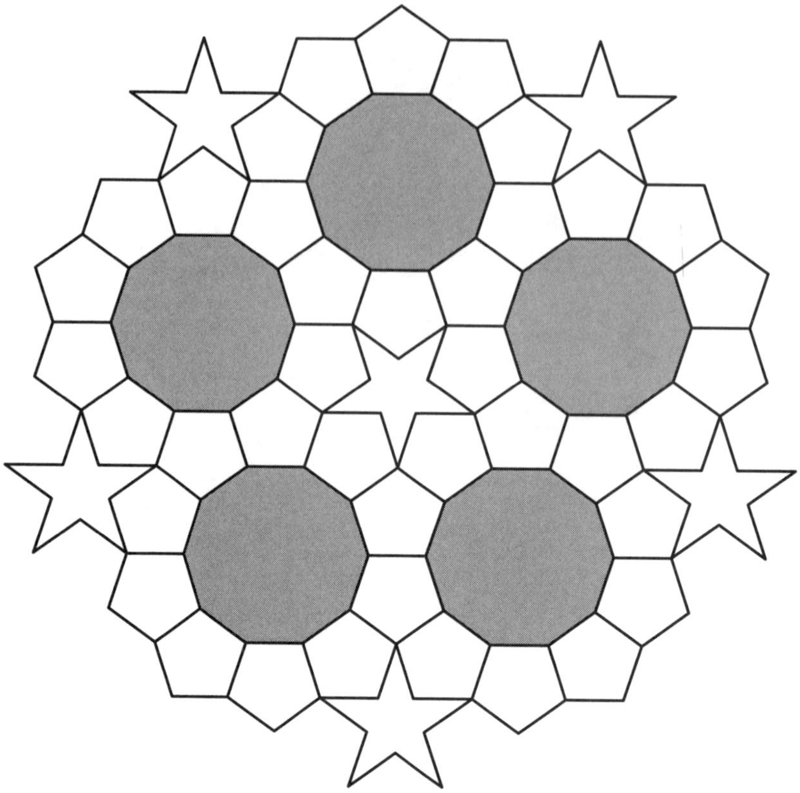

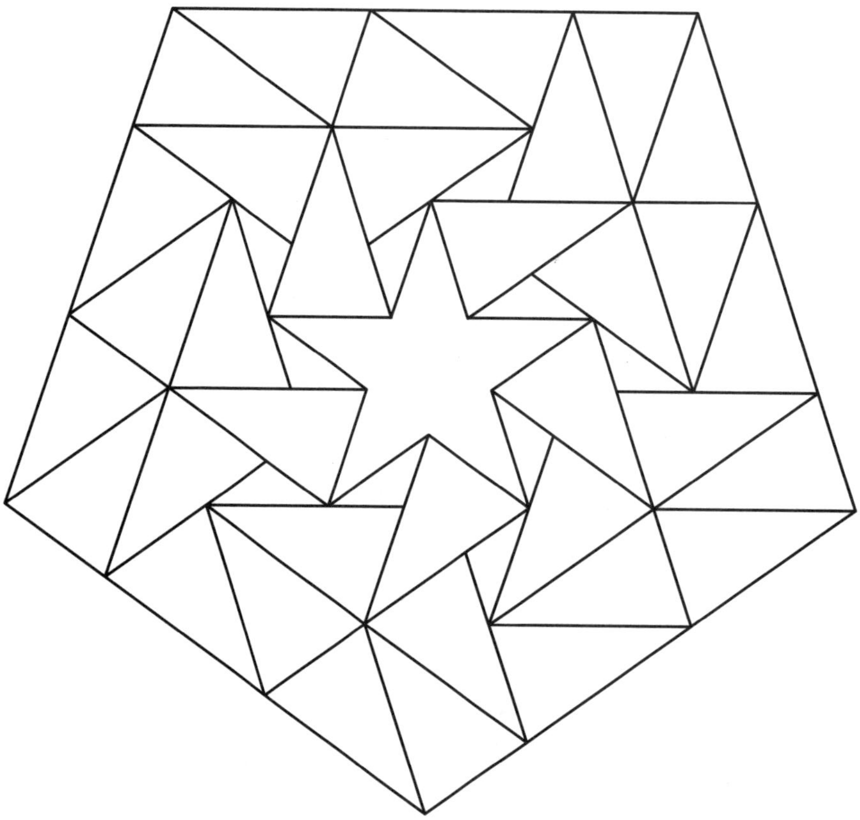

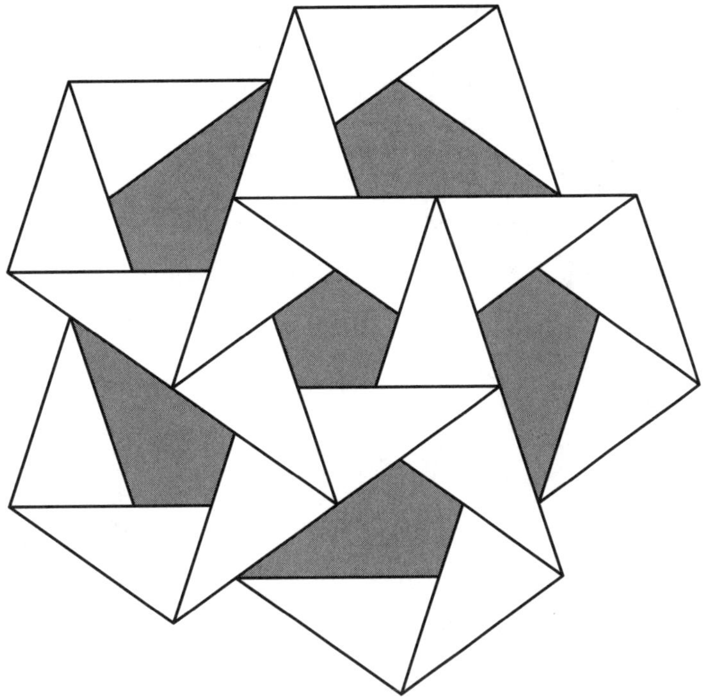

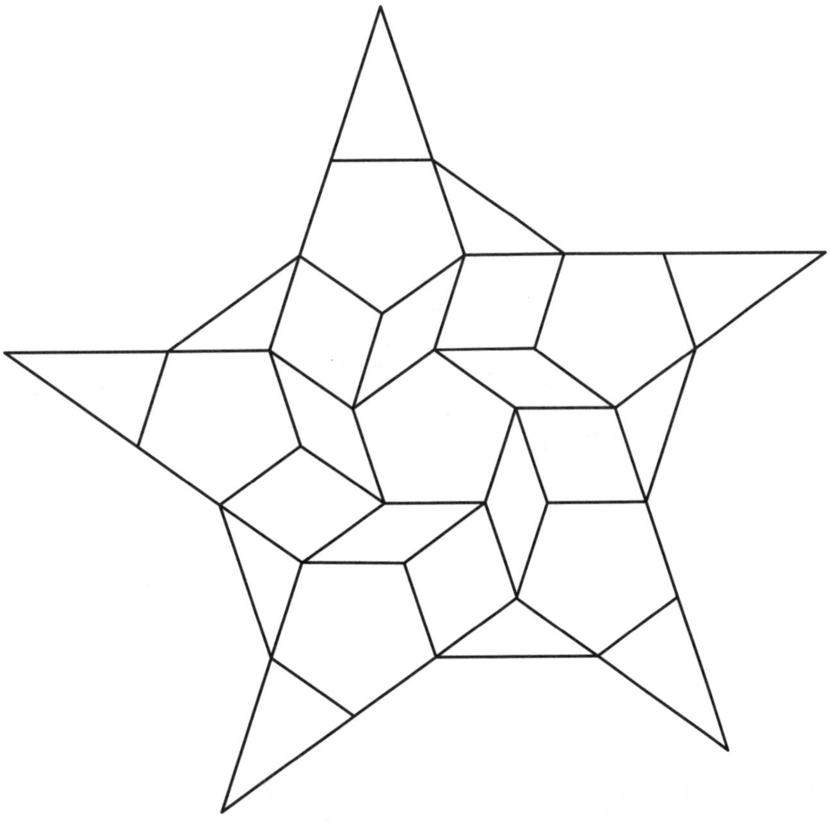

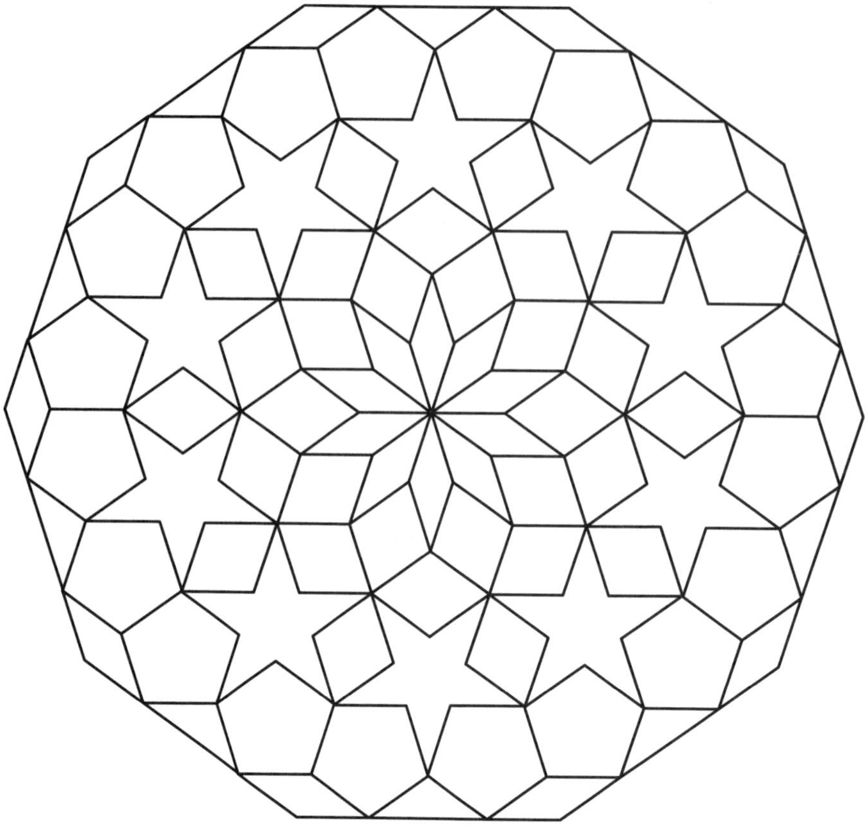

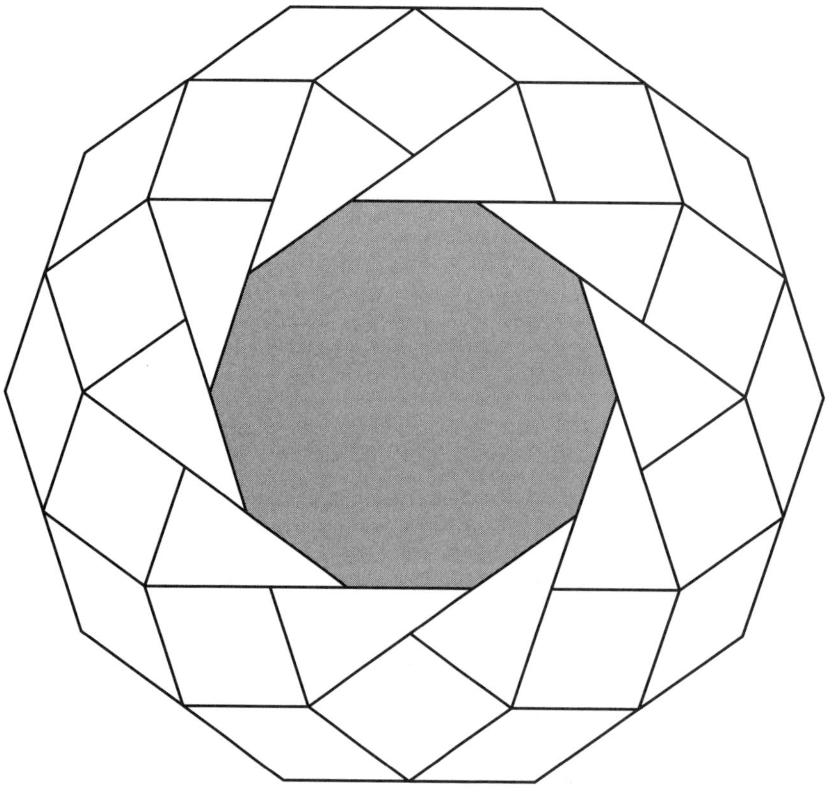

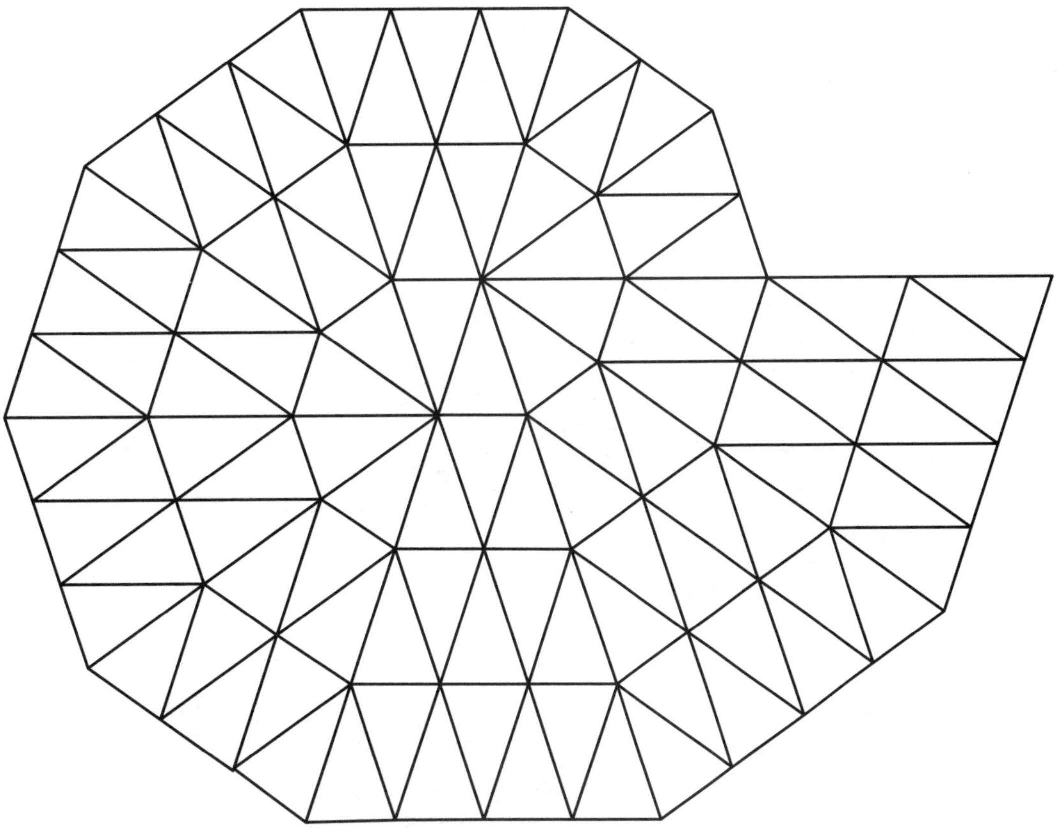

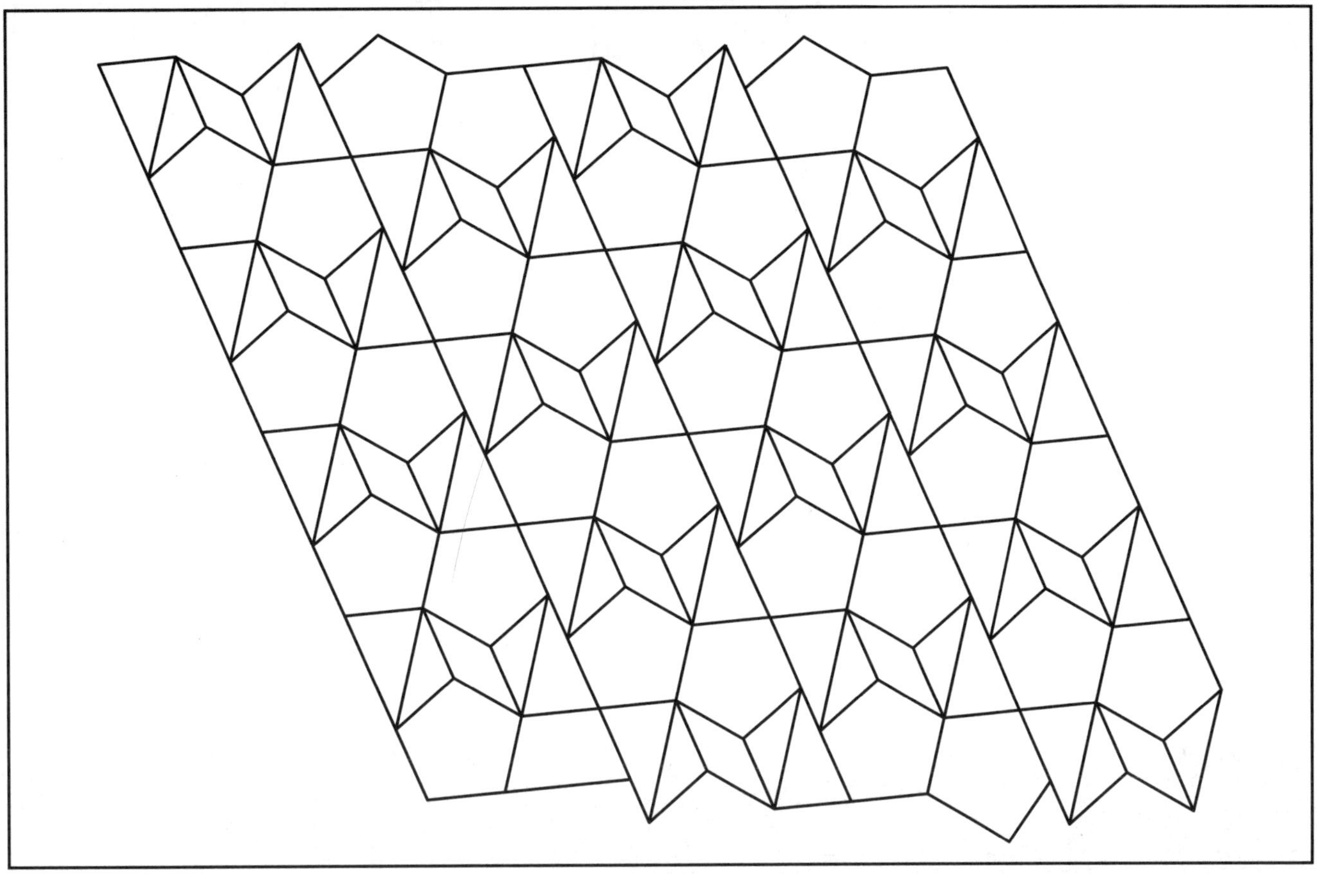

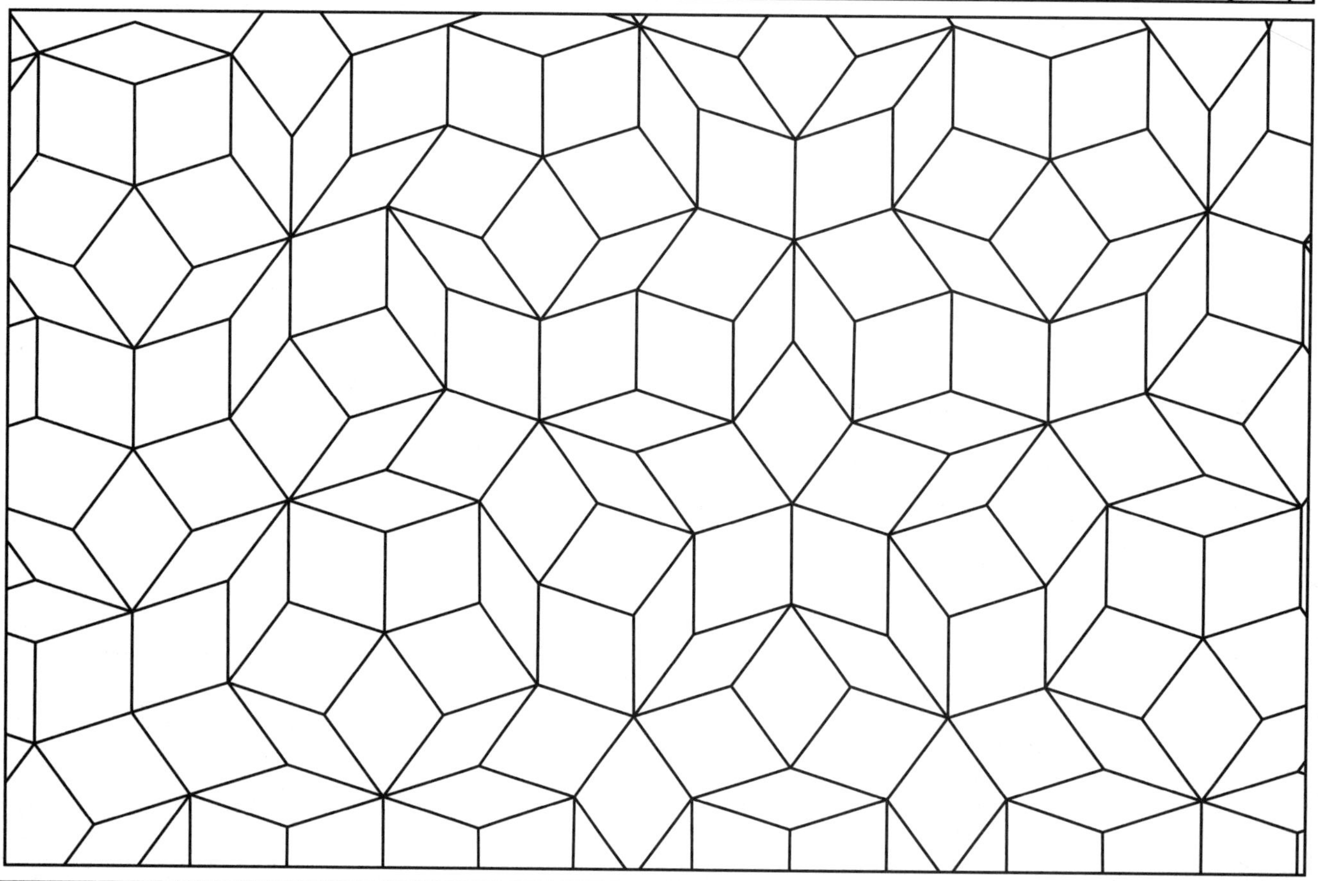

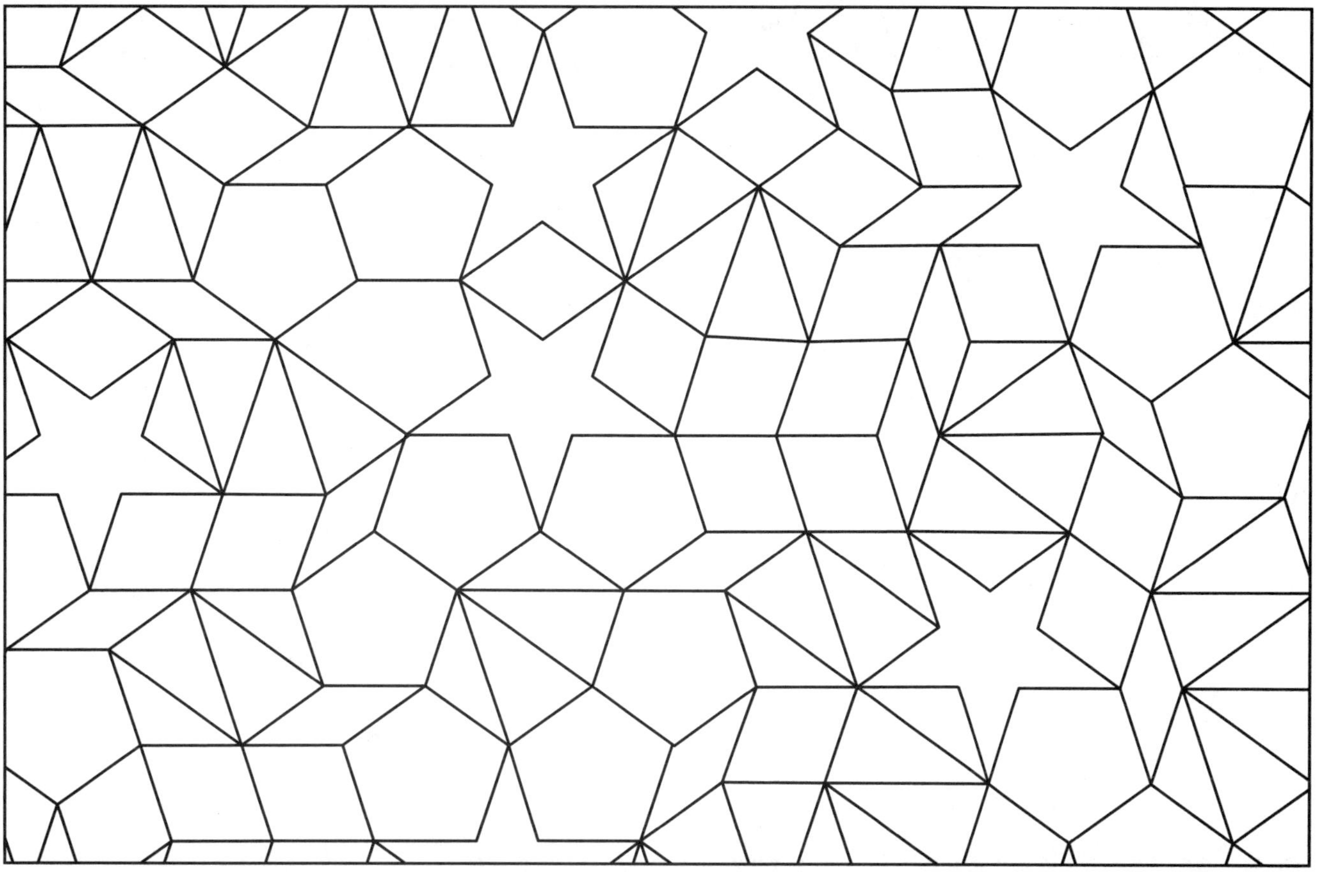

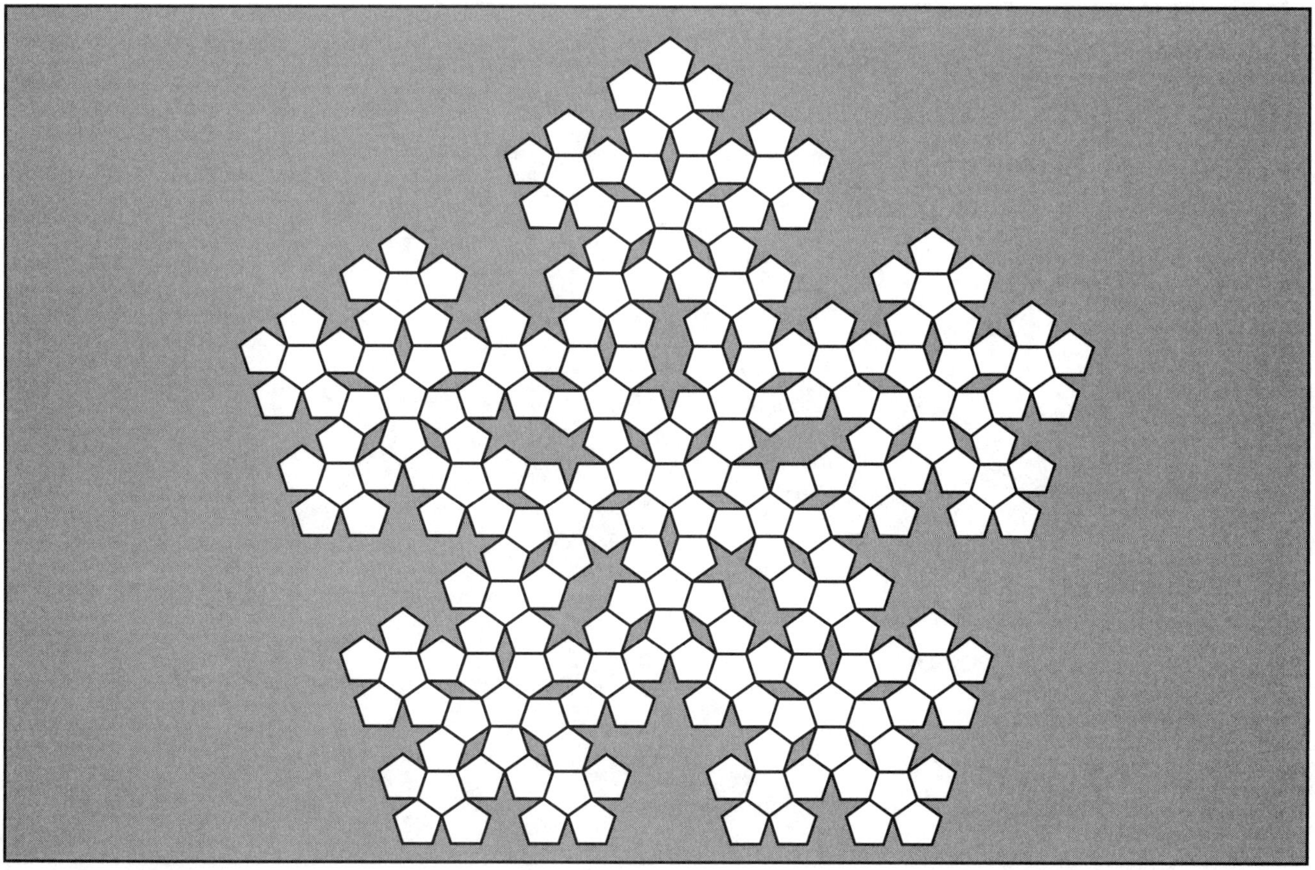

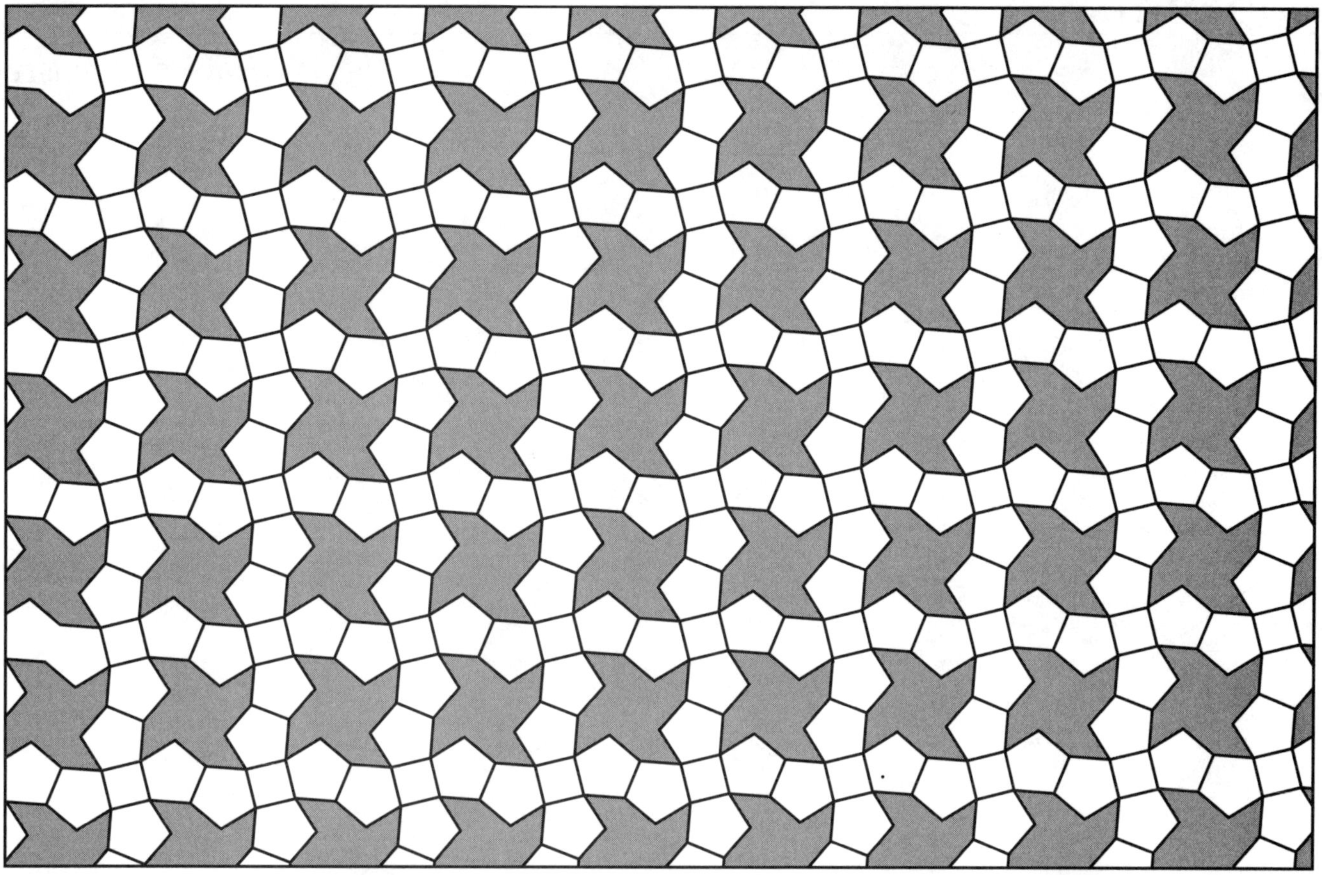

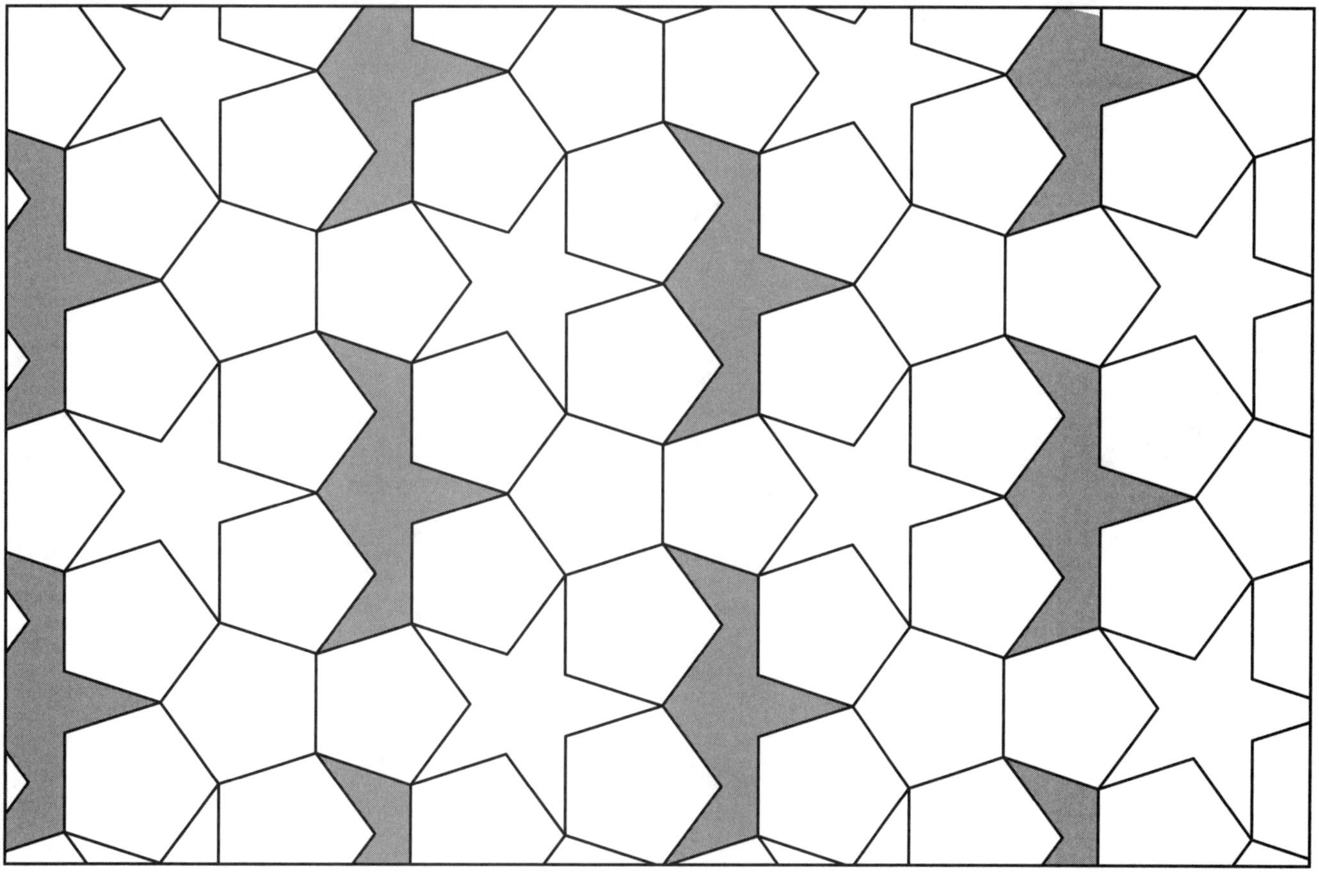

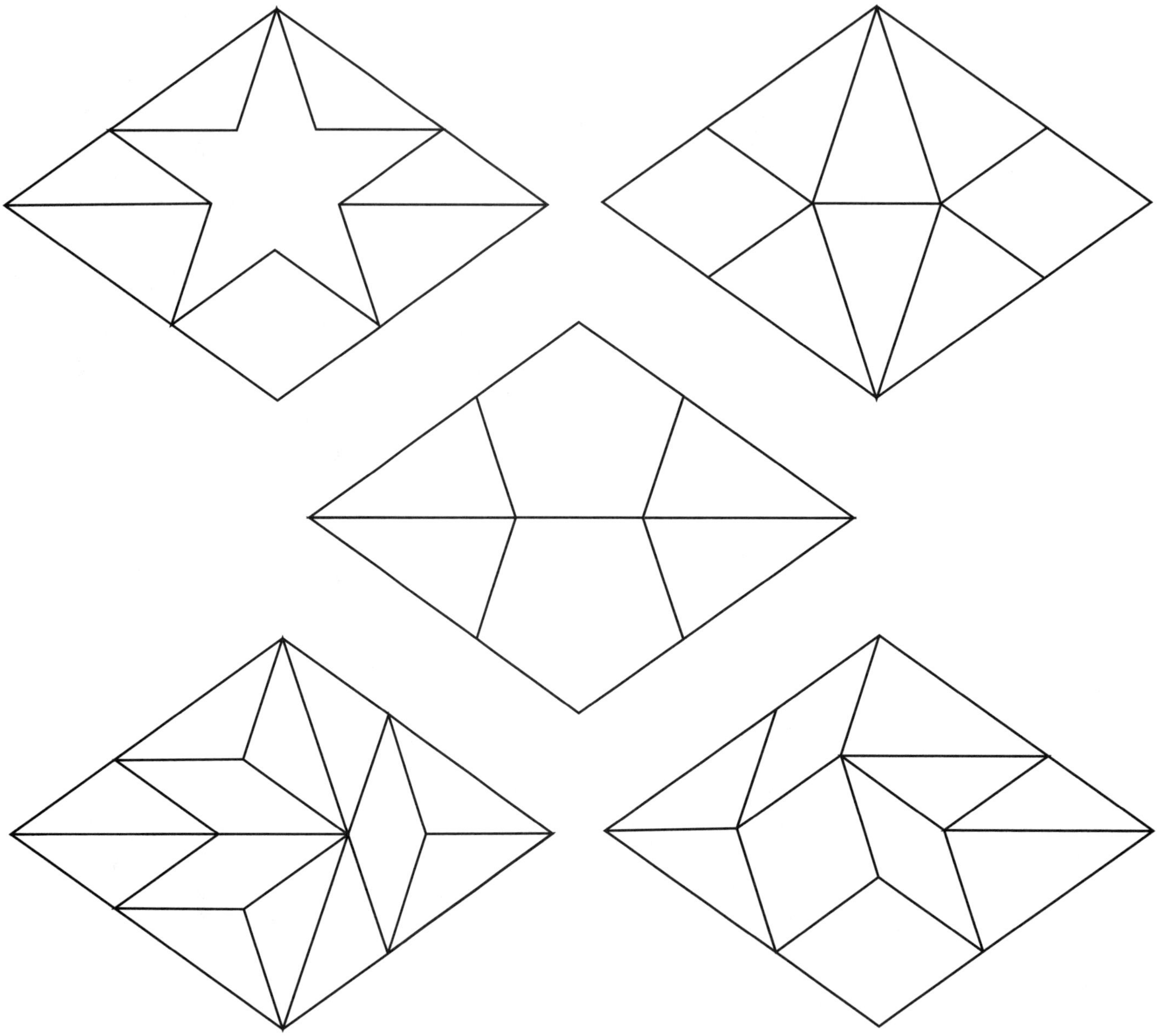

Blackline Master 1 (Investigation 6)

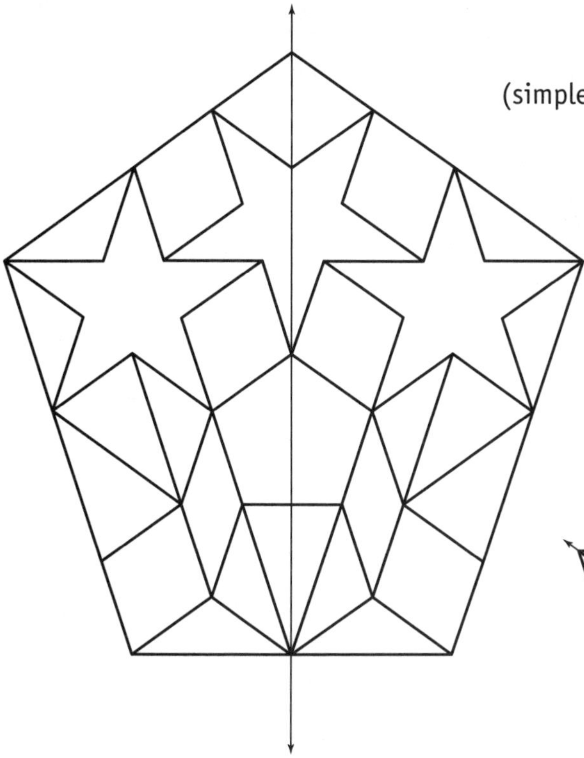

1 mirror
(simple bilateral symmetry)

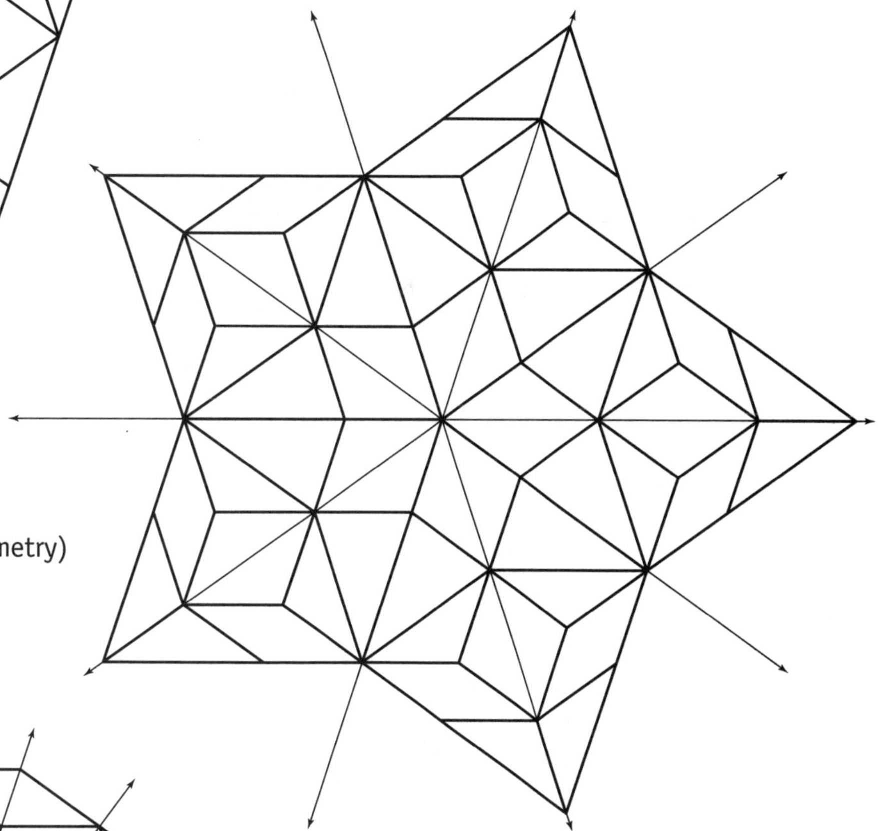

5 mirrors
(5-fold rotational symmetry)

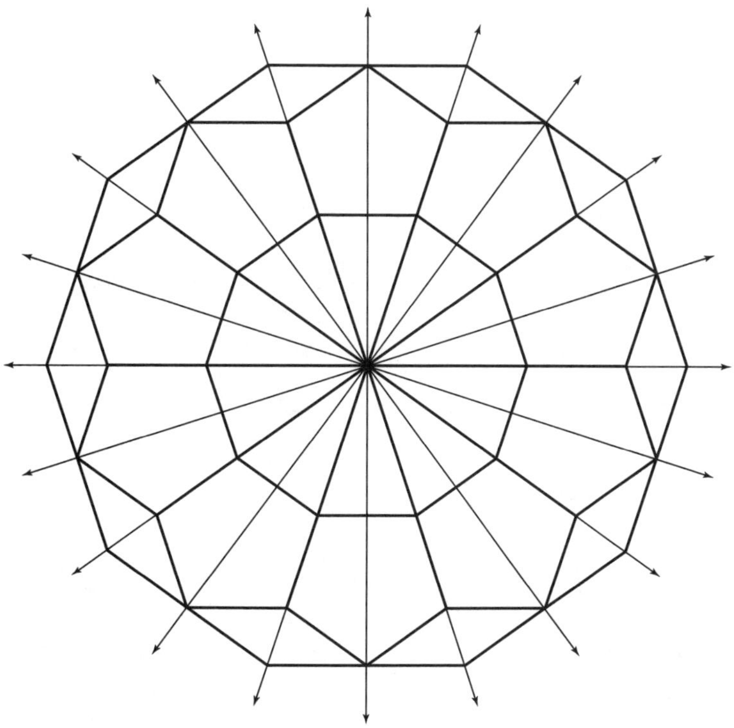

10 mirrors
(10-fold rotational symmetry)

Blackline Master 2 (Investigation 7)

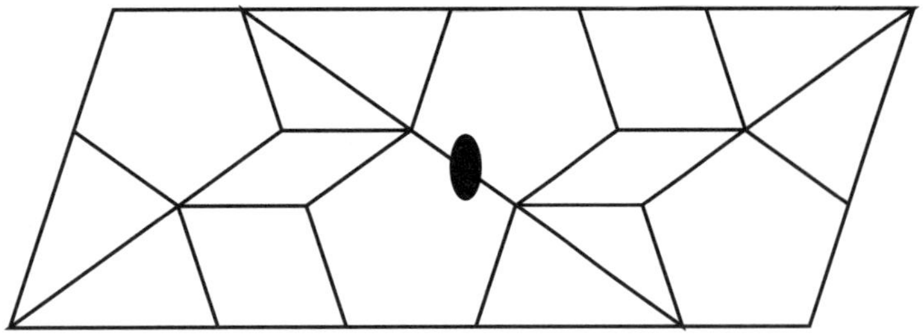

2-fold rotational symmetry
(no mirrors)

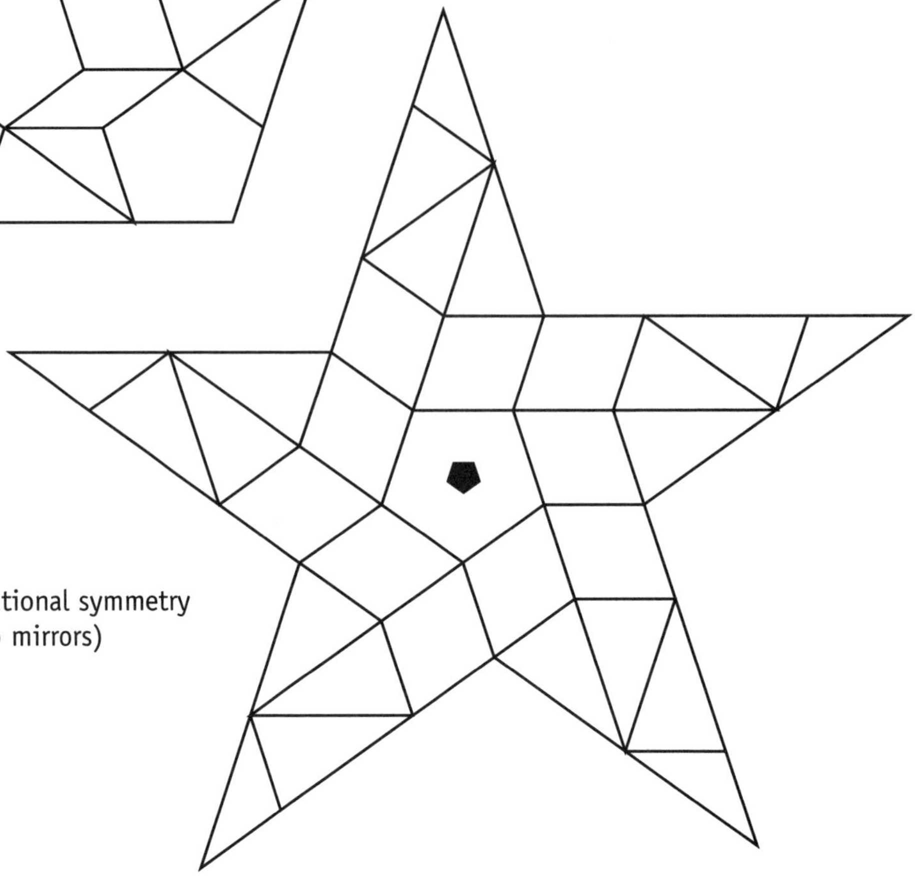

5-fold rotational symmetry
(no mirrors)

10-fold rotational symmetry
(no mirrors)

Blackline Master 3 (Investigation 7)

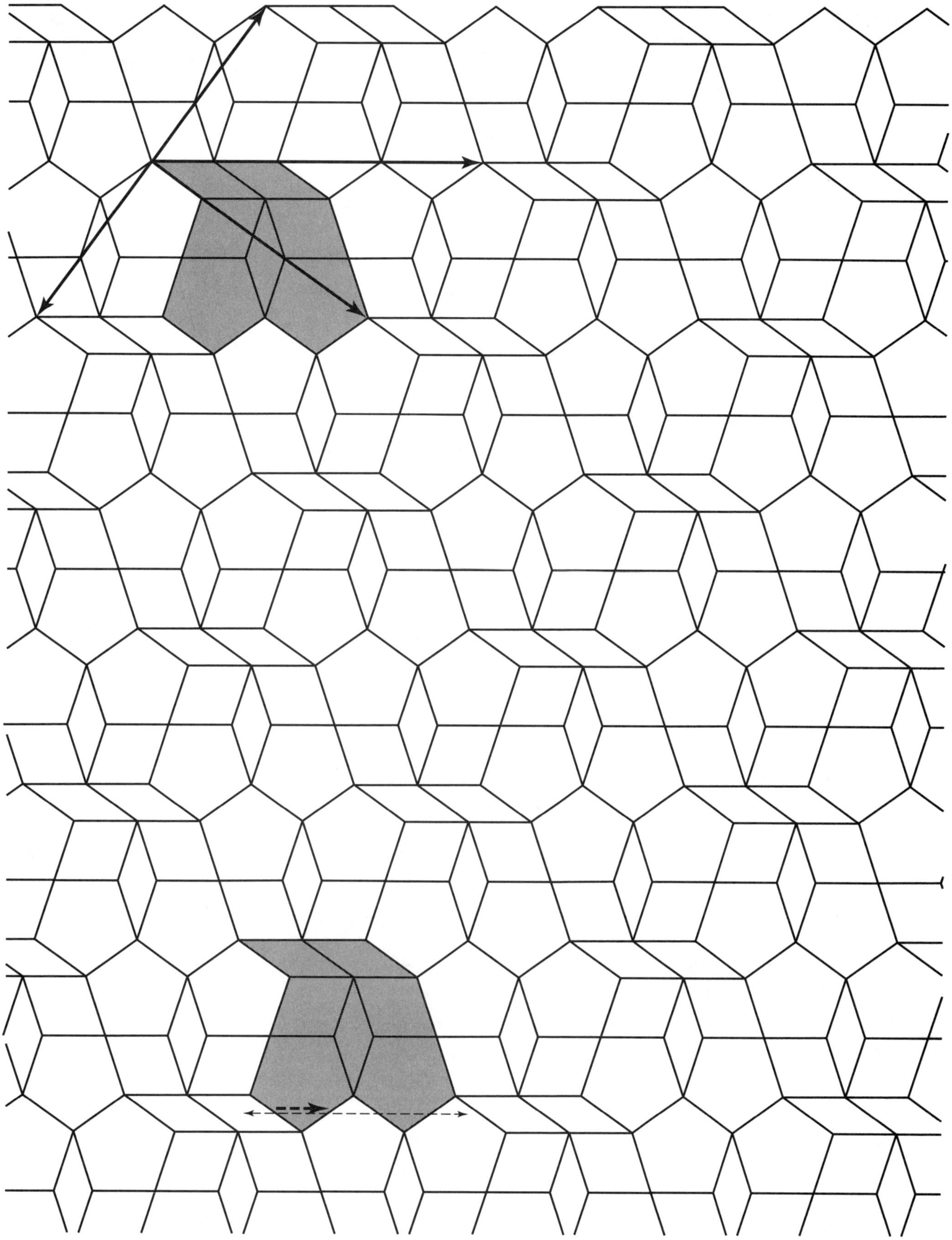

Blackline Master 4 (Investigation 8)

Appendix 6

Advanced Research Topic Possibilities

1. Classifying 2-dimensional patterns: the 36 basic types
2. Defining symmetry groups: closure, identity, and inverse
3. Deeper explanations: fundamental regions, unit cells, and Dirichlet regions
4. A deeper look at polygonal tilings: aperiodic tilings, duality, spiral tilings, Islamic tilings
5. Relationships between 2-dimensional tiling and 3-dimensional space-filling
6. Hyperbolic symmetry and the Poincaré circle
7. Similitude and the similarity operations and transformations
8. Lattices, networks, and graph theory
9. The pentagon in nature: flowers, fruits, leaves, and animals structures
10. Quasicrystals: a "quazy" character in materials science

Suggestions for Improving Student Thinking

(adapted from *Developing Minds,* ASCD, 1990)

1. Ask broad, open questions.
2. Wait before calling on students.
3. Ensure that students process information in a variety of ways.
4. Model and describe your own thinking in resolving problems and practicing other metacognitive processes.
5. Help make students aware of their own thinking and the thinking of their peers.
6. Follow up on student responses by asking for clarification, elaborational evidence, and details of their thinking processes.
7. Have a clear set of ideas and/or skills that you want students to get. Plan a sequence of activities appropriate to the contexts that engages students with these targeted ideas/skills.
8. Encourage students to think more deeply about ideas and relationships, and to give voice to their curiosity by developing their own penetrating questions.